UNA
# TROUBRIDGE
## The Friend of Radclyffe Hall

Let me not to the marriage of true minds
Admit impediments. Love is not love
Which alters when it alteration finds,
Or bends with the remover to remove:
O, no! it is an ever-fixed mark,
That looks on tempests and is never shaken . . .

SHAKESPEARE

UNA
# TROUBRIDGE
## The Friend of Radclyffe Hall

## RICHARD ORMROD

Carroll & Graf Publishers, inc.
New York

Dedicated
To the Town and People of Rye,
without whose hospitality,
help and encouragement this book
could not have been written

and
To Shirley,
with love

Published by arrangement with Jonathan Cape Ltd.

First Carroll & Graf edition 1985

Carroll & Graf Publishers, Inc.
260 Fifth Avenue
New York, NY 10001

**Library of Congess Cataloging in Publication Data**

Ormrod, Richard.
  Una Troubridge: the friend of Radclyffe Hall.

  Bibliography: p.
  Includes index.
  1. Troubridge, Una Vincenzo, Lady, 1887–1963.
2. Hall, Radclyffe—Relations with women—Una Troubridge.
3. Authors, English—20th century—Biography.   4. Singers—
Great Britain—Biography.   5. Sculptors—Great Britain—
Biography.   6. Lesbians—Great Britain—Biography.
I. Title.
PR6015.A33Z83   1985        821'.912 [B]        85-12800

ISBN 0-88184-193-5

Manufactured in the United States of America

# Contents

# Contents

*Note:* The titles of chapters 6, 8, 10, 15, 17, 18 and 19 are quotations from Una Troubridge's writings, and those of chapters 9, 13, 14 and 16 from Radclyffe Hall's.

# Acknowledgments

Firstly I wish to thank Barbara Fearon for unfailing encourage-
ment, help, and accommodation at 'The Forecastle', Rye; then
the following organizations or officials: the Public Record Office,
Canada, for photocopies and microfilm; the Humanities Research
Center, University of Texas, for copies of letters; Remo
Morbideli, Roma, for details of Una Troubridge's burial; *The
Times* newspapers; the British Newspaper Library; the Royal
College of Art; the Department of Education and Science; Mr
Collins and the staff of Tunbridge Wells Public Library, for their
help in obtaining books and microfilm; the Central Chancery of
the Orders of Knighthood, St James's Palace; Lt-Col. T. Crump,
Superintendent of the Corps of Queen's Messengers; Mr Michael
Rubinstein, solicitor, for access to his father's letter file of 1928;
and A. M. Heath & Co., Literary Agents.

For help with photographs I wish to thank: the B.B.C. Hulton
Picture Library (plates nos 16 and 19); The Friends of Highgate
Cemetery (plates nos 28 and 30, photos by Ian Tanner); Mr Tony
Halstead, for photography in Rye and London (plates nos 4, 21,
22 and 23); Mr Felix Hope-Nicholson, for permission to reproduce family photographs (plates nos 1, 4, 14 and 24) and to
photograph the bust of E.C.T. Troubridge, 1909 (plate no. 4); the
*Illustrated London News* Picture Library (plate no. 11); Keystone
Press Agency Ltd (plate no. 17); Remo Morbidelli, Roma (plate
no. 29); the National Portrait Gallery, for permission to reproduce
photographs of Radclyffe Hall (plates nos 18 and 20); Mr Nicola

*Acknowledgments*

Rossi-Lemeni, for permission to reproduce plates nos 15, 25, 26 and 27; the Theatre Museum, for permission to reproduce Una Troubridge's bust of Nijinsky (plate no. 8); Sir Peter Troubridge, for access to family albums and permission to reproduce plates nos 2, 3, 5, 6, 7, 9, 10, 12 and 13; and Mr and Mrs L. Baker, for permission to photograph at 'The Black Boy', Rye.

For comments, reminiscences or other help, I am indebted to: Sir John Gielgud; Mr H. Montgomery Hyde; Dr E. J. Dingwall; Mr John Wyse; Gordon Stannus; Mrs M. J. Lancaster; and Mrs J. R. Mumford. And at Rye: Miss Mabel Bourne; Mrs G. Bligh; Mrs James; Mrs Fisher; Donald Hughes; Mrs T. Pitcher; Mrs Wethey; Mrs E. Goldsworthy; and Miss Ann Hamilton.

For secretarial or research assistance, I wish to thank: Mrs T. L. Ormrod, for typing, book loans and comments; Miss D. M. Mayo, for research assistance; Mr Michael Smith, for invaluable secretarial assistance and helpful suggestions.

For permission to use quotations: Nicholas Vincenzo Troubridge Warren, for permission to quote from his grandmother's unpublished letters; Mr Nicola Rossi-Lemeni, for permission to quote from Una's diaries; R. Lovat Dickson, literary executor, for permission to quote from the works of Radclyffe Hall and Una Troubridge; Messrs Barrie & Jenkins, publishers of the only hardback edition of *The Well of Loneliness* available when I was writing the book (London, 1973); the Society for Psychical Research, for permission to quote from their published and unpublished papers. The extract from a letter from Geoffrey Faber to Michael Rubinstein is reprinted by permission of Faber & Faber Ltd. For permission to quote from other unpublished letters (authors listed in brackets), I wish to thank the Bodley Head (Lascelles Abercrombie); the Trustees of the Galsworthy Estate (John Galsworthy); Sir Rupert Hart-Davis (Hugh Walpole); R. G. Medley (Harley Granville-Barker); Alexander Murray (Gilbert Murray); and A. P. Watt Ltd (Arnold Bennett).

Lastly, but not least, I wish to thank Monica Still and Marya Burrell, for much stimulating discussion, friendship and other communications.

*Tunbridge Wells, Kent*
*February 1984*                                           RICHARD ORMROD

# Introduction

Anyone looking, as I did, in any twentieth-century biographical dictionary, and in *Who Was Who*, will find no mention of Una, Lady Troubridge, this now half-forgotten figure, although she is still listed in the *Dictionary of British Artists 1880–1940*. She is remembered in the popular imagination, if at all, because her name is coupled with that of Radclyffe Hall, who in turn is popularly remembered for having written the once-notorious *Well of Loneliness*.

Strangely, little has been written of either of them, and almost nothing about Una, apart from Lovat Dickson's *Sapphic Chronicle* of their lives together, published in 1975.

This is the first full-length biography of Una, Lady Troubridge, in her own right. The story of her life falls into three main parts: from birth to the age of twenty-eight; the middle twenty-eight years with 'John'; the last twenty years, after John's death.

Her extraordinary story is worth telling: in her late youth she married into a famous naval family, becoming for a short time an Admiral's wife; she was a painter and sculptor (the *only* sculptor of Nijinsky); a talented translator from the French, Italian and Russian languages (Colette's first English translator); a friend of many famous writers, artists and actors; biographer of Radclyffe Hall, whose consort she was for nearly thirty years. Their love story is as compelling as that of the Brownings, whom they much admired, and was the most vital and important relationship in both their lives.

*Introduction*

When she died at the age of seventy-six, twenty years after John's death, part of the inscription she had instructed her executors to put on her coffin read:

Una Vincenzo Troubridge,
The Friend of Radclyffe Hall

The word 'Friend' here sadly typifies the inadequacy of language to express kind and quality of relationship: she dedicated herself body and soul to Radclyffe Hall (John) as lover, companion, comrade-in-arms, social and domestic organizer, secretary, and latterly nurse. 'Wife', 'consort', or even 'lover' might be more appropriate epithets.

She effectively relinquished husband, child, mother, friends and social approval for John; and this self-description on her coffin implies that, in her view, the one significant thing she had done in her life was to love Radclyffe Hall. For her, this was true.

Because she typifies something of the womanly, devoted being in the background, supporting and encouraging, but rarely thrusting herself forward, Una is in many ways an enigmatic figure: many of the people who met, knew, or worked for them, remember Radclyffe Hall vividly but Una only vaguely, if at all. She is seen so often as a secondary, shadowy figure behind or at the side of the dominant, memorable John. She allowed herself to be eclipsed, seeing her role as supportive and subordinate to that of the central protagonist's.

This presents the biographer with a problem, particularly regarding the primary testimony of those still living who remember them. However there is abundant biographical material in the extant volumes of Una's diary, her many letters, and in unpublished material of a clearly autobiographical nature.

The question of why she did not write an autobiography is an interesting one. It seems clear both from implications in her Will, and from the fact that she left all the above-mentioned material when she could have destroyed it, that she wanted both their lives together, and her own life, to be written about: but she did *not* want to write it herself.

In the Foreword to her *The Life and Death of Radclyffe Hall* she says, 'I have hesitated . . .' and she did: the book was written in 1945, two years after John's death, and left unpublished until 1961, two years before her own death. She explains that she did not want to write either an 'expurgated' or an 'idealised' biography; but that 'a perfectly truthful biography must of necessity involve others and include indiscretions . . .' Here we have a clue, and the nearest we get to an answer. Her reluctance to write about John was only exceeded by her reluctance to write about herself, and presumably for the same, or similar, reasons. Thus the task falls to others.

In the *Life* she cannot avoid mentioning herself, as she explains: 'As from August 1915, the story becomes also my own story . . .' but she makes it quite clear that her mandate is to write John's and not her own life: 'I am afraid it may be far from easy, to continue making this as I wish it to be, the story of Radclyffe Hall and not of Una Troubridge . . .' Further to ensure her own relative absence from the book, she states: 'I shall . . . try to omit, so far as possible, my personal concerns and history.' Those very same 'personal concerns and history' are the subject of this book.


'In my craft or sullen art' as biographer, my primary duty is to my subject: to represent her truthfully and impartially; my secondary duty is to the reader: to bring my subject alive in an interesting and readable book. Neither of these tasks is easy! I am partial in that I have chosen to write about her at all; and could certainly not do so without some measure of personal empathy.

The biographer's role is twofold: evidential and interpretive. One must marshal the evidence and documentation, gathering new information or testimony where possible. To do this one is, to some extent, a licensed voyeur: 'licensed' by one's office as biographer to pry into and unearth many normally private areas of a person's life and experience. Even so, anyone can gather 'facts', whether old or new: what is important is their interpretation.

To interpret a book is a work of criticism: the act of assessing and evaluating. To interpret a human life, to attempt to assess and evaluate its meaning and significance, is an act of presumption normally confined to theologians and psychiatrists!

However, I offer no apology for this act of presumption, in the hope that it will justify itself; and help, in the words of her close friend, the opera singer Nicola Rossi-Lemeni, to 'revive and perpetuate her memory'.

Lastly, I hope that I may both do justice to my subject and tell her story in a manner of which she would have approved.

# I

# Genesis
# (1887–1916)

# 1

# *Childhood (1887–1900)*

In a quiet Kensington square on an early spring day in the heyday of the British Empire a girl child was born into an upper-middle-class family. She was placed in a black japanned cot with high railings in the day nursery, under the charge of her first nurse, a Frenchwoman who was to treat her none too kindly. The day was March 8th, the year 1887. Her legal name was Margot Elena Gertrude Taylor, but she was to be better known and remembered by the name carved on her tombstone in Rome seventy-six years later: Una Vincenzo Troubridge.

Two mysteries surround her at the outset. The first is how, despite half a century of legislation, her birth came to be unregistered for forty-six years;[1] and the second is why, disregarding her baptismal names, she was called Una from her earliest days. It was an ancient Irish name perhaps suited to her maternal ancestry, and also the name of a paternal aunt; and as a literary family they would have known of the Una in Spenser's *Faerie Queene*. Yet none of these suggestions solves the mystery, which is compounded by time and documentary silence. If there is any truth in the psychology of names it was to be strangely appropriate: the feminine of the Latin *unus* and the Italian *uno*, it means one, singular; and she was destined to become a person of marked singularity.

It was a good time to be born. Queen Victoria, whose full titles ended with 'Empress of India', celebrated her Golden Jubilee that year, which also saw the first Colonial Conference. It was an era of prosperity at home and peace abroad. Basic human rights and social conditions had improved more in fifty than in the previous five hundred years. Although women did not yet have the vote, a girl born in 1887 grew up, unlike her mother, with a right to higher education; and the Married Women's Property Act of five years before made it possible for women to contract, divorce, inherit, and earn a living in their own right. Seventeen years of free state education were breaking the link between poverty and illiteracy, though the Workhouse was still a grim reality haunting the nightmares of the poor. Popular living writers included Kipling, Hardy, Yeats and Bridges; Tennyson had been Poet Laureate since Wordsworth's death thirty-seven years earlier.

Such was the world into which the child who lay peacefully in her cot was born. In another part of Kensington not far away, a thin little girl of seven lived unhappily with her mother and step-father. They were to meet twenty-seven years later and to change the course of each other's lives.

Some time that day Viola, aged five, was told that she had a baby sister, and may even have been taken to see her in the nursery. Her birth was to complete the family of Harry and Minna Taylor.

The Taylors were a family who experienced a marked degree of social and financial dichotomy, in an era when annual income was still an index of status in the gradations of the social hierarchy. Although Una was to know 'regularly recurring breakfast, luncheon, tea and dinner . . . warm clothing and nursery fires . . .'[2] money was 'none too plentiful'[3] and there was a 'limited and overworked household staff.'[4] It has been said that at this time, 'The great dividing line between the upper middle-class and that immediately below it was the possession of a carriage . . .'[5] Although the Taylors did *not* keep a carriage they none the less clung – at least as regards her mother – to their correct status in society.

Minna Gordon Handcock, small, fair and beautiful, had been just twenty when she married Harry Ashworth Taylor on August 2nd, 1881. She was Irish, one of the seven children of the Hon. Robert French Handcock, seventh son of the 2nd Baron Castlemaine of Westmeath, and Isabella Louise Gordon. An ancestor, William Handcock, MP for Twyford in the first Restoration Parliament in 1661, obtained a patent to erect his estates into a manor, calling it the Manor of Twyford. Following two further generations of MPs and a Dean of Achrony, the Rt Hon. William Handcock was created 1st Baron and Viscount Castlemaine in 1812, and Rev. of Ireland. The Viscountcy expired on his death and the Barony devolved to his brother Richard, MP for Athlone, who was Minna's grandfather. Their arms were '*Vigilate et Òrate*', or Watch and Pray.

Through her mother Una was related to the Florentine families of Tealdi and Vincenzo, and to Mabel Veronica Hatch (later Batten), who were to figure importantly in her later life.

On the Taylor side Una's ancestor William Taylor had inherited in the early eighteenth century the 717-acre estate of Swinhoe-Broomford in Bamborough, Northumberland. William, though an inconsiderable squire, had been an educated man and enjoyed reading Latin. His son George, born in 1732, inherited the estate, but a lawsuit resulted in its becoming entailed. George married Hannah Forster of Lucker, whose father Thomas Forster 'was condemned in 1715, and escaped out of Newgate by an exchange of clothes with his wife . . .'[6] George's eldest son broke the entail on the estate, then died; and his third son, another George, sold it, married Eleanor Ashworth, a Durham ironmonger's daughter, and took a farm at Bishop Middleham. Their son, Henry Taylor, was Una's grandfather, and a plan of the estate was all he inherited!

Educated at home despite a family tradition of Trinity College, Cambridge, Henry Taylor went to sea as a Midshipman at thirteen and a half but only for a year, due to 'languid' health. He started his political career with a clerkship in the Colonial Department, was much preferred, and left after thirty-five years, having served under eleven Secretaries of State. In 1848, 'circumstances' and 'health' led him to decline the office of Under-Secretary of State.

5

Like his granddaughter, born after his death, he was 'subject to nervous depression and lassitude', and 'constitutionally liable to fits of oppression and dejection'.[7]

Gladstone said of him that he 'wanted nothing but ambition to have been a great man'; but he said of himself, 'What ambition I have . . . is poetical and not political.' Both his elder brothers, his father, and his grandfather, had written poetry; and he first saw himself in print at the age of twenty-two, with a verse tragedy called 'King Don Philip the Second'. This was followed by many others, including 'Edwin the Fair' and 'Philip van Artevelde'; Murray published his essays, and Moxon his verses; and he also wrote numerous articles and reviews. Nothing of his is remembered today, but like many another fleeting star he was highly regarded in his day.

Wordsworth praised his poetry; Southey described him as '. . . a most remarkable person for strength of character as well as for intellectual powers';[8] and Macaulay wrote to him: 'I am more and more struck by . . . the resemblance between your poetry and Schiller's.' His plays were acted by Macready; he was a friend of Coleridge, Tennyson, Browning, and Carlyle; and acquainted, 'amongst statesmen with all . . . that were conspicuous except Canning, Brougham and Disraeli.'[9] He was given an honorary degree by Oxford University in 1862; accepted a Knight Commandership in 1869; and was awarded the Order of St Michael and St George.

He married Alice Spring-Rice in 1839, the year her father was raised to the peerage as Lord Monteagle. Alice's eldest sister (Una's great-aunt) had been attached to the Court as Maid of Honour to the Queen, and her first cousin was Aubrey de Vere, the poet. Their second son, Harry Ashworth Taylor, born in 1854, was Una's father. At the time of his marriage it was said that Henry Taylor possessed a collection of thirty-two embroidered waistcoats which had been presented to him by various female 'friends'!

Alice Spring-Rice was a charming, beautiful and vivacious woman, of unusual character, who died when Una was three. It was humorously said later that Una, 'may be said to have been a less successful edition of her grandmother'![10] Certainly Lady Alice was, like her granddaughter, a capable and spirited woman. In 1852 when a new family house was needed, *she* designed it; she also had charge of all money matters, which had always been a 'trouble and inconvenience'[11] to Henry Taylor!

Henry said of her: 'Alice has always been with myself subject to captivation by girls and women . . .' It was a characteristic that their second granddaughter was to share with them, but in ways they could never have anticipated.

Harry Taylor came under his father's literary influence from the outset. In 1860, whilst ill, Sir Henry wrote of Harry, aged five and a half: 'Harry comes to me in bed at half-past seven and we read the *Arabian Nights* till breakfast; and in the course of the day, whenever he can spare half an hour of his valuable time, he comes for a few chapters of the *Morte d'Arthur* . . .'[12] In addition, Una recorded later that her father, 'had been one of those children who had known the kindly friendship of Lewis Carroll.'[13]

As a little boy he neglected his lessons and 'When . . . his Mother . . . told him he would be much happier if he did them as he ought . . . he replied, "Oh Mother . . . if *that* is what you think, you need not mind . . . for it is impossible for me to be happier than I am." '[14]

He was sent to Rugby, then 'crammed' for an examination before going up to Oxford, where he was said by his father to be 'improvident'. He wanted to become a professional pianist but Sir Henry would not permit it and put him in the army instead. Accordingly, on January 20th, 1875, aged twenty-one, Harry joined the 22nd Foot, 2nd Royal Cheshire Regiment as a sub-Lieutenant, being promoted full Lieutenant on November 29th, 1876. By 1877 he had transferred to the 47th Foot, 1st Battalion, the Royal North Lancashire Regiment, where he was Instructor of Musketing. In 1881, aged twenty-seven, while stationed in Dublin, he married Minna in Christ Church Cathedral. The following year the 1st Battalion went to Gibraltar, where Viola was born.

Sir Henry had reservations about his son's 'ways with money', and observed that, 'his Minna, her Mother says . . . is not fitted for making a poor man's wife . . .'[15] but commented with relief later that, 'Harry is exceedingly happy in his marriage . . .'

adding, 'The only thing that is wrong is that Harry's profession is not the right one for a young married couple.' He tried to use his influence to procure Harry a place in the Consular service or 'any other employment that would be fitted for him'.[16] He was obviously successful as Harry was appointed a Queen's Foreign Service Messenger on March 17th, 1883, resigning from the army on April 14th with the rank of Captain, as it was then customary for army officers on retirement to be given the honorary rank one above that held whilst serving.

At the time there were twelve such messengers, who were appointed by the Secretary of State for Foreign Affairs. The duty of a Queen's Messenger was 'to preserve, secure and inviolate, to the utmost of their power and in all circumstances and in every emergency, the diplomatic bags and other matters entrusted to their charge.'[17] They wore a uniform, had to be physically fit, aged between twenty-five and thirty-five, able to render simple accounts, and good horsemen! The annual salary was between £250 and £400.

Harry Taylor stood six feet two inches in his stockinged feet. His thick and longish hair was snow-white from early youth. He had a broad, square forehead, vivid blue eyes, and was a very striking-looking man. His face portrayed the most concentrated nervous energy. Like his father Sir Henry, he had distinguished intimate friends and literary abilities. His influence was to be crucial in the intellectual and psychosexual development of his second daughter.

Many mixed strains therefore went into Una's making: Irish nobility, sunken English squirearchy, clergymen and Members of Parliament, ironmongers and poets, Jacobites, ·rebels, and recluses. Many of these forebears were well-educated and avid readers. In particular she was descended from spirited, intelligent women, and was to be truly their heir.

To capture the full flavour of an upper-middle-class, late-Victorian childhood we have to make an imaginative backward leap, leaving behind our modern, more relaxed, relatively classless society. Such a childhood, though 'privileged', had its own privations, certainly in terms of parental time and personal freedom; but it was structured, disciplined and secure. Child psychology hardly existed, and Freud's observations on the dynamics of the infant psyche were not to disturb parental complacency for some years.

The new-born child we have left sleeping in her cot was, her mother told her later, 'an affectionate infant'. Not surprisingly, several of her earliest memories concerned this cot. Recalling later her very 'first pet' she remembered: 'I was found nurturing a black beetle in my cot . . .'[18] Left largely in the charge of her first nanny, the Frenchwoman, who dutifully slept beside her cot, Una's only language until she was three was French. Although not fond of this nanny she remembered at the age of three: 'standing at the foot of that cot, wearing a dark-red flannel dressing-gown, holding on to the railings and shrieking with mingled misery and fury . . .' when she left, and greeting her successor, Mary Ann, 'with yells of "*Allez-vous en, sale chienne! Voleuse, voleuse!*"'

This memory of herself at four seems equally typical: 'I had been extremely naughty; not . . . an unusual occurrence. I stood in the middle of the night nursery stamping and bellowing with fury, deaf to the expostulations of my nurse and my mother . . .' She was not a docile child!

When her sister Viola was seven and a half her parents decided that she must have dancing lessons, and Una, aged three, was taken along as well as there was only one nanny. For nine years she was to be 'an undistinguished and rather unwilling pupil'[19] at the literarily-named Mrs Wordsworth's select dancing classes at Queensbury Hall, South Kensington, where the assistant was a drab, equally literarily-named spinster, Miss Pope. Dancing, perhaps as a consequence of these early ordeals, was to be a social grace she acquired comparatively late in life.

If she was a poor dancer, Una showed from the beginning an aptitude for drawing. In the same year, aged three, she produced an extremely naturalistic rendering of Adam and Eve in watercolours, which first opened her parents' eyes to her talent, and led to immediate drawing lessons.

As a small girl she developed a peculiar idiosyncrasy – a passion for making tiny objects. She would knit with cotton upon sewing needles, and she contrived a very minute harness for a very minute horse; and just after she learnt to write she managed to write the Lord's Prayer on a threepenny bit. These qualities of ingenuity and patience were to stand her in good stead.

Reared at home by parents who disapproved of girls' schools, Una soon had her day nursery turned into a schoolroom and when she was seven two new people entered her life. The first was Miss Salmen, a remarkably capable young artist who undertook the task of guiding the first steps of an art student still in muslin frocks, white socks, and ankle-strap shoes.

Una was something of a child prodigy, and her appearance on students' days at the Victoria and Albert Museum aroused a good deal of astonishment. Other students and casual visitors would collect round the high stool on which she was perched and try to see what she was doing. Miss Salmen's methods endeared her to Una because she would lighten the hours of rather dry copying from the antique or from anatomical studies, then current practice, by telling her fairy stories or tales of ancient Greece which Una then had to illustrate from her own imagination before the next lesson.

Encouragement came also from other sources. Her father's friend Sir Edward Poynter wrote to the seven-year-old Una: 'Dear Bébé, I liked your letter and your pictures very much. I never saw such beautiful hair as your fairies have . . .'[20]

The second new person was not so affectionately regarded: a Belgian governess, Mademoiselle Polaert, kind but dull, who came daily for 'three tedious hours' to instruct Una and Viola in French, reading, writing and arithmetic. The French consisted of grammar, literature and history; dictation and reading aloud; and *La Mythologie* strictly censored for French scholastic use! The governess was 'tall and gaunt and long-suffering . . . wore brightly-coloured glacé silk blouses with enormous puffed sleeves and a small watch hung like a decoration . . . above her left nipple . . .' and being 'devoid of diplomas and deficient in discipline, the results of her tuition were as meagre as the salary she received.'[21] Yet Una *did* learn, her tendency to laziness counterbalanced by her innate intelligence, curiosity and retentive memory.

When she was eight she wept despairingly on being told that she was now considered 'too old' for a nurse, and that Mary Ann her 'slave and refuge' was to leave. Some time in her early childhood the family moved from Hereford Square to 23 Montpelier Square, Knightsbridge, which was to be the family home until 1907. Una was a reluctant city child, hating streets and longing for fields, farms and the seaside. The annual holiday was supplemented by 'the existence of relations and friends with country houses, who were generous in their invitations.'[22]

As a very young child she was at times 'privileged to be a member of a then considered extremely illustrious colony at Rottingdean', where her parents' friends included Sir Edward Burne-Jones, Sir Edward Poynter, Rudyard Kipling and Stanley Baldwin; but she was to retain 'no memory . . . or any vivid recollection of that brilliant company.'[23]

What she did remember more vividly were the annual August holidays at Brighton, Bournemouth, or some other seaside resort. They took 'rooms' or lodgings consisting of two bedrooms and a sitting/dining-room in a side street off the front, as sea-front prices were beyond the Taylor finances. Harry and Minna endured the privations of this ordeal in order to give their children the benefit of a change of air, but must have been glad to get back to the comparative comforts of home.

Not so Una, for whom it was 'the dingy London house with two rooms on each floor, steep stairs in between, and a bare soot-encrusted cat-run behind it,'[24] her only personal garden four flower-pots in each of the two barred nursery windows. Apart from this there was the communal square garden, a large rectangle of grass, trees and pathways, where she 'grubbed for dingy shells in dingy gravel' or sat decorously on a green-painted iron chair carefully dusted beforehand by her nurse or governess. As a variant there were the 'abominated' daily walks with Mademoiselle Polaert in Hyde Park or Kensington Gardens; their only excitement being sometimes allowed to 'buy something for tea' on the way home.

She rebelled against what was considered 'suitable clothing' for these jaunts: shoes and stockings, 'stuffy coats and white cotton gloves . . . or lumpy woollen gloves in the winter . . . and . . . thick gauze veils worn in very cold weather to protect the

11

complexion.'[25] Her sister Viola seems not to have minded these things.

Children, like servants at this time, had their place. They were not allowed to sit around in the drawing-room, or in the dining-room after meals; if their parents had visitors, they were not to be seen or heard unless they were called for. The day nursery, which became first the schoolroom then later 'the young ladies' sitting room', was where Una and Viola were expected to spend their time when not at meals or out. They were to emerge only if and when summoned by the specified number of peals on the call-bell which hung above their door, operated by a lever on the drawing-room landing below. They had supper upstairs by themselves, which consisted of the soup course from downstairs dinner, and a chunk of cake or an orange. Visitors arriving or leaving could be watched from the nursery windows. Una was to remember that on one occasion Prince Albert of Schleswig-Holstein dined at their house. Of visitors they *were* allowed to see, maternal uncles and aunts who were 'frequently good for half a crown or at any rate a shilling' were understandable favourites, but she was less enthusiastic about relations who did not offer such 'tips' but 'had to be kissed all the same . . .'![26]

Though treated respectfully by the servants, and called 'Miss Una' and 'Miss Viola', the girls were scarcely freer in the household hierarchy, at least on formal occasions. Informally, her 'highbrow pre-Raphaelite family'[27] seem to have been fairly happy and harmonious, although her parents had quite different values. Minna was very class- and society-conscious, and concerned with manners and appearances and the means to maintain these. She was naturally sociable, and had many friends. Her relations were richer than Harry's, who was often away from home on his missions for Her Majesty, keeping in touch by letter. When at home he was 'a companionable and gregarious person . . . thoroughly enjoyed a good talk, and discussions upon literature, music, or more personal subjects . . . but outside this immediate circle he was certainly not inclined to give himself trouble.'[28] An avid reader, he spent much of his day happily alone with a book, or went for solitary walks. He had studied music, was devoted to it, and played very well, influencing Una in both her early love of

books (which was later to become positive bibliomania) and
music. He also took a keen interest in her drawing.

He was 'an intensely sympathetic parent to Una, they being
more like devoted brother and sister'.[29] In her baby French she
had humorously christened him 'le Petit', which later degenerated
into 'Petchiot'; but most of the time she called him 'Harry',
very unusual for that time. 'A great mutual devotion and affinity
existed between Una and her father, who was much more deeply
devoted to her than to his elder daughter . . . and there was no
affinity or bond between Una and her mother.'[30] This is very
revealing, and although written with hindsight by a third person
its veracity is not in question. This abnormally close and exclusive
attachment to her father, from her earliest years, was to cause
problems later in her life, and may well have remained an
unresolved 'Electra complex'.

As this statement also reveals, she seems never to have been
emotionally close to her mother; and certainly there was little
empathy between them later. She called her 'Mother' and only
occasionally 'Minna' in her adult years. As a child she was subject
to her mother's domestic authority, which covered clothing,
behaviour, discipline, lessons, use of leisure time, friends, and so
on. This authority must have been considerable on occasions, as
Harry when away could not be called on to mediate, or modify a
decision. Una found it irksome and her innate rebelliousness often
asserted itself.

Clothes, which she came later to love and used to express her
personality and attitudes, were a bone of contention in her
childhood. Una was a pretty child with dark hair and grey eyes.
Compelled to display her mother's tastes in the matter, until Una
was seven she and Viola were dressed in Kate Greenaway clothes:
muslin or cashmere dresses of first Empire style, with short puff
sleeves, sashes under the armpits and skirts terminating in three
flounces and reaching nearly to the ground. They were the sport of
other less aesthetically garbed children, which Una never forgot.
As the girls grew older Minna met with and assimilated pre-
Raphaelite ideas, and Una and Viola found themselves clothed in
turkey twill or butcher blue linen of spartan fashion, sparingly
adorned with lace or relieved by a necklace of cloudy amber, coral,

or Venetian glass beads. This style of clothing went with Minna's enthusiasm for Morris wallpapers, linoleum floors, unstained oak furniture, blue pottery, uncomfortable chairs, and with an in-ordinate sense of superiority! Her mother's artistic evolution was deprecated by Una very early on in her life.

Although Harry seems to have felt a natural empathy with his youngest daughter there is no evidence to suggest any blatant favouritism on his part, or any resentment on Viola's. The two sisters, despite the age-gap, seem to have been treated very similarly until they were thirteen and eighteen respectively, when Viola outgrew the schoolroom. Having a sister with a five-year head-start made Una intellectually precocious and competitive, and in terms of innate talent she superseded Viola at an early age.

Viola had a protective attitude to Una, most obviously manifest during their teens in time of family troubles. She was also the more docile of the two, less rebellious against parental authority, and early became religious, following their paternal aunt Ida's example and embracing Roman Catholicism. She tried in vain to interest the young Una in the rosary and Catholic ideas. She was less impulsive than Una, who was prone to enthusiasms for things and people, and apt to let these run ahead of her judgment. Of the two, it was Una who was the natural leader and often the instigator of their activities.

They had a trapeze in the schoolroom and early on gave their parents very unacrobatic acrobatic displays; then magic lantern lectures; and later, scenes selected from their favourite dramatists. In that particular brand of parent-torture Una was the self-admitted 'prime mover'. Gifted with a prodigious memory, su-preme self-confidence, and having at that time little sense of humour, she would, when they had lured their audience to the schoolroom, take the floor as Hamlet or King Henry the Fifth, and strut about declaiming 'miles upon miles' of Shakespeare . . . Her long-suffering audience never attempted to deflate her egoism, but politely endured and applauded with exemplary patience![31] Viola, neither so gifted nor so egotistical, appears to have taken a back seat in these proceedings; perhaps acting as announcer or quite superfluous 'prompt'. Unexpectedly from such beginnings it was to

14

be Una herself who ultimately gave stage to a more central protagonist, content to take a supporting role.

There is little evidence that the rivalries and resentments so common between sisters existed between Una and Viola. Their temperaments seemed to work together like electrical positive and negative, without causing a fuse to blow. However, Una was well aware that certain visitors preferred her sister to herself. One of these was Sir Philip Burne-Jones, son of the painter, who had a delightful way with children: '. . . he much preferred my sister to me, but an invitation to a pantomime or to a day at . . . the Zoo generally included me as well . . .'[32] she recalled later.

One thing Una did hate, in relation to her sister, was bed-sharing. From the age of eight, when Mary Ann left, she had had her own room, but when staying with relatives or on holiday, she and Viola were often 'delivered defenceless into the talons of the double bed.'[33] She was to remember, 'the sinking at the pit of the stomach that had been wont to greet the . . . announcement that my sister and I were expected to share a double bed.' Eventually they learnt to put the bolster down the middle to divide the bed into two, which 'robbed the sharing nightmare of some of its horrors.' Why this reaction was so extreme is not clear, but it shows an early preference for sleeping alone which was to some extent life-long and to affect her later relationships.

From the very beginning Una was intensely fond of animals, and after her unusual 'first pet' came a series of more conventional ones: a tortoise called Atalanta, a dormouse, Japanese waltzing mice, Esau the hedgehog who fed from her hand. She liked to have something alive and responsive to care; and, as later, she needed to be needed. One of her more unusual pets was a twelve-inch-high brown owl called Merlin, who was never caged but allowed to fly round the house despite his droppings which whitened the furniture! He was purchased by Una and her father in conspiracy, for three shillings, during a weekend when for some reason they were left to keep each other company. Doubtless Minna was none too pleased on her return!

Although the Taylors' was not a religious household they had both High Anglican and Roman Catholic relatives with whom they went to stay. There was no pressure from either side, and in late childhood Una declared herself an unconvinced sceptic; yet strangely conscience played an active part in her early days. She was a sensitive child and would often undergo torments of conscience on the slightest provocation. This childhood conscience, unlike her later adult one, was a capricious tyrant, who would leap out at her at any place or moment, and magnify some small transgression into gigantic and overwhelming proportions.

Theirs were not religious Christmases but they followed traditional lines. The day began with stockings at the end of the bed, containing a host of small things, with bigger presents round the tree later. 'Miss Una' and 'Miss Viola' would be given books by the servants, to whom they in turn would give some little thing like an embroidered handkerchief. They spent the morning in their 'lair' poring over their 'spoils' before Christmas dinner, eaten either at 1 o'clock or at 7 p.m. This consisted of turkey, sausage and chestnut; plum pudding, brandy butter, and the ritual mince pie; tangerines and glacé fruits, plums and raisins. It took at least two hours, being followed by crackers and much laughter and shouting . . .

One of Una's great enjoyments at Christmas was pantomime, which she went to until she was ten; being allowed to go to her first 'grown-up' play at eleven. At ten she lost her heart to 'a splendaciously ample and properly upholstered Principal Boy . . .' whose 'sex was never for a moment ambiguous. She was not chosen for any boyish characteristic, but because she was a strapping buxom lass with large shapely thighs, well developed hips and bust, a handsome, roving eye, a flashing smile and a rich contralto voice . . .' Una 'sat in silent worship before the well-filled silken tights . . . the debonair gait, the clustering curls . . . of this peerless wonder . . .'[34] It is revealing that Una saw the object of her adoration in such erotic terms; and indicative of things to come that she found the combination of the male role and the unambiguously female body so compelling so early. At least part of this description was to fit the woman who did become Una's Principal Boy later.

In this connection, there is perhaps an even earlier indication. At six years old the object of her 'passionate admiration and devotion was . . . a young girl in her teens. She had blue eyes . . .

and masses of glorious wavy auburn hair that reached almost to her knees . . . she was peerless . . .'³⁵ On the face of it this is an ordinary childish admiration for an older girl; but on a deeper level shows an early response which may be seen as a milestone in her erotic evolution.

An important emotional influence on Una's childhood was one of her mother's friends, Mrs Audre Eaton. She first entered Una's life when she was eight, and grew to love her as her own child. Una on her side gave 'the utter and selfless adoration of childhood and adolescence . . .' and 'she was the one thing that mattered, the one effectual inducement to effort, to the breaking of bad habits and the cultivation of good ones. She was the one beautiful, admirable and entirely satisfactory being,' and she wielded over Una 'an absolute power in all things . . .'³⁶ Mrs Eaton, knowing her power, wisely used it to Una's advantage and not to her own. As the primary female influence she took the place of her mother, and Una gave her a ready affection she had never given Minna. They met infrequently as Mrs Eaton was a globe-trotting grandmother whose numerous progeny were widely scattered, but the two of them kept up a spirited and affectionate correspondence for many years.

Una was not a strong child in terms of health and had 'relatively serious illnesses' at 'fairly frequent intervals'. The unusual thing about these is that they were experienced by Una as pleasurable and rewarding events: 'serious doctor-and-nurse illness . . . was not to be despised . . . even convalescence had its advantages . . .' for it 'gave one an enjoyable sense of added importance,' and was accompanied by 'much petting and indulgence'. As much as anything these bouts of illness relieved 'the monotonous weave of daily existence'; providing not just extra attention but 'additional luxuries and comforts', including more 'succulent diet', and often an unexpected extra seaside or country holiday. Not surprisingly the end of illness was seen as regretful and anti-climactic: 'gradual improvement ceased to be punctuated by praise and rewards, and began to elicit suggestions anent personal effort . . . and a resumption of normal existence.'³⁷

This pattern of gratification was early established and was to become life-long and perhaps subconscious: illness providing

17

temporary escapism from problems, or unwanted duties; disarming criticism; gaining attention, forbearance, and special treatment. In a basically hysterical personality-type anxieties may be conveniently converted into symptoms: real enough in themselves but psychosomatic in origin.

Although Una heard much talk of the need for economy at home, she did not realize until she was nearly twelve how the extra expense of illness affected the precarious family finances: doctors' bills, nurses' fees, medicines, special foods, convalescence. Before that she had just accepted philosophically the limitations that differentiated her life from that of richer friends and relations. She was beginning to emerge from some of the blissful ignorance of childhood into an awareness of grim economic reality.

At twelve she was on the brink of many important developments and changes in her life; a lanky girl 'in faded brown stockings and outgrown well-worn cotton raiment', and, in her parents' estimation at least, 'already destined . . . to be an artist', with marriage 'a comparatively unimportant factor'.[38]

# 2

# Youth
## (1901–7)

When Una was thirteen and Viola left the schoolroom, Mademoiselle Polaert left also, and in her place, for six months, came a Miss Watson, who looked like Jane Eyre and sported a good university record. She was one of the new breed of academic women unknown before in English history, who became tutors rather than governesses, won respect by their brains and often ended their careers as valued members of a women's university or teacher-training college. On her first morning Una greeted her with the pencil-sucking, dawdling, conversational tactics that had succeeded so well in whittling down Mademoiselle Polaert's nominal three hours; but she quickly found herself tackled, routed, and finally subjugated by the small tyrant whom she then christened 'Bricks and Mortar'. This no-nonsense approach was just what was needed, and Una learnt more in those six months than in the previous six years.

At the same time Miss Salmen, her art teacher, gave way to a Mr Rooke, whom Una described as 'a twittering little man with a stutter and pre-Raphaelite yearnings'.[1] From a cosy one-to-one situation with a teacher she had liked, she now found herself in a class with half a dozen other children. Mr Rooke's teaching made no mark on Una at all; but a fellow pupil most certainly did. She was Cicely Horne, who later became Mrs George Lambton. Her beauty at fifteen years old was such that Una, at thirteen, neglected all study for the pastime of staring at her face. She accompanied this admiration with 'a painfully passionate devotion' to which its object did not respond.

Life at home continued otherwise much the same. To the emerging adolescent there naturally arose 'red-letter or black-letter days connected with the realization or disappointment of ambition . . . with joyful meetings and sorrowful partings . . .' and in addition there were, 'lovely places visited, enchanting things read and all the joys of art and music to absorb one . . .'[2] Her father, who had unsociable habits when at home, although giving her much of his valued companionship, also at times aroused her criticism. During their frequent discussions she sometimes accused him of caring very little for anyone 'except us three' and 'Willy Richmond,[3] and I don't believe you'd break your heart if he died!'[4] She was at an age when she thought it right to exchange affection and ideas with the largest possible number of people, and her father resolutely held the opposite view. He avoided society with a passive determination.

His contribution to the arena of ideas was largely through the press. He studied his daily papers and various periodicals and thoroughly enjoyed entering into any argumentative correspondence that happened to be going on at the time. Many of his letters to the papers were more witty than serious, including funny little efforts sent to *Punch*. His letters to Una when abroad often showed the same flair, for example one dated September 2nd, 1902 is addressed to 'Miss Jane Austen' and begins: 'Dear Madam, Mrs Hall has informed us that you are well in health: I hope I need not tell you I am glad of it . . .', and ends: 'I am, Madam, Yr. most humble servant, Sam. Johnson.'

Harry had at the same time a keen social conscience, and did engage in at least one serious press campaign. He sympathized deeply with the outcasts who, then as now, sleep out in the London parks and embankments, and on various occasions spent the entire night among them; he fed them daily with bread rolls which he carried round the park in a string bag before breakfast. Having visited almost every foreign capital he considered it a scandal that no provision was made throughout the winter months in London for giving heat to these unfortunate people. He wanted to establish, on the model of those he had seen abroad, large open-air coke braziers around which the freezing vagrants might keep warm. He studied statistics in favour or disfavour of this scheme and fought an inflexible opposition on the part of the London police. He once told Una that but for the fear of appearing a self-advertiser he would have provided the necessary materials, established his brazier on the embankment, and allowed himself to be arrested by the police. Every fresh case of suicide in the river, or death from exposure, was unfailingly taken up by him in the press as part of the campaign for more socially humane treatment.

This attitude extended to matters nearer home. His generosity is shown by his attitude to one particular visitor – an elderly gentlemen, one of Minna's old admirers who still loved her dearly and inflicted himself upon her with clockwork regularity for two hours every Sunday afternoon. Minna herself greeted his announcement by the maid with groans, but Harry was amused at the fidelity of her ancient admirer! The reception of another guest at this time also tells us that the Taylors put loyalty and friendship above petty social sanctions. A beautiful woman friend of theirs, who had been ostracized by most of her friends for divorcing a brutal husband, was still received by the Taylors; but to save her embarrassment she was never allowed to meet any other guest, so if she arrived first they were not 'at home' to other callers; or, if they already had other guests, they were not 'at home' to her if she called. This worked well until the occasion when, owing to a parlourmaid's error, she was shown into a tea-party . . . some guests froze, while others, ignoring Minna's attempted introductions, swept past the beautiful victim, out of the room and the house!

Despite the liberalizing influence of Harry, Minna still tended to inquire of every new acquaintance of her own or her daughters', 'Who *is* she?' and was addicted to studying the *Peerage* and the *Almanac de Gotha*. A woman of good birth, still young and exceedingly pretty, with no money to speak of and two penniless daughters to launch, she felt that she had a duty to herself and them to see that they should be reared in gentility, come out, be presented at Court, and perhaps even marry some desirable sprig of nobility with adequate means.

To this desirable end 'calling', as then universally practised among the middle and upper classes, was a necessary preliminary means. Harry, declaring that he was too poor to 'keep up' with the aristocracy of birth, declined to take any part in this proceeding, and spent his time hobnobbing with his cronies, the aristocracy of brains, instead. Financially, it seems that he was right: 'At the turn of the century it was generally reckoned that a couple who married on £600 a year would be able to keep a carriage and two maids.'[5] Harry Taylor's annual income at this time was £400 and he had a large house, two children, a wife, and several servants to support, and did not keep a carriage! Because of this, Minna would go to the livery stable in Sussex Place and hire a carriage for the afternoon at 10s. an hour, complete with driver and cockade, on days when she went 'calling' between the sacred calling hours of 3.30 and 6 p.m. Viola and Una, dressed in their best, would accompany her. Strangely, the point of the exercise was *not* to find people at home, but to find the largest possible number of them out! Visiting cards would then be left, which would produce, in due course, either 'return' visits or invitations to tea or dinner.

First on Minna's visiting list would be HM Queen Victoria – not that she actually 'received' such visitors, but Minna, and many others, at regular intervals wrote their names in her visitors' book and were as regularly invited to attend one of Her Majesty's garden parties. Next would come several owners of strawberry-leaf coronets, who would later 'request the pleasure' of Minna and Harry's company at an evening reception to which Minna would always go alone. She must have had a fund of excuses for her errant husband! After that would come people just above, on their own level, or just below them; distant family connections, or people associated with Harry's chiefs at the Foreign Office.

If the people visited were 'at home' there followed ten to fifteen minutes of polite conversation, including the offer of tea. This would be refused where possible, as Minna would want to get maximum use from the hired carriage! Una would often be left in the carriage, regarded as too young to accompany her elders into the houses, her job being to act as unpaid footman. She was always glad to get home to shed both best clothes and 'company' manners; and so it seems were her elders, who would entertain Una and Harry with a humorous post-mortem of the afternoon's events: 'Did you hear Miss Thomas scolding the maid before she came down for having said she was at home? . . . Did you hear Lady Johnson's false teeth clicking whenever there was a silence? . . .'[6]

At about this time Una met a girl slightly younger than herself who was to become a life-long friend. She was Jacqueline Hope, daughter of Laura (née Troubridge) and Adrian Hope, who had been the guardians of Oscar Wilde's children during his imprisonment. Their grandson [7] has suggested that his mother and Una met in a hotel whilst on holiday, and this may well be correct. The family lived, as they still do, in the huge, rambling mansion, More House, in Tite Street, and Una soon became a frequent visitor there.

In an age of family music-making, parlour games and amateur dramatics, friends and relations with the skill and the space got together to make their own entertainments. One of these, a private performance of a play called *The Teraph* by Hedworth Williamson, united Una's new friends and one of her mother's cousins, Mabel Batten, a beautiful society hostess and talented amateur singer who was then in her forties. 'Ladye', as she was known, took the principal part, other parts being played by Mrs Adrian Hope, with Jacqueline as the child attendant; and Una, with her dramatic flair, must have had a part in it somewhere! Una had always known Ladye as a family visitor, and had sometimes been taken out by her. She was well-connected, of idiosyncratic character, and later became one of the confidantes of Una's youth.

Another new friend Una made at the age of thirteen was the veteran painter G. F. Watts, then aged eighty-five. He had painted the portraits of her paternal grandparents which still hang in the National Portrait Gallery, and had known her father since he was a boy. Like Harry's other artist friends he took an interest in Una's artistic development, and wrote to her: 'My dear little Una, As a fellow student though a few days older I may call you so, I have been delighted by the drawings you have sent . . .'[8]

He invited her to spend a few days at his country house in

Surrey, but on the very night of her arrival she developed diphtheria, and remained his guest for eight weeks, together with her parents, a maid, and a hospital nurse. Like her other illnesses it proved to have hidden advantages, although for weeks she was so seriously ill that her life hung in the balance. In the days before mass immunization diphtheria was potentially and not infrequently fatal. She was given, amongst other edible delights, large black hothouse grapes, peeled and seedless; and ate pink stewed pears as she lay by the open window at dawn, looking out at the snow-covered garden and listening to the hooting of the owls. A country convalescence was ordered by the doctor, and Una was taken to the home of Mrs Emily Muirhead Campbell,[9] an old friend of her father, at Salcey Lawn, Northampton. It was to be a momentous experience. The large old house, where guests were said to have included Henry VIII, Charles II and Nell Gwyn, features prominently in Una's scrapbook, and she was to visit it many times before the First World War. On this occasion, as she recorded later: 'I found kindness and beauty and peace and understanding, and there I found experience and sorrow also and much that went to the making of me and much that I shall never forget . . . And there I knew for the first time the happiness of an utterly selfless love; of a devotion that knew no jealousy or criticism, that was content simply to love and humbly . . . accept that mede of affection that was offered in return.'[10] Exactly who the object of this affection was remains an enigma; she gives no names, but obviously saw the experience, in retrospect, as a significant stepping-stone in her emotional development.

Her father wrote to her, firstly from Cercle Dorient, Constantinople:

> Darling,
> Don't you think we might start a book of 'Rhymes of Salcey Lawn' . . . Viola could translate from French . . . you and I could do the doggerel . . .

then from the Club de Constantinople, Peru:

> My own sheer darling,
> This should reach you through the Salcey post on New Year's

Eve. Darling, the Orient Express was dull, deadly dull. Noisy men and unspeakably ugly women . . . one . . . with such a cavern of a mouth as has only come to me in nightmares. I wonder so what you and the little Madam are up to – no good, I expect. Tell her I'm writing to her. Much love to you darling . . .

and later, when she was getting better:

My own sweet little Una,
I saw Harvey[11] this afternoon and he has most *most* satisfaction in his account of you . . . he said just a question of comparative rest and as much open air . . . as you could get . . . if straining your head with work, the work . . . would become bad, whereas if you lie fallow for a bit you would pick up any lost time . . .

She seems to have been fretting over her art work and anxious to get on with it, no doubt with thoughts of the imminent future in mind. She had quickly outgrown the calibre of the Rooke classes, and several artist patrons had suggested the Royal College of Art to her father.

Viola wrote to Una as well, in strangely cloying emotive terms, more like love-letters than purely sisterly ones to a modern ear:

My Una,
It does not matter to me . . . how you feel or where you are, as long as you are happy. Even if you didn't feel a grain of affection for me . . . I should not care . . . if you were happy. Your happiness – the happiness of your splendid young life is everything to me. It is your heritage, your birthright – my gratitude to Emy[12] can never be great enough for having given it back to you at Salcey. Nothing else matters in the least, my Una . . . I should be quite content to go softly all my years if you could live in a state of continued and extatic joy . . . I pine to see you . . . I feel as if only half of me was alive without you – can't you draw me? . . . I hear you have done such divine drawings . . .

In September 1900, at the age of thirteen, Una competed in the stiff entrance examination for the Royal College of Art. Designed for adult candidates, it consisted of the submission of: '(1) A drawing from the antique. (2) A drawing from life. (3) An anatomical rendering in pencil (bones and muscles) of No. 2.'; and an examination at the College: 'Modelling a bust from the antique. Time allowed: 6 days.'[13] These entry requirements were designed to eliminate 'dilettante students'. On October 25th Una received a handwritten letter:

> Madam,
>     I am instructed to inform you that you have been successful in passing the Entrance Examination to this College. You will be required to report yourself to the Head Master on Monday next 29th inst. at 10 a.m.
>     Yours faithfully . . .

The signature is indecipherable but was probably that of the Principal, Mr Augustus Spencer.

The Royal College of Art, founded in 1852, had become 'the chief centre of State-aided Art education'.[14] A typically Victorian institution, its object was to produce art teachers for state schools, craftsmen and industrial designers, *not* painters; and its emphasis was heavily practical, particularly towards 'Architecture, Manufactures, and Decoration'.[15] The college became the subject of heated arguments, letters to *The Times*, and several Commissions, and underwent considerable reorganization in 1900, the year Una entered it. The length of courses was cut from seven to five years; fees were raised from £10 to £25 per session; and 'the former separation of classes for male and female students is . . . dispensed with'.[16] In addition students could elect to qualify in either all four schools of the college: Architecture; Sculpture; Painting; and Ornament and Design, gaining the full Associateship, with the letters ARCA[17] after their names; or, alternatively, they could elect to qualify in one school only, gaining the Schools Associateship, without the letters after their names.

Una decided to study for the Associateship of the Modelling School only, and, not having any award or scholarship, entered as a fee-paying student. There were two hundred and ten students at the time, of whom seventy-two were female. It was said that 'The age range of the students on admission is a wide one, extending from 15 to over 40,'[18] so at thirteen years and seven months Una was exceptionally young, and by implication exceptionally able.

The whole college at that time was situated behind the Victoria and Albert Museum, with which it was closely associated. The head of the Painting School was Harry's old friend Sir William Richmond; and Edouard Lanteri was Professor of Sculpture and Modelling. Lanteri's school had an excellent reputation, and his views had reformed the courses taught. He had been instrumental in removing the compulsory one-term introductory course in house-planning, arguing that it had no relevance to modelling specialists. But he did consider that 'there was a great need for instruction in history and mythology, similar to that given in the Ecole des Beaux Arts, Paris.'[19] He introduced classes for marble- and stone-carving; and his course included, 'the armature of the bust and figure, anatomy from the round, treatment of various reliefs, and simple figure composition'.

Edouard Lanteri was an Italian, born in Burgundy, who became a naturalized Englishman in 1900. He had exhibited at the Royal Academy since 1876, and executed bust portraits of members of the Royal Family, ambassadors, admirals, and famous artists; and also statuettes, statues and groups. When Una entered his Modelling School he had already been teaching there for twenty years; and was that rarity, the born teacher who brings his whole heart into his work. He was a striking-looking man who bore a resemblance to St Paul in the Raphael cartoons.

Before Una had been a week in his charge he spotted her unusual talent and began to nurture it. She was then a child of great promise who thought she would one day conquer the art world. Lanteri thought so too, and he devoted many hours of his valuable spare time to the child who began to haunt his studio in her insatiable quest for knowledge. He became a great influence on her life, his teaching going beyond the province of art or sculpture: he became not only an instructor but her 'philosopher, guide, and friend'.[20] Mr Clemens, formerly a pupil, then for many years Assistant Professor to Lanteri, said of him, 'He was a man who took an unusually fatherly interest in his pupils.' All her life Una was easily able to relate to older men, possibly as father-surrogates, and her appeals to them for help were rarely refused. Lanteri was to figure later as Einar Jensen in Radclyffe Hall's third novel, *A Saturday Life*.[21]

Una probably walked daily from her home to the college carrying her sketch folders, one of which, dated 1902–7, shows book-plates for friends, life studies, a series of book illustrations for *Jane Eyre* and preliminary sketches for statuettes. She must have greatly enjoyed her new freedom from the schoolroom, and the prematurely adult status she now had as an art student. The only complaint she seems to have had was that working in clay had ruined her nails!

Between the ages of twelve and seventeen Una, like many adolescents before and since, went through a stage of 'hero worship': engineering a series of mental and bloodless love affairs with inaccessible people ranging from long-dead historical figures and characters from literature to contemporary actors and actresses. Her 'number one' historical god was Napoleon, and she wore round her neck day and night a medallion bearing his image; decorated the walls of her room with portraits of him, and read about him with encyclopaedic zest.

In 1902, at the age of fourteen, her 'number one' theatrical idol was Sarah Bernhardt. She collected photographs of her, drew, painted, and modelled her; imitated her, and went frequently to see her perform at His Majesty's Theatre where, thanks to the kindness of Sir Herbert Tree, she was allowed to come and go as she chose.[22] She also saw there Henry Irving, Ellen Terry, and Beerbohm Tree; and saw Sir Herbert himself twenty-six times as Malvolio! Una was never to forget that Sarah Bernhardt graciously accepted some pencil drawings she had made of her, and in doing so thanked her with a kiss.

Judging from the contents of her sketch book at this time, it frequently accompanied her to the theatre where she 'drew from the life': Viola Tree in *Richard the Second*; Basil Gill in *Oliver Twist*; Cyril Maude as Toddles; 'Signor Caruso as Ottavio'; Irene Vanbrough in *The Admirable Crichton*; and many others. One of her great heart-throbs of the time was Fred Terry, whom she saw in *The Scarlet Pimpernel* nineteen times, each time wishing herself in the part of Julia Nielsen, his leading lady. He in turn, like Sarah Bernhardt, was presented with sketches of himself done by Una during the many performances she attended; and like her, he was kind to the young artist: 'The sketch is most flattering and greatly appreciated by Yours sincerely Fred Terry.'[23]

Una also saw Adeline Gene[24] in *The Debutante*[25] and wrote to her. She kindly replied giving Una times for sketching her in preparation for a sculpture, which was duly executed and later exhibited. She wrote, on its completion: 'Dear Miss Taylor, Ever so many thanks for that dear little statuette I am awfully glad to have . . .'[26]

Her training at the Royal College of Art was such that from the age of sixteen onwards Una began to achieve some success as a sculptor, and to receive commissions, which gave her a partial financial independence. These usually came about through her friends recommending her to other people who then approached her directly, as in the following letter from a Spencer de Holsey of HMS *Blake*, Devonport, dated March 2nd, 1905:

> Dear Miss Una,
>     You are a business woman. I will try and elevate myself . . . to a business man.
>     Statue – Female.
>     Size      ⎫
>     Subject  ⎬   Left to you.
>     Taste    ⎭
>     Price £15 to £25.
> I have heaps of room here . . . 2 large and 3 small cabins. Also . . . don't hesitate re. price. Later on when you are famous I shall say the 'creation' was given me years ago when the artist was 'quite a girl'.

This letter is additionally interesting as it implies that Una, then barely eighteen, had already met Captain Troubridge, her friend Jacqueline Hope's Uncle Ernest, a handsome widower with three children. It must have been on his recommendation that a naval man commissioned Una; or alternatively it is possible that Troubridge himself had introduced Holsey to Una at Tite Street.

Whether these commissions were modelled in the workshops of the Royal College of Art, or whether she hired a studio is not clear; but it may well have been the latter as a Thomas Brock wrote to Sir Edward Poynter[27] recommending Mr P. Bartholomew of Balham as 'an excellent founder' to do Una's castings.

Una's new-found independence manifested itself in various ways. At seventeen parental authority was looming less large, and she defied it first by bringing home from a visit to Bedfordshire a red dachshund bitch, despite an emphatic letter and three telegrams from her mother forbidding her to bring another dog into the house! The second obvious defiance of her mother was in the thorny matter of clothes; for as Una now earned her own dress allowance she felt quite entitled to spend it as she chose. Sick to death of low-cut square necks, primary colours, and Art with a capital A, she found relief in extreme contrast and became a tailor-made girl, style early 1900s. She collected her abundant hair into a stiff pompadour, and took to flannel shirts with stiff collars, cuffs with links, and a narrow ribbon bow-tie, severely-cut coat and skirt, and specially-made patent-leather Oxford shoes with low heels. This throws up an image of the early Suffragettes; but she loved variety and after a brief flirtation with this fashion went for a softer look, with lace collars and cuffs and large, flat hats with sweeping ostrich plumes. This was followed by voluminous trailing silks, barely draped shoulders, velvet throat bands and buckled shoes, *circa* eighteenth century! For outdoor wear she adopted Fred Terry's highwayman's coat, white stock, and plain three-cornered hat, completing the outfit with a gold lorgnette. (See plate no. 1.)

These elements of play-acting and adamant independence must have been a source of mild amusement to her father, but of intense dismay to her mother.

As well as her art studies and commissions, Una was devoting herself to singing and having her voice trained. She was a mezzo-soprano, and like her father played the piano. At what age these lessons began is not absolutely clear but in all probability it was in her late childhood or early teens. A letter from her first singing teacher, Ivy McKay, to Minna, accompanied by a page of detailed instructions, implores her to watch Una's 'tendency to wobble or quiver' and when this happened to '*stop, and begin again*', to ensure 'a smooth and free emission of that lovely tone'. Although the letter ends on a complimentary note calculated to please any mother, it does not inevitably follow that Miss McKay was being insincere; indeed her real interest in her pupil is obvious throughout: '. . . she is very young and we must nurse the plant . . . she is a lovely girl, has a lovely heart and a lovely voice . . .'[28]

Mrs Eaton showed a characteristically generous appreciation, writing from Folkestone: 'I want to hear your voice, what a gift it is!' and again from Dublin: 'I have never had your Great Gifts dear child, but . . . thank God for . . . one priceless gift, the power to appreciate . . . Your devoted and understanding old friend.'

Harry was staunch in his support of her musical ambitions, perhaps remembering his own; and writing from Marienbad in early September 1905:

> My little darling,
>     My hopes are all with you when you sing on Monday, but I know you will be a success . . . Anyhow you have the best part of life before you, and 3 devoted people wanting to help you all they know . . .

In the same letter, he added: 'the King's coming is all they think of hear [sic] . . .' and referred to 'Viola's reforming revolutionist, who let's hope will come home covered with honour . . .'

This was presumably a reference to Maurice Woods, the journalist to whom Viola had become attached, who may have been sent to Marienbad by his paper to cover the King's visit. In the event it was Harry who came back 'covered with honour' as he was made a Member of the Royal Victorian Order, Fourth Class, on September 8th, on the occasion of the King's visit. He was by that time the longest-serving King's Messenger, with twenty-two and a half years to his credit.

Harry's health weakness was his chest. He had had a bad bout of pleurisy which left him very weakened; but tuberculosis was not suspected until he had his first severe pulmonary haemorrhage in August 1906. King Edward VII sent him to Midhurst Sanitorium in Sussex, where he wrote his first letter to Una after the haemorrhage:

> My little Una,
> Don't worry about me I'm pulling along – I was miserable at bringing M[inna] back but she will tell you I couldn't help myself.
> G[od] B[less] you my own darling.
> H[arry].

Weeks later he wrote:

> Darling little Una,
> I know I haven't been answering your constant letters, but you know the one home letter exhausts the little material of this place . . . One of you's to come down on Fri . . . I don't think I ought to be without either of you for long when I want you both so much – I know there is the money question, and how that darling Min has kept from me all worrying letters etc. and borne the whole herself – That Min is a crowned Saint . . .

The 'money question' was, as always, uppermost in times of illness; and *how* Minna, who had no money of her own, 'bore the whole herself' is uncertain. Perhaps she was assisted by some of her better-off relations.

After leaving Midhurst supposedly practically cured, he was sent to Pau in France, on November 22nd. The journey worsened his condition and the doctor in charge of the case told Minna, on their arrival, that he marvelled that she had not allowed her husband to die peacefully in England. She must have been very shocked by this comment after the optimistic pronouncements at Midhurst; but she kept calm and cheerful. Harry had nothing but praise for her in his letters to Una and Viola: 'No one but you two can realise what she is, the darling, never cross or impatient for a second and, God knows, she has enough to make her so.' And later: 'My Darlings, Min is about the only thing you will not have heard about and so I write about her. She is quite wonderful as usual . . .'

Ironically, it was *her* health and happiness he was worried about: 'I tried her temperature . . . just as a precaution but she had none.

The food is so good it must do her good . . . She has found friends, and I expect will know all worth knowing in the place . . .'

Harry and Minna were alone at Pau, leaving Una and Viola at home. Early in the new year, 1907, there was a panic because they had lost touch with Viola, who had apparently gone to stay with a cousin in Athlone. In very shaky writing Harry wrote to Una on January 2nd:

> My blessed,
> We simply can't get any knowledge of Viola. M[inna] was getting miserable as post after post came in without a line from her, and as it is even more than usually important to me not to have her fretting I wired yesterday but am still [20 hours] without an answer . . . She [Minna] *is* so sweet to me. Oh! Una, French doctors do want such a lot of samples! Samples of me engage the attention of the whole analysing staff of . . . Pau . . . My arms are round you darling. Yr. Harry.

The note of humour despite adversity is characteristic of the man.

Four days later Minna wrote to them jointly, sending a progress report: 'As to my beloved H. his temperature is very unsatisfactory and he is allowed to take no exercise at all . . . he is appallingly thin . . . this fever consumes him . . . on the other hand he eats very well, sleeps well, and coughs very little . . .' Then chiding Viola: 'Viola must not fritter money away – you see by not writing she cost two expensive telegrams . . .'

Most of this six-page letter, however, concerns her narrative about her 'bolt from the blue' which, they are warned, *'You are to keep . . . to yourselves.'* She relates at length how a fellow-guest in the hotel, a Mrs Barham, had been told all about their circumstances by Minnie Hatch (Minna's aunt and Ladye's mother) and being wealthy herself, pressed Minna to accept £40 towards their hotel expenses. She is obviously afraid that her daughters will disapprove of her taking charity, and constructs an elaborate justification for herself. They are to go and see Minnie Hatch to say how kind people have been, but are not to mention the money directly; and they are to 'drop in' to see Edward Poynter's picture for although 'it is a nuisance . . . he would be a dreadful bad enemy.' She adds, 'I long for you both out here, you would love it and the people . . . I know heaps of people now.' Her social instincts are always uppermost, even in this extremity.

Viola went to Pau before Una, and wrote on her arrival:

> Cher Amour,
>    I got here at 5.30 last night after a long journey . . . all the time I wanted you and Maurice . . . I do want you so the whole time . . . H. is perfectly cheerful . . . Minna is trying heat now for a change, and keeps the windows shut . . . I am in a voluminous flat with white carpets that terrify me – fearful good food – all the things, in fact, that make me unhappy – it is all *too* good and too much . . . Mother seems to have made masses of friends . . . Yr. V[iola].

The sisters obviously had quite opposite feelings about good living. The financial problem had been resolved, as a Mr Herbert saw to it that the Foreign Office would keep Harry on indefinitely.

When Viola had been there a little while, she wrote to Una: 'I do not think if you saw him you would feel very unhappy – you would just feel the impossibility of feeling anything at all.' Such emotional anaesthesia is often defensive; and the hopelessness of the situation was rapidly becoming evident: 'now we do not even have the distraction of going out together as we think it wisest not to leave him.'

She shows her elder-sisterly concern for Una: 'Of course selfishly I want you, yet I do not really advise your coming out till it is necessary. You are so young for the unutterable gloom and though you may be unhappy in London, yet you have your work and many friends. Here you would have neither and I cannot bear to think of you dragging through the interminable days.'

And of Harry himself: 'often he dozes for hours . . . sometimes he is a little better, sometimes a little worse.'

Viola reveals that, like Una, she has no illusions about her mother, and her statements are the antithesis of Harry's:

> She would not admit it, of course, but she is very well and eats about treble what I do. You know exactly . . . At times M. tries to remember the tragedy of it and says, 'Isn't it awful – I can't bear to think of it.' It is not that she doesn't care – but it's all

grown into a grey groove of custom. She was shocked because I asked if I might go to the Opera, in the next breath she says, 'Why don't you make more friends and go about.'

Harry's letters to Una remained cheerful:

My dearest,
    The Doctor came and reported improvement in me – so we had a cheerful morning. Weather just the same and cold . . . [but] the end of that must come and then comes my chance. Til then I must be on the shelf and make the best of it . . . Viola is invaluable to Min as a companion but no use of course in taking any [?work] from off her hands, and Min won't let her try . . .

One senses the man of action and optimism champing at the bit of his circumstances; and despite the Doctor's reports he became steadily weaker and more emaciated.

    At last Una herself went to Pau in February. It had become just a matter of time. They kept from Harry the knowledge that he was dying, to prevent his worrying about them; and during his last illness he talked quite cheerfully about plans for the future.

    Una wrote to her close friend Jacqueline Hope: 'Father was not so well again yesterday which made me busy but he is better today . . . all day I help mother . . . go for walks and errands. But of course most of the time I am with Father who wants me and likes to have me, though he doesn't speak much . . .'

    The daily fluctuations in his condition deceived no one; and Una was with him when he died on March 5th, three days before her twentieth birthday. What natural grief she felt has gone unrecorded, but it must have been very considerable.

Following hard upon her father's death came the break-up of the family home and financial hardship. It was the end of an era. There was a small pension, but the house, which was leased, had to be let. Harry's total estate, willed to Minna in ten lines dated 1884, amounted to only £671.19s.7d. (multiplying by ten, this would be roughly equivalent to £6,000 today; not a lot between three people).

When Viola later married Maurice Woods, Minna went to live with them at 41 Eaton Terrace; and afterwards kept an antique shop. In 1909 she still owed Una and Viola £225 each,[29] 'this payment not to commence till the letting of 23 Montpelier Square.'

Una herself had left the Royal College of Art during the term ending in February 1907, in order to go to Pau; and after her seven years of study and success as a sculptor, it is surprising that like 'a very large number of students'[30] she left without obtaining the Schools Associateship. Professor Lanteri must have been disappointed in his star pupil, although she was still sculpting professionally and ambitiously.

On the same day that Harry died, March 5th, 1907, Captain Ernest Troubridge was appointed captain of the battleship *Queen*, and Chief of Staff on the Mediterranean, based at Malta. Like Harry he had been awarded the MVO in 1905; and like Una's grandfather Sir Henry, had been made a Companion of St Michael and St George. Between 1905 and 1907 Una had met him at Tite Street a number of times and liked him. He was manly and charming, and was interested in art as his sister Laura, Jacqueline's mother, was a talented artist who had been asked to paint portraits of the royal family in 1892. He was also keen on music, liked opera, and sang and played the banjo. Una's involvement with the Troubridge family was such that she appeared in their photograph albums and was making drawings of Ernest's sisters in 1907.

Shortly after her father's death Una went to Florence to stay with her cousins, the Tealdis, in their palatial villa, Sant Agostino. They had eight children, two of whom drowned together while bathing in a lake in Switzerland; and this family was the model for the Ferraris in *A Saturday Life*.[31] The children's governess was a striking and unusual Italian woman called Marguerite Michel, with whom Una struck up 'a short but intimate friendship'.[32] What first attracted Una to her was her cheerfulness and courage despite unhappy circumstances and ill-health. They soon became 'very intimate indeed' and Una 'her confidant as regards the most private matters of her life.' During these discussions Marguerite, who was of a demonstrative nature, 'would hold, and as it were play with, her [Una's] hand'.

Marguerite was thirty-eight, six feet tall, with dark hair and a deep voice; and despite the hot climate, always wore white stocks, [33] or ties. She was obviously a masculine type, and seems to have been fond of Una in a way which Una herself did not at that time fully understand. Una made a statuette of her, complete with stock; and Marguerite gave Una a ring which she specially wanted her to wear. The Tealdis did not approve of this close friendship with the governess and tried to influence Una against her. Marguerite could be domineering, and significantly Una 'felt a distinct resistance against being in any degree overwhelmed or managed or in any way dictated to by this very dominant person.'[34] As a return of confidence Una told her about Captain Troubridge. 'I called him Ernest to you and to no one else,' she wrote later. She usually called him either 'Troubridge' or 'Zyp', his childhood family nickname.

They shared much laughter and pleasure together, conversing in French as Marguerite's English and Una's Italian were at that time rudimentary. Marguerite made such an impact with her 'so salient . . . personality' that even Viola, so much less prone to enthusiasms about people, used to say to Una long afterwards, 'Well, if we have done nothing else in life, we have known Marguerite Michel.'

At the same time as this ambiguous friendship, Una was falling in love with Florence itself, and was having singing lessons with Signor Salvati, an opera singer. Also in so Catholic a country, the religious question began to absorb her mind again. Earlier in her adolescence she had cultivated exoticism, studying Bushido, Shinto, and Buddha with conscious superiority. She was now ready to modify that exoticism and admit that there might be something to be said for Christianity, but was still volubly critical of all established churches.

Beginning to feel that her Italian friends secretly pitied what they considered her misguided ideas, she one day asked her singing master where he thought she would go to after death. He flushed crimson with confusion, then grudgingly admitted that as he and his wife Emilia liked her so much they tried to feel that while there is life there is always hope! Una realized, despite his subtlety, that they thought she was damned. Shortly after this incident she was received into the Roman Catholic church.

Her stay in Florence lasted many months, and early in 1908, on her way back to England, she visited Troubridge in Malta. 'Don't fall out with dear Louise[35] over religion; remember she finds great consolation in it all,' Viola had warned Una earlier, adding, 'Of course, Capt. Troubridge would not take *that* tack.' It seems likely that Una told Troubridge of her conversion, and that his own conversion, defying family tradition, was a direct result; which may account for some of the Troubridge family's subsequent animosity towards Una.

On March 8th, 1908 Una attained her majority, but had nothing to inherit. Her only fortune consisted of her abilities, looks, and ambitions – their fulfilment was to take some unexpected twists and turns.

# 3

# Marriage
# (1908–12)

'Almost before I knew it I was grown-up . . .'[1] Una said in later
years; and Harry's death, changed family and financial circumstances, and her majority, combined at this time to precipitate her
fully into adulthood. This was the real thing, not a precocious
taste of it. She took a studio and continued her art work intermittently, but found it difficult to settle down to life in England after
her long sojourn in Florence.

   Shortly after her visit to Malta she became engaged to Captain
Troubridge, and went frequently to talk to her cousin Ladye[2]
about him. Whether this was because she was unsure about it, or
just bubbling over with an enthusiasm she wanted to share, can
only be surmised. He was forty-six, with three children then aged
twelve (Chatty), thirteen (Thomas) and fourteen (Mary), and
had been a widower for seven years. Una was twenty-one and
sensible of the difficult task she would be undertaking. Ladye
herself had married a man twenty-five years her senior[3] and was a
sympathetic listener and a wise counsellor, who took a great
interest in the engagement. Una had known Ladye since her
childhood and trusted her; and they shared many interests,
notably singing and a love of Italy, especially Florence. A versatile
woman, Ladye was at that time fast becoming close friends with

39

'John' Radclyffe-Hall[4] who lived near by in Shelley Court. Although both John and Una constantly visited Ladye at this time at her house in Ralston Street, they never met.

Feeling the call of Italy again Una went with Viola on a protracted holiday to Levanto during the summer. From the Hotel Savoia she wrote to Jacqueline Hope on August 25th, 1908: 'I've had a heavenly time at Levanto . . . a nice non-interfering chaperone and knew everyone but was independent which I liked, bathing twice a day . . . ' Then she adds with an almost schoolgirl enthusiasm: '. . . and Jacqueline I really swim just like a man now and used to go out in all the big seas and so lovely swimming through the breakers . . .' She describes her sun-worshipping: 'I'm so *brown* you wouldn't know me and my hair bleached by the sun as in it all day without hat or gloves and love it.' Every night there was: 'dancing – which you would have loved, with scores of young men over from Lysezia but I don't ever dance and the young men failed to interest me which was sad as I might otherwise have had a better time . . .'

It seems that young men always failed to interest her in any serious way, despite many admirers and some closer friendships, as with the Florentine Guilio Santasilia. She found maturity more attractive: she could trust herself to it and feel secure; the brashness and posturing of young men would have left her cold and critical. No definite date had then been set for the wedding, as she concludes her letter: 'I think we[5] shall begin to talk about going home in October but don't know. I can't bear the thought of leaving Italy and yet while we wonder I can't do serious work and I want to . . .'

In the event Una went to Venice where she met Troubridge, and they were married at the British Consulate on October 10th, honeymooning at the Pension Chiodo Toffoli. Unusually for a woman at the time, Una's 'rank or profession' was stated on the marriage certificate as 'Sculptor'. Whilst they were there she sketched Wanda Ulanowska, and even if this was not 'serious work' it does prove that she *was* still working even on honeymoon. Among the wedding presents was a very large Italian bed given by Mrs Dodge of the Villa Curonia in Florence, one of Una's friends; and Ladye gave Una a pair of silver shoe-buckles. Two and a half months later, on December 23rd, 1908, Viola married Maurice Woods in London; but this marriage, like Una's, was not to be a lasting one.

The question must be asked why, despite the disparities of age and circumstances, this marriage seemed viable to Una; why she so confidently took on, at twenty-one, a ready-made teenage family and a husband old enough to be her father. Was she simply swept off her feet by falling in love with a handsome older man, whose personal charms were much enhanced by a naval uniform? Or in terms of an unresolved 'Electra complex' was she unconsciously 'replacing' Harry in a more exclusive and intrinsically 'incestuous' relationship? Two small points hint in this direction: both had white hair, and there was only eight years' difference in their ages.

Una gives one rather flippant hint of her ostensible motives for marrying him: 'I met Capt. Troubridge, and married him, chiefly, it must be admitted, because I discerned in his snow-white hair and rather Terryish cast of countenance a likeness to the beloved and for ever unattainable Scarlet Pimpernel of my dreams.'[6] John stated later, on Una's authority, that it had been a 'marriage of affection'[7]; and certainly it was *not* a marriage of financial convenience, as has been erroneously suggested.[8] She seems to have been very happy to marry into this old and distinguished naval family, with several members of which she already had close, affectionate relations. She became Jacqueline's aunt by marriage.

Ernest Charles Thomas Troubridge was born in 1862, the third son of Colonel Sir Thomas St Vincent Troubridge, 3rd Baronet, a hero of the Battle of Inkerman, where he lost his right leg and left foot. Both the Colonel's father and grandfather were Admirals, and the latter, 'a close friend of Nelson', was created 1st Baronet in 1799 for services in the Mediterranean. The Troubridges had inter-married four times with the Quaker Gurneys[9] and with the Cochranes, another distinguished naval family who were also Earls of Dundonald.

Ernest's mother was Louisa Gurney, who died when he was five. His father also died a year later. His elder brother Thomas succeeded their father as 4th Baronet at the age of seven. The family of six young orphans was left to the care of old Daniel Gurney, their maternal grandfather, at Runcton, an old house of forty-three rooms, in Norfolk. 'Grandpapa', then seventy-seven, was soon christened 'the Ancient' by his grandchildren, who were cared for by 'Guddy' Gordon the housekeeper who had been there for fifty years, several maids, and Mrs Quick the cook who had served twenty years.

Ernest, his elder sister Laura said in her journal,[10] taught himself to read at three years old. She described him at eleven: 'He is . . . simply lovely. He has dark brown awfully thick *clots* of rather curly hair and a very white skin, red cheeks, blue eyes, a lovely little nose, angelic mouth, and an awfully pretty-shaped face – altogether the sort of face that one longs to kiss.' He was adored by his three sisters, as the tone of this entry shows, and is frequently referred to in Laura's journal in gushingly endearing terms; but occasionally a more detached note creeps in: 'He has no character hardly, he is entirely governed by Tom. He does *whatever* Tom does and has also *dreadful* manners . . . he is . . . selfish, but very affectionate.' He was also frequently angry and sulky, with a tendency to flamboyance. At thirteen he entered the navy as a cadet after coming first out of sixty-eight candidates in the entrance exam. After three years he was promoted to Midshipman aboard the *Temeraire* in the Mediterranean; three years later he was made acting sub-Lieutenant, Seamanship Class I, then full sub-Lieutenant aboard *Liberty*. The following year, 1884, he was promoted Lieutenant aboard *Agamemnon* in the China seas, and later that year was appointed to the Royal Yacht. In 1888, while serving aboard the *Sultan* in Crete, he saved the life of a young signalman who fell overboard in the dark from a torpedo boat at full speed, and was awarded the silver medal of the Royal Humane Society. That same year he was appointed Flag Lieutenant on the staff of Vice-Admiral Watson aboard *Bellerophon* in North America and the West Indies. When he docked at Halifax, Nova Scotia, he met and married the prettiest girl there, Edith Duffus, in 1891. In 1892 he was appointed to the Training Squadron aboard *Volage*; and in 1895 promoted to Commander, serving aboard *Revenge*, the Flagship of the Rear Admiral in the Mediterranean. In 1897–8 he took part in the international blockade of

Crete and in 1901 was promoted to Captain. Between 1901–4 he was Naval Attaché successively to the Courts of Vienna, Madrid and Tokyo; he was serving in Tokyo when the Russo-Japanese war broke out in 1904, and by special permission from the Japanese government embarked on one of the Japanese warships, being the only non-combatant European officer to witness the Battle of Chemulpo. He was able as a consequence to give the British Admiralty reports of the highest value in determining naval policy, and was made CMG and MVO. These reports excited great interest and enhanced his reputation. In 1900 his wife died, shortly after the birth of their fourth child, Edward Godfrey, who died on December 28th, 1899; his three surviving children being cared for by his sisters Helen and Amy.

Troubridge had been called 'the handsomest man in the British Navy'; and even his family admitted that he liked the ladies and had 'escapades'. He was an extrovert and generally popular, and 'his robust temperament and his genial character made him friends wherever he went . . .'[11] Given his nature, celibacy would not have agreed with him; nor would the 'wife in every port' traditional to sailors have been as rewarding as settled married life. Una was young, attractive, talented and sociable; and he would expect her to be an asset to his position as well as to his home. It would allow him once more to provide a family home for his children, with their new step-mother. He probably felt that a pretty young wife would enhance his own prestige. There were good solid reasons for marrying her, and in addition he may well have been in love with her.

What sort of a husband was he? It is clear that during the first months of her 'new life'[12] Una was still basking in the euphoria of her Venetian honeymoon, and was blissfully contented, as she had obviously told her friend Julia Neilson (now married to Fred Terry), who replied: 'how delighted I was to know you were married and so happy – splendid.'[13] The rocks which lay ahead were sufficiently well-hidden, and characteristically Una devoted herself to her new husband and way of life with that exclusive dedication she always brought to fresh enterprises. They had only been settled in Malta a matter of weeks when Troubridge was made Commodore 2nd Class at the Royal Naval Barracks at

Chatham, on December 22nd, 1908. He was a sailor who loved the sea and could not have been pleased by a land-based appointment. One of its few advantages would be a small financial one, for although his annual pay of £1,095 (a fortune compared to Harry Taylor's £400 p.a.) remained the same, he received additional 'table money' of £185.10s.

At Chatham Una lost all interest in her sculpture, and ceased to work regularly, almost sinking her identity in that of her husband. This was a great surprise to those who knew her well, and looking back on it herself later she was amazed at her own behaviour. She willingly subjugated her personality to Troubridge's, her needs and interests to his. This process was aided by an unfortunate occurrence in mid-1909, a near-fatal ectopic pregnancy which left her very weakened and confined for some months to the Commodore's House. Its long-term physical consequences were to include recurrent bouts of salpingitis, about which nothing could be done.

In her appearance she set about trying to look her husband's age, taking to sweeping black velvets and purple 'facecloths' in her altruistic effort. She did not realize until afterwards that this occasioned intense amusement in those who beheld it; and could have pitied her husband in retrospect – although he was a willing party to her tactics – for the ridicule she had brought upon him by her well-intentioned masquerade.

The monopolizing of Una's entire personality by Troubridge reached its culmination by the winter of 1909. The bad weather kept him more at home during his leisure hours and did not favour visitors, and Una herself, still convalescent, was barely able to go further than her own garden. Troubridge grew to take it as a matter of course that Una should be always there, awaiting his return, interested only in his interests, and scarcely having an opinion that was not a reflection of his own. Una herself did not foresee the consequences of this state of affairs.

Such a self-eclipse is in the nature of things temporary, and in Una's case a resurrection of individuality and activity was inevitable. Two things helped to bring this about: an improvement in her health, and an unexpected turn of the naval wheel early in 1910 which took Troubridge to a London-based appointment as ADC and Private Secretary to Mr McKenna, the First Lord of the

Admiralty. Just prior to this, whilst still at Chatham, Una had started exhibiting again, being registered in the *Dictionary of British Artists* as a sculptor; and in addition had written to Lanteri for a testimony to her busts and figures, which he duly wrote, in French as usual.

On their return to London her resumption of mental independence and activity really got under way, as she took an interest in her old pursuits. Taking up music again she started daily singing lessons, and made new friends. Troubridge's complete monopoly of her time and energy began its wane, and brought about the first crisis of her marriage. The consequences of those early months when she had allowed him to monopolize her to the exclusion of all other interests now became apparent: not unnaturally perhaps, having become accustomed to her undivided attention, Troubridge disliked her following other interests with sustained energy or enthusiasm.

Una again went to Ladye to discuss this new situation and its complications; and Ladye, aware of all the circumstances, would often remind her that it was all her own doing, saying, 'You mustn't forget, Una, that you yourself accustomed him, when you first married, to your having no occupation but him.'[14] It is small comfort to know that you are the author of your own distress! Another grave consequence of the move to London was the proximity of the very large Troubridge family. Ernest's three sisters ('all of whom were in love with him,' his great-nephew[15] told me), who had loved his first wife Edi,[16] never liked Una. To them she was younger, unconventional, strangely dressed, and they resented her. To her they were stuffy, irritating, sanctimonious, and part of that 'tyranny of kinship'[17] to which she was now, for the first time, subject.

They were then living at 107 St George's Square, and with them were Troubridge's three children, now aged fourteen, fifteen and sixteen. They were too young to remember their mother clearly, having been four, five and six when she died, but they were old enough to resent Una being in her stead. She tried to be kind and understanding, and was interested enough in them to paint them all in 1910, the year of her very fine statuette of Troubridge. (See plate no. 4.) Nevertheless they never liked her, and later Chatty (Charlotte Edith Annette) accused Una of spending their dress allowance on her own wardrobe. They portrayed her to their friends and descendants as the classic wicked step-mother, though clear reasons for this do not emerge: 'My mother and my aunt didn't like her,' I was told. 'She was heartily disliked by my mother's family.'[18] Tom, the younger brother of the present Baronet, Sir Peter Troubridge, who often went to stay with 'the aunts' (Mary and Chatty) as a boy, remembers that they had 'cordially disliked' Una. His father, Thomas, Ernest's only surviving son, used to call his first cousin, Jacqueline Hope-Nicholson, 'old Jack-pots' because she was sympathetic to Una.

This problem with her step-children vexed Una, and added another problem area to her marriage; then in February 1910 she became pregnant again. This time it was a normal pregnancy, though she was unwell during its progress.

Lord Fisher, one of Troubridge's naval colleagues, wrote to Una on March 23rd, 1910: 'What a nice letter you have written me from a bed of sickness . . . don't fail to write and tell me when it will be convenient to stay here . . . Yours till the Angels smile on us, Fisher.'

Five months later her father's old friend Sir Edward Poynter wrote to her from Como:[19]

> Dear Una,
>     I am longing to hear how you are and whether your stay by the sea has done you good. I thought when I saw you that you were looking stronger, but you are so brave and make so little of your ills that it is difficult to know how you really are . . .

Whether she 'made little' of her ills to Troubridge, and how sympathetic he was, is a matter of conjecture; as are her feelings at the prospect of motherhood. She may well have felt that a child of her own would strengthen her position, and deflect some of Troubridge's paternal attention from his own to *their* child. On November 5th, 1910 Andrea Theodosia was born. She was to develop Troubridge's looks but Una's personality. Una was especially gratified to find that the child had a slight cleft in the chin, a feature she had always thought very attractive.

For Troubridge this was his fifth child, so some of the novelty of fatherhood had long worn off; and at forty-eight, with his other children nearly adults, he may not have been exactly overjoyed to hear again 'the patter of tiny feet'. Andrea was quickly called 'the Cub' or 'Cubby', and the hour in the evening when they had her to themselves was called by Una 'Cubby time'. Although Troubridge, like many men, was not very interested in small babies, finding them more interesting as they get older, Una's maternal instinct seems to have been at its strongest during Andrea's earliest years. Even when Andrea was seven Una was said to have 'an unreasonable tendency . . . to morbid anxiety where the child is concerned . . .'[20] These facts must be balanced against later Troubridge family allegations of neglect and lack of maternal feeling on Una's part.

On March 6th, 1911 Troubridge was promoted to Rear Admiral, his annual salary remaining unchanged but with 'table money' increased to a maximum of £1,642 p.a. in addition. He remained Private Secretary to McKenna, and then to Winston Churchill when he became First Lord of the Admiralty in October 1911. 'Rear Admiral Ernest Thomas Troubridge CMG MVO and Mrs Troubridge' were duly invited to the Coronation of King George V and Queen Mary at Westminster Abbey on June 22nd, 1911, which must have pleased Una as she kept the large, elaborate invitation afterwards in her scrap-book.

In these London years one of the 'tyrannies of kinship' Una had to endure was the annual Christmas dinner at her sister-in-law's, where there would be eighteen seated at a large round table, seven adults and eleven children. She describes one of these occasions under a thinly veiled fiction, where 'Henry' and 'Elsie' are undoubtedly Troubridge and Una herself:

[there were] critical asides: 'What a pity it is that Elsie is bringing up that child so badly – but then I always knew when Henry married her . . . Poor darling Henry, and he thinks her an angel! . . .'

Henry is supposed to adore his sisters, anyone would think so to see him with them, jocund and jovial and understanding. Only Elsie the wife of his bosom knows of the scene that preceded this family dinner: 'I tell you, Elsie, I'm damned if I'll go; they treat you like hell and they bore me stiff – let's have our Xmas all to ourselves . . . or ask someone lovely that we really care for . . .'[21]

This shows a division in Troubridge himself between new and old loyalties, between personal will and corporate expectation; and rather than break with family tradition he is willing to be hypocritical himself and to subject his young wife to discomfort and antipathy. This loyalty to the family also shows itself in his 'choice' of career, and in the names given to his first four children. This was one of his weaknesses. One wonders whether he would have defended Una against direct criticism as distinct from the veiled variety. She had few friends amongst the Troubridges, most of whom closed ranks against her. She found herself in an isolated position, and at many disadvantages.

Always a favourite with older men, she kept up her correspondence with Lord Fisher, at that time very pro-Troubridge in his sentiments. Fisher described Troubridge to Una as 'your dear husband' and 'a good friend in adversity'. At times the letters became mildly but always respectfully flirtatious: '. . . *You are a philosopher after my own heart!* Let Troubridge take care I don't elope with you!'[22]

Fisher, aware of Una's keen opera interests, urged her to come to Venice for the music; and 'let his hair down' a little on official matters. In a letter from the Excelsior, Naples, dated December 28th, 1911, marked PLEASE BURN at the top in capital letters, he confided: 'I had a hectic time in my two visits to Winston . . . we moved on here as Winston intimated another pilgrimage and I said I'd see him d——d first! . . . I think you ought to send me one of your lively letters soon and your photograph . . . Yrs. till we part at the Pearly Gates. (You'll get in all right – I shan't!) Fisher.' Winston Churchill had just been made First Lord of the Admiralty and Fisher was First Sea Lord; but relations between them were to change, to Troubridge's detriment, within six months.

In January 1912 Troubridge was appointed Chief of War Staff, after four months as Churchill's Private Secretary; and spent all of

48

that year organizing this newly formed department. Rumblings of international discontent had made it necessary. In May 1912 Churchill arranged a meeting of the Committee of Imperial Defence in Malta. This committee included Lord Kitchener, Fisher, and Troubridge. A full inspection was made of the island and the debate which followed at Valletta was a heated one. Churchill wanted all the Mediterranean battleships in home waters to defend Britain; but Troubridge argued strongly that Malta and the Mediterranean squadron must be retained. Churchill was supported in his arguments by Fisher, against Troubridge; and although Troubridge's viewpoint swayed the decision to keep the squadron, he had crossed swords with a powerful man who did not forget such things. Two years later, in altered circumstances, Churchill was to have his revenge.

In November 1912 long-standing step-mother–daughter dissension reached an impasse, and Troubridge asked his sister Laura Hope if she would take his daughter Mary (then aged eighteen) to live with her and Jacqueline at Tite Street, as 'she and Una are like oil and vinegar.'[23] This not proving a satisfactory arrangement, Troubridge took 1 Durham Place, not far from St George's Square, for his daughters and two maiden sisters. By this time Tom, the son, was in the navy following in his father's footsteps, and was to serve with him in Malta. This solution was the best for everybody, and a blessed relief to Una who had done her best but never secured the affection of her step-children, although their resentment did not extend to Andrea.

After four years of marriage and the altruistic effort to be what other people wanted her to be, Una had managed to re-emerge to full individuality whilst remaining relatively successful as a wife and mother. She had had her failures, and made her mistakes; but she had her husband's measure, and his affection. 'Cubby' was a source of pride and pleasure, and she now had her marital home to herself. The future seemed secure, its main uncertainty Troubridge's possible future appointments and their relocations accordingly. In a general way she was happy enough, her discontents vague, undefined. Other naval wives were perhaps not the most interesting of people, but she had her art and her music; and life in the London she knew, where she could meet family and friends, was better than that of a naval station.

She never anticipated that within less time than she had already been married, her life was to be altered utterly and irrevocably; the old order swept away by a new.

# 4

# The Melting-Pot
# (1913–15)

On January 6th, 1913, Rear Admiral Troubridge was appointed Commander of the 1st Cruiser Squadron, aboard the Mediterranean Flagship, HMS *Defence*. The squadron's base was Malta, and for Troubridge it must have been a welcome return; in addition it was the end of four years of being land-based. There would be exercises and manoeuvres at sea, patrolling, inspecting. For Una it meant going back to a naval stâtion, with entertaining, social obligations, the company of other naval wives. She was less tolerant than average of the social round, resenting inroads into her private time, and never tolerating fools gladly. As wife of the Squadron Commander it would mean many new duties.

Una was already showing signs of marital stress in the form of nausea, frequent headaches and insomnia. Before they returned to Malta she consulted a bright young psychotherapist and neurologist by the name of Hugh Crichton-Miller. He specialized in psychosomatic disorders, particularly 'Neurasthenia', a fashionable word at the time to describe a state of excessive fatigueability, physical and mental, of unknown aetiology. He had a profound, almost hypnotic influence on women patients, charged exorbitant fees, and was later to found the Tavistock Clinic, among others. She first went to Crichton-Miller on January 10th, explained her

*Genesis (1887–1916)*

'symptoms' and noted in her diary: 'He said he would cure me if I would stay in England and give him time . . .'

She took Troubridge to see him, and they discussed it and decided to accept his help, and made their plans accordingly. On the 13th she went to Crichton-Miller again, who 'talked psychology'; then the next day, the 14th, she was hypnotized for the first time, and 'felt much better and more cheerful all day.'[1] Troubridge left for Malta on January 18th, leaving Una and Andrea behind. Una saw him off, then went home to lunch. Reading between the lines, she was not heartbroken to be left alone in London. She divided her days between socializing with Viola and Maurice, her mother, Laura and Jacqueline Hope, doing a drypoint etching called *The Wicked Voice*, and frequent, almost daily, visits to Crichton-Miller. She also read his book *Hypnotism and Disease*, published the previous year. On January 23rd she recorded: 'Crichton-Miller – *epoch making visit!* Wrote to Zyp[2] all about it . . .' Exactly what this visit revealed she does not say, but it may well be that Miller had discussed 'inversion' with her and that she had gained spontaneous insight into her own latent nature. Certainly they did discuss it at some time. He taught her to hypnotize herself, which she did successfully on February 2nd, making herself light-headed. Despite the obvious dangers of such a procedure, its object was to relieve tension and produce thought-control by auto-suggestion.

She had Andrea with her, went to the opera often, and seems to have been generally happy. She wrote frequently and warmly to Troubridge from a safe distance, and he at first replied in like, sympathetic vein: '. . . two letters from Malta made me *so so* happy . . .' she recorded on February 3rd.

Diaghilev's Russian Ballet was in London at the time, and Una had haunted Covent Garden and made many drawings of Vaslav Nijinsky. Through the daughter of General Sir Ian Hamilton, Una was introduced to Nijinsky's instructor Enrico Cecchetti, and obtained his permission to attend his classes in the Drill Hall in Goodge Street. Nijinsky took his daily lessons there, and consented to sit for Una in his rest intervals. She began sculpting him as Debussy's Faun (see plate no. 8) on February 5th, without Diaghilev's knowledge as he invariably refused to allow such sittings. Nijinsky was very co-operative and kind to her, even allowing her to stand in the wings before his stage entrances. She spent many hours and days sketching for and making the bust, initially in wax then casts in marble, bronze and clay.

Una started going to hypnotherapy classes at Crichton-Miller's clinic, Bowden House, in Harrow, and read much psychology including William James (the brother of Henry), whose writings later inspired the 'stream-of-consciousness' writers. Her sister Viola was not happy in her marriage to Maurice Woods, and Una took her along to see Crichton-Miller, who began to treat her as well.

Troubridge had taken the weeks away from his wife in good part, and sent her some 'lovely' earrings and a bracelet for her birthday on March 8th; but three days later Una recorded in her diary: 'Got unhappy letter from Zyp and went to Miller about it . . .' and later that same day: 'Afraid another unhappy letter from Zyp – wrote to him . . .' Whatever it was blew over, for on the 15th she: 'found happy letter at last!' Another letter on the 17th was such that she: 'Settled to go to Malta and return later . . .' cutting short her treatment with Crichton-Miller.

On March 23rd she sailed for Calais, leaving the Cub with Norah the maid, and stayed overnight in Paris. The next day she went to Rome via Geneva and Pisa; then to Naples on the 25th, finally arriving in Malta on the 27th, where Troubridge met her in his barge and took her to the Osborne Hotel, where he was staying until their house was ready for occupation.

They had not met for over two months. Whether their reunion was happy is not clear, but they celebrated it by an evening at the opera.

Una was immediately plunged into the hectic social round: the opera, dinner parties, luncheons and teas, guests and visits. Troubridge spent a lot of time playing tennis and golf and going to the races. On April 8th she and Troubridge talked over plans, but left things pending, with Andrea still in England. Una began to develop her symptoms again, particularly headaches and fatigue. On April 11th she was: 'In bed all day –' then 'up for dinner party [at] Admiralty House.'

She took up her singing again with new vigour, joining the professionals at the Malta Opera House. The following diary entry is typical of her days in Malta: 'Sang with Quarti [an Italian tenor] in Opera House . . . worked at etchings. Lunch aboard [HMS] Defence. Drove to Marsa for tea. Evening opera – Carmen.' There was little time for herself, or for home-life; the social round dictated every part of the day. No wonder she exclaimed with relief, and by implication exasperation with the opposite: '. . . we spent for once a quiet evening!' (April 14th).

On the 25th she dined at the Palace to meet the Duke and Duchess of Norfolk; and on the 26th went to see a polo match between the army and the navy . . . and so it went on. On April 29th the programme for the 21st Grand Annual Concert at the Theatre Royal, Malta, included:

> Songs. Madam Butterfly's farewell to her child. Puccini.
> Annie Laurie.
> by Mrs Troubridge . . .
>
> Duet . . . Madam Butterfly. Puccini.
> Mrs Troubridge & Signor A. Quarti.

The *Daily Malta Chronicle* recorded the event several days later:

> The honours of the evening were apportioned in large measure to Mrs Troubridge who invaded the hearts of her hearers in a succession of achievements which dethroned each other in grandeur of perfection. 'Madam Butterfly's farewell to her child' and the old-time ever-favourite song 'Annie Laurie' were replete with pathos and impressiveness which embellished a cultured voice of remarkable range and sweetness . . .

Another paper said of the same occasion: 'It was the first public appearance of Mrs Troubridge, and her rendering of "Madam Butterfly to her Child" followed by "Annie Laurie" was the signal for such a demonstration as has rarely been witnessed before in Malta.' Una was evidently pleased with this journalistic acclaim as she kept the cuttings in her album; and continued to nurture dreams of an operatic career.

On May 1st she went to Cooks to see about a ticket back to England, but on the 7th, after packing, she: 'Dined on board [i.e.

*Defence*] and decided *not to go to England* . . .' and went early to Cooks on the 8th to return her ticket, wiring Norah to bring the Cub to Malta. What made her change her mind at the last minute is not clear, but it may be that Troubridge managed to persuade her. Crichton-Miller wrote to Una later: 'when you decided not to come home it was just because you felt so much confidence in yourself and your own health that no further treatment seemed necessary at the time . . .'[3] but that seems too simplistic a view.

Andrea left London on May 17th and arrived on May 25th. On May 23rd Una and Troubridge had tea at Marsa with the Churchills and the Asquiths. On June 3rd Andrea became 'seedy', then 'ill', then 'very ill', with a serious intestinal illness of which she nearly died. Una's tendency to panic when the child was ill came naturally to the fore, and when she was finally pronounced convalescent after three weeks Una took her away, although Troubridge himself was 'not well and lying up'. They went from Syracuse to Rome, Milan, and on to Montreux. Two days later Troubridge wired to say he was well again and leaving for England.

A week later: 'Zyp wired us to come to England and I answered Yes.'[4] Troubridge met them at Dover and they went to Eaton Terrace. The next day Una took Andrea to a Dr Still and Troubridge went to Devonport. Una later went again to Crichton-Miller; sang at her mother's party; and continued her Nijinsky bust, going again to watch him at the Drill Hall and at Drury Lane. She worked each day at the bust, sometimes until 3.30 in the morning, taking advantage of Troubridge's absence. After nearly a month he returned, on August 4th, and they stayed at Harrow to continue Una's treatment; taking their annual holiday from the 18th at Hunstanton in Norfolk, the Troubridges' family home in succession to Runcton. On September 1st Una saw Troubridge off at Paddington, returning with Andrea to Harrow. On the 15th she took Andrea and her step-daughters Mary and Chatty to London; and on the 22nd she went to Columbia Building and made a test record. What the outcome of this was we are not told, but it is another indication of the seriousness of her interest in a musical career.

One day during this time she went to an afternoon reception in one of the old houses in Cheyne Walk, meeting there her cousin

Ladye and her friend 'John' Radclyffe-Hall. The three of them sat and talked in the garden, then they drove Una home to St George's Square. Of this first meeting with John Una was to remember nothing at all; it made no impact and had no sequel. As she said of it later, 'nothing warned us of what the future held in store.'[5]

She wrote long letters to 'Zyp', and on October 10th recorded in her diary, 'Our Wedding Day 1908', which although recorded as a fact rather than as a sentiment, implies that she is not altogether unhappy to record her fifth anniversary. He sent her buckles as a present.

On October 18th the Nijinsky 'Faun' was finished and Lanteri, her old professor, came to see it. On the 23rd Una recorded: 'Packed. To Miller's for last treatment, making 57 treatments in all. Evening – Nanny, Cub, Chatty and I left for Malta.'

They arrived on October 29th, were met as usual by Troubridge's barge, and went to tea at Marsa. The normal social round had begun again. Troubridge was away at sea for two spells of ten days each during November, but the routine continued in his absence: the races, many afternoon calls, singing practice . . . On his return things went on as before. The widening gulf between Una and Troubridge was becoming clearer, and she began to realize that his nature and interests were incompatible with hers. One day serves to illustrate their divergence: on December 21st she had singing lessons, a walk with Cubby, a matinée of *Rigoletto*, and he played golf all day. They were sharing less and less, and there were occasions when Troubridge slept aboard *Defence*.

They had moved from the Osborne Hotel in Valletta to 'our house' at 22 Piazza Maggiore, and kept servants, a coachman and their own coach. Una's life-style was now more like that of her richer Handcock relatives than it had ever been, due to Troubridge's high income and the many 'perks' of life in Malta, yet she was not happy. She was well provided for, and had social status; but she was not free. She had responsibilities and obligations which often prevented her from being herself; the role in which she was cast frustrating many aspects of her highly evolved and individual personality. Troubridge treated her as a showpiece, but was not attentive to her real needs. She threw herself into her opera singing, having daily lessons from Salvati who was in Malta with the professional opera. She also wrote to a Minnie Stevens for advice about her singing and received the reply that 'you yourself must work out your own salvation . . . must work out the problems by yourself . . .' It was an answer which she would have to apply to *all* her problems.

She was still writing to Crichton-Miller about her headaches, and he astutely assured her, 'I doubt very much whether they are entirely due to the spectacles.' They began when she got up in the morning and sometimes lasted all day. Viola, it appeared, was having similar problems and was 'not quite certain whether she [was] going to be cured or not,' Crichton-Miller informed Una, doubtless to make her feel less alone in her predicament. He had, he said, had a talk with Viola's 'surprising husband who is an odd contrast in every single particular to yours,' adding as an after-thought, 'I wonder if two sisters . . . ever married men so astonishingly different as your respective husbands.' Viola had by this time had a son, Oliver Woods, who was more or less Andrea's age; but she was finding marriage no easier than Una.

In late November Crichton-Miller wrote to Una referring to conversations earlier in the year saying, 'I am so glad you "got light" upon the knotty point that made your last days in town so turbulent,' and that he looked forward 'to hearing . . . that your mind has been at rest on the subject.' The 'subject' referred to is tantalizingly obscure, but its effect on Una was obviously crucial.

The year 1913 closed with an eleven-item opera programme at 22 Piazza Maggiore, Una's own party at which she inaugurated the practice of engaging the opera singers to sing for a fee. She, of course, sang with them, both arias and duets, and the band of HMS *Defence* was borrowed for the occasion. She finished the old year feeling 'very seedy' as a result!

In early 1914, as her diary records, she was frequently feeling 'seedy' and took to her bed; and when she records her husband's departures one senses her relief. When he had gone she got up and carried on the usual social round, particularly opera-going; and wrote her diary in Italian, partly because she was learning it, and partly, one suspects, so that Troubridge, if he found it, would be unable to read it. Yet its contents are fairly innocuous, with many references to sports, opera and the movements of HMS *Defence*; although it is clear that Una is skating faster and faster on thinner and thinner ice in order to escape painful facts about her life and herself.

Crichton-Miller wrote in March, in response to one of Una's letters: 'Well, the devils are on you, are they? I am frightfully sorry to hear it – is it worse than nausea? It means that you are repressing some big complexes . . . you remember that I nearly finished you off before you left by suggesting one possible factor.'

She was experiencing 'distress not only physical but also mental'. Viola was also going through a period that was 'horribly tragic' as she was being 'sacrificed and broken to a thing that is all brain and no heart' – presumably her husband.

Exactly what it was that so 'nauseated' Una that she experienced it as a physical symptom she may not have fully known herself; but reading between the lines of the situation, she was becoming steadily more alienated from Troubridge and the life she had to lead with him. There is a suggestion of an increasing sexual dysfunction, and an attempt to deflect this with a range of psychosomatic symptoms. An invalid ceases to be a sexual object for the period of their invalidity, and becomes instead an object of care and concern. It was a way of dealing with difficulties which she found rewarding, and comfortingly escapist. When away from Una, Troubridge was not averse to extra-marital adventures; and she was to discover later that due to one of these, he had passed on to her a venereal disease.

On May 1st the 22nd Grand Annual Concert took place at the Theatre Royal and the programme again included airs by Una and duets by Una and Salvati. Advance notice of this concert advertised: 'The entertainment to be given under distinguished patronage, will have its attraction in the appearance of Mrs Troubridge . . .' After the event, the *Daily Malta Chronicle* recorded:[6] 'Mrs. Troubridge who was received with applause, gave brilliant emphasis to the beautiful airs . . . which were realised in dramatic power and touching tenderness . . . Mrs. Troubridge and Sigr. Salvati . . . sang with exquisite effects duets from . . . Donizetti.

In response to prolonged applause, which repeated acknowledgements failed to appease, the duet . . . was repeated.'

Despite this obvious success her dreams of an operatic career were fast receding: it began to be apparent that permanent harm had been done to her voice by one of her trainers. She was deeply disappointed. Troubridge, by way of 'consolation', said to her: 'Never mind, I am just as pleased that you should only sing for me and our friends, I never have really wished you to work at anything that would occupy you away from me. I would much rather you only did things as a diversion for yourself and me, and were not engrossed in anything.'[7] He was of a dominating disposition, which Una always reacted strongly against, as she had with Marguerite Michel; and she resented being treated as an adjunct of her husband rather than as an equally valid person in her own right.

In July Una and Andrea went to Florence with the Salvatis and stayed at Berchielli's Hotel; photographs show her looking strained and unhappy. Then in August she went to Levanto with friends Leo and Eva Rigoletti, and Ninetta Massola, a relation of May and Cencio. Andrea, aged nearly four, was photographed on the beach happily playing with the younger men or being hoisted up on their shoulders: a marked contrast to what she was used to with a father who, old enough to be her grandfather, took comparatively little interest in her. Una herself began to look more relaxed.

At the outbreak of war in August 1914, the First Cruiser Squadron was ordered to watch the entrance to the Adriatic where the whole Austrian fleet lay before their anticipated entry into the war. The German Commander in the Mediterranean, Admiral Souchon, had two fast new ships, the battlecruiser *Goeben* and a light cruiser, *Breslau*. He received a wireless message from the German Admiralty in the early hours of August 4th telling him to proceed at once to Constantinople as a treaty had been concluded with Turkey on August 3rd, but this order was immediately cancelled. Souchon decided to proceed towards the open sea. Both the French and British Admiralties were carefully watching the *Goeben* and *Breslau* as potential threats to the French troop transports of over 80,000 men. Troubridge's brief was to follow and intercept these ships and if possible prevent their reaching open sea; but he had also received instructions via Sir Berkeley Milne, Admiral of the Mediterranean Fleet, but emanating from Winston Churchill, the First Lord of the Admiralty, that the forces in the Mediterranean were not to be brought to battle by a superior enemy force. The *Goeben* had a speed of nearly six knots above that of the cruiser squadron, and an effective gun range of almost double theirs. Both these facts made it difficult and dangerous to engage her; for if she turned, the squadron would be sitting targets within range of her guns, whilst she was outside their own. Troubridge was astute enough to realize that without favourable weather conditions such as mist or fog, or very narrow straits, he could not get the ships within range of his guns. They shadowed the two German ships during the night, but rather than risk the squadron, Troubridge allowed them to pass unmolested from Messina to the Dardanelles. It has been said that 'No other single exploit of the war cast so long a shadow upon the world as [this] voyage . . .'[8] which brought about a chain of death and destruction.

On August 18th Admiral Milne, Troubridge's immediate superior, was recalled to London; and although the Admiralty endorsed his conduct 'in all respects' he was retired from his post. Three weeks after the 'crucial misfortune'[9] of the ships' escape, Troubridge was also called to London. He and Una travelled on Sunday September 20th, arriving at Southampton at 8 a.m. and at the Charing Cross Hotel at 11 a.m. Andrea had been left with friends in Florence, where she was to stay for the next few months while things were sorted out. It was a very worrying time, and within a week of being back in London Una was again consulting Crichton-Miller. She relied on him for moral support as much as anything, although anxiety always produced an exacerbation of her 'symptoms'. On September 21st, 1914 the Secretary of the Admiralty announced, via the Press Bureau, that 'Rear-Admiral E. C. T. Troubridge has been recalled to England from the Mediterranean in order that an inquiry may be held into the circumstances leading to the escape of the *Goeben* and *Breslau* from Messina Straits . . .' The preparations for this inquiry took up most of October, and Troubridge himself, mindful of the possible slur on his distinguished naval family, requested a court martial to clear his name.

Una confided her fears to her old friend May Massola, who replied from Levanto in October: '. . . so awfully sorry you and your man are having worry and trouble . . . I had seen mention of it in the English paper – then there were your photos in the *Tatler* . . . I am glad to think that at least in London you are in the midst of friends and not isolated as in Malta . . .'

On November 4th Una recorded succinctly in her diary: 'Zyp left 10pm for Weymouth,' and on Thursday 5th: '10am. Court Martial began. Cubby's 4th birthday. In bed.'

The court, consisting of nine Admirals and senior Captains of the fleet, sat at Portland and was held in secret on the insistence of the Admiralty. Troubridge was assisted in his defence by Sir Leslie Scott, KC, MP; the charge against him being that he had failed to pursue the *Goeben* and the *Breslau*. (Though not part of the 'charge' there is a heavy innuendo of 'cowardice in the face of the enemy' of which Troubridge would have been keenly aware.) The court sat each day, including Sunday, until Monday November 9th. During this time Una was alone at home, without even the consolation of Andrea; and her diary entries, in English for the first time since January, are brief and repetitive: 'Court Martial all day. In bed.' She had taken to her bed as usual in times of stress, and remained there until the 13th.

On Monday 9th she recorded: 'Court Martial till 8pm. Zyp fully and honourably acquitted. In bed.' and on the 10th: 'Zyp home 12.50 pm. In bed. Telegrams and people.'

On the 12th she recorded: 'In bed. Announcement evening papers.'

The headlines read: 'Admiral Troubridge Acquitted. Result of Court Martial,' and continued, 'The result of this inquiry . . . will be as satisfactory to the country as it must be to Rear-Admiral Troubridge himself that his conduct has been vindicated by a competent and impartial tribunal . . .'

Una was as relieved as Troubridge, and at last on the 13th she records: 'Got up. Morning papers.' She read the various press accounts, as they were favourable. May Massola wrote to her shortly afterwards: 'Really dear, I can't say how glad both Cencio and I are to know that your worry is ended and that your man has come out well – what I want to impress upon you is our delight at the good news and hopes of your speedy convalescence . . .'

But the difficulties were not over. After his acquittal Troubridge naturally expected either to return to his command or to receive another one, but nothing happened and 1914 closed very uncertainly indeed. One of its few personal delights for Una had been the display of her bust of Nijinsky at a big international exhibition in Venice.

The first four months of 1915 passed without any new command for Troubridge; but in late January Andrea returned from Florence, so that at least they were united again as a family. Churchill, still First Lord of the Admiralty, refused to see Troubridge although they had previously worked together so closely. Although it was his orders which Troubridge had obeyed in not pursuing the *Goeben*, Churchill was deeply angered at the outcome, for as Asquith said earlier, 'Winston with all his war paint on . . . is longing for a sea fight to sink the *Goeben.*' Four times it had escaped, and although only one of these concerned Troubridge, Churchill was not in a forgiving mood.

As Una wrote later[10] it was not 'until it was widely mooted that Lord Curzon purposed at question time to ask the House why a distinguished Flag Officer, tried and fully exonerated and acquitted by a court martial . . . was not being employed in time of war,' that Churchill at last sent for Troubridge. On his return from this interview he told Una that, 'he had found the First Lord at his desk writing, and had not been greeted or asked to sit down for an appreciable time. Winston Churchill then addressed him . . . "Troubridge, I have an appointment to offer you, but as it is in the forefront of the battle, I think you may not care to accept it." '[11]

Una asked Troubridge what reply he had made to such an insult, and he answered, 'I simply told the First Lord that I was ready to accept any appointment that would be useful to my country in time of war . . .' otherwise he preserved a disciplined and dignified silence. This treatment must have hurt his sense of professional pride; but an even more bitter blow was that he was not – then or later – to have another sea command. Instead he was sent as Head of the British Naval Mission to Serbia, with naval forces and guns based in Belgrade to keep the Danube open for the allies.

He went in May and Una was left alone in London with Andrea. It was understood that, transport and conditions permitting, she would join him there later. She was living in a small house at 40 Bryanston Street, Marble Arch, and to occupy herself as well as to do something useful for the 'war effort' set about organizing a British Eastern Auxiliary Hospital in Belgrade. The first contingency of helpers left London in early April and arrived in Belgrade at the end of the month. Una was organizing the delivery of supplies through the Director of Transports at the Admiralty, who wrote to tell her that the 'case of gauze wire' she wished to send to Serbia could go to Salonika on June 3rd. On June 4th her old friend Lord Fisher wrote from HMS *Iron Duke* sending a £1 donation for her hospital; on May 31st she had written to the Admiralty setting out the financial position of the hospital unit, and asking for a grant towards its maintenance. The Commissioners were 'unable to accede to' her request, but offered six shillings a day for any naval officer or rating given hospital accommodation in Serbia, provided that 'the expression *Naval* Hospital is not used,' or any reference made to naval personnel serving in Serbia.

Her Tealdi cousins wrote to her: 'How perfectly splendid your hospital work is! I knew you would do it well when . . . you were undertaking it, for whatever you do you do it well . . . and give it heart and soul.'

Although busy with this project, Una could not deny to herself that she was both lonely and desperately unhappy, and that the 'heart and soul' had gone out of her marriage. Whilst Troubridge's troubles were at the forefront of their lives she had sympathized, and supported him, but now that he was abroad and she had time to take stock of herself and her feelings, she realized that her marriage had been a great disappointment. It had been an 'altruistic effort' that had not worked. There were too many incompatibilities and the gulf between them had widened. He had made her unhappy, and as she was to state later, she 'could not write in defence of him as a husband.'[12]

One of Troubridge's descendants told me that he thought this had been 'A marriage of sexual attraction which went sour,' and as far as Troubridge is concerned this may well have been true; but from Una's point of view, it had been more of a 'therapeutic' marriage which had gone wrong – an attempt to compensate for the deep emotional loss of her father. On this basis, psychologically, it was bound to fail, as no human being can 'replace' another, and certainly not in a vastly different kind of relationship; and a woman 'marrying' her father invokes an automatic incest taboo. Quite apart from this complicated substrata, her marriage had neither fully engaged her passions nor utilized her intelligence, education, or powers of devotion and dedication. She *had* used her social and linguistic abilities, and had continued to sculpt and to sing, but overall more of her was frustrated than was fulfilled.

At twenty-eight, she had a husband of fifty-two in whom she was emotionally disinterested, and who was many miles away; a daughter of four and a half of whom she was fond; a trained mind, a trained voice, and an as yet untapped reservoir of deep feelings. Almost as a symbol of her desire for independence she cut off her abundant hair to a short, page-boy style, and reverted to a practical, slightly more tailored style of dress, though not as extreme as in her youth.

More out of duty than desire to be with her husband, Una had made inquiries about travel to Belgrade. She was unhappy in London but hardly because of Troubridge's absence, and was deeply reluctant to go to Belgrade. On July 30th a letter to Una from the Admiralty referred to the 'provision of a passage' to Serbia . . . but she was never to take it, or to see the hospital unit she had been instrumental in founding.

She had been seeing some friends and relations in order to take her mind off her problems and to get out of herself; and feeling depressed and intensely lonely she accepted an invitation from her cousin Lady Clarendon, Ladye's sister, to have tea with her in Cambridge Square on August 1st, a day which was to change the course of her life.

# 5

# The Game
# of Love
# (1915–16)

In significant relationships the first meeting tends to make a deep impact and to be vividly remembered. August 1st, 1915 remained enshrined in Una's memory, and was afterwards celebrated as an anniversary, being carefully circled in her diary for many years. Una and 'John' Radclyffe-Hall were introduced by Emmy Clarendon at her party, and although it was actually their second meeting, it was the first time that they 'realised one another's existence'.[1] They and their circumstances had changed in the two years since 1913: Una's marriage had broken down, and John, though devoted to Ladye, was erotically disinterested in her and exercising a roving eye.

Each was immediately struck by the other, and if 'love at first sight' is possible, this was one of its instances. Una was to recall this meeting thirty years later, after John's death:

I can still see John as I saw her on that day, as clearly as if she stood before me now . . . She was then 34 years of age and very good indeed to look upon . . . her complexion was clear and pale, her eyebrows and very long lashes nearly as golden as her hair and her eyes a clear grey blue, beautifully set and with a curiously fierce, noble expression . . . Her mouth was sensitive

and not small . . . [she had] the most infectious, engaging and
rather raffish smile . . . Her face and the line of her jaw were an
unusually pure oval . . . she had . . . an aquiline nose with
delicate, tempered wings to the nostrils . . . it was not the
countenance of a young woman but of a very handsome young
man . . . she was only of medium height but so well pro-
portioned that she looked taller than she was and the very
simple tailor-made clothes which she wore . . . fostered the
illusion. Her hands, and here again they were not feminine
hands, were quite beautiful and so were her feet. Altogether her
appearance was calculated to arouse interest. It immediately
aroused mine . . .[2]

Here at last, in the flesh, was her 'Principal Boy': the strange,
compelling combination of the masculine principle in the handsome, androgynous body, for Una so emotionally and erotically
right. But as well as this chemical attraction there was a rapport,
and

> Some compelling force of will,
> Sprung from sympathies complete –[3]

The attraction, Una knew, was mutual; and she was quite aware of
its nature, having discussed inversion with Crichton-Miller. The
superficial similarity to Marguerite Michel must have struck her
also, especially as John shared the same baptismal name and
sartorial preferences. Whether Ladye sensed the undercurrent of
feeling between Una and John on this occasion is uncertain, but
she was soon to do so since from this first day of their meeting they
were to be 'at first much together, and soon afterwards scarcely
ever apart . . .'[4]

Una went home from this meeting happier than she had
arrived, with her feelings animated, and the promise of further
meetings to look forward to. She felt that something momentous
had happened, and she was right: the game of love had begun.
They were fated to be the most famous lesbian couple of the
century. Another couple, Natalie Barney and Romaine Brooks,
whom they were to meet later in Paris, also met each other in
1915.

Ladye and John had by this time been settled together for some years and had a town flat at 59 Cadogan Square and a country house, The White Cottage, at Malvern. Due to falling incomes and wartime economy they disposed of their flat and put The White Cottage up for sale, moving into a suite of rooms at Vernon Court Hotel in Buckingham Palace Road temporarily, whilst deciding where to fix a more permanent and cheaper abode. They had been fairly happy together, but Ladye at fifty-eight was indolent, accustomed to being petted and spoilt (partly by John), and lived a slow, sedentary life, out of keeping with John's comparative youth and natural vigour. She was a woman of great self-control, not given to displaying her feelings, and John was of a restless, passionate disposition. Several years earlier John had had a passing fancy for another woman, which Ladye had on that occasion 'dismissed with a tolerant smile', but she did not particularly welcome Una's increasing incorporation into their daily lives, or John's obviously increasing interest in her.

In September Una took Andrea and her nurse to Brighton and John and Ladye joined her there, before they all went on to Watergate Bay in Cornwall. Andrea was looked after by the nurse, and Ladye, none too well, was confined to the hotel; which left Una and John, as they wished, much time alone. If John ever asked herself, as in one of her earlier poems,

> How may I kindle the soul of this woman,
> With what torch may I touch it to flame?[5]

the answer was simply by proximity and familiarity, as she soon discovered. Watergate Bay, wild, beautiful and isolated, was a perfect setting for the 'long walks and talks and drives'[6] essential to their escalating intimacy; and there they developed the mutual interest and attraction spontaneously begun in August. They had plenty of opportunity for stealing off by themselves for moonlit walks on the beach, where no one could overhear their earnest conversation, or see the first outflow of feelings into tentative physical expression. Alone together in a Romantic setting, they may have had intimations of what was to be between them.

Day by day Una 'fell more completely under the spell of her

enthralling personality.' John 'was so intensely alive . . . could be so kind and so tender . . . was also so wilful, so humorous . . . so intelligent and yet so naive and simple . . .'[7] In Cornwall Una saw John in collars and ties and country tweeds, and began to succumb to her physical as well as her mental attractions.

'Life's but a game, Love is the same . . .'[8] John had written, and she was accustomed to taking her flirtations or attractions lightly, and did not at first realize that this 'game of love' with Una was different from her previous ones. She said to Una, 'How do I know if I shall care for you in six months time?'[9] which must have disconcerted Una considerably. She had tried to push unpleasant realities from her mind and 'thought little', but 'felt a great deal'. She was 'swept along on a spate of feeling . . . and all [she] knew or cared about was that [she] could not . . . having come to know [John] imagine life without her.'[10] In other words, she had fallen deeply in love, 'quite simply and naturally . . . in accordance with the dictates of her nature,' and 'it seemed an inevitable thing . . .'[11]

She was greedy for happiness after the unhappiness of her marriage, and 'had, at 28, as much consideration for Ladye or for anyone else as a child of six.' The 'anyone else' included her husband and child. She knew what she wanted, although 'there seemed so many factors against it at the time'; and, emotionally aroused and focused, was not to be shaken off, even by John's inability to predict the duration of her own feelings. On some deeper level of feminine instinct than John could understand, Una *knew* that she had found her emotional home, her right mate at last. Quite apart from being in love, they were well suited in other ways, having much in common: both had been middle-class Kensington children; neither had been emotionally close to her mother; both were known by names which were not their baptismal ones; both their fathers had been to Oxford, and were artistic; both their paternal grandfathers had been eminent, self-made men in their day; they were both Roman Catholics and adult converts; and were both 'attached' in relationships which had begun at approximately the same time, and were in different ways unsatisfactory. Una was more widely read and generally better educated than John, but they shared musicality, sensitivity to the fine arts and poetry, and a love of Italy. In addition, their general values and life-styles were quite compatible. On a less rational level, 'Fate was throwing them continually together . . . they could not have escaped this even had they wished to, and indeed they did not wish to escape it.'[12] During these weeks their relationship reached the point where they had either to turn back, or to go on in full knowledge of the consequences. They could not go back: John's strong sensual instincts were aroused; and Una, like Mary in *The Well of Loneliness*, was 'quite . . . openly in love . . . she had said, "All my life I've been waiting for something . . . I've been waiting for you."'

Una had written to May Massola in September, from Brighton, and as they were in the habit of writing frank, informal letters to each other, it seems likely that Una may have mentioned her meeting and subsequent friendship with John. May replied on September 16th, 'I have such a long letter from you to answer . . .' but did not mention John at all, filling her letter with news about the opera season. May's subsequent letters make no reference to John either, so it may be that, after all, being unable to say *everything*, Una said nothing about this new development in her life. Unfortunately, none of her letters to Troubridge, or his to her, survive, so it is impossible to know exactly when and how Una broached the subject with him.

She had asked Crichton-Miller to take the Cub to live with his own family at Bowden House, Harrow, for a time, presumably so that she could go on to Watergate Bay unencumbered; but Miller, using the excuse of overcrowding, declined decisively, making an alternative suggestion of a residential school run by three old ladies. Una decided against this, but later boarding schools were to figure prominently in Andrea's life, and in Una's and John's discussions.

After their return to London from Watergate Bay Una and John continued to see each other frequently, unwilling to let anything interrupt their mutual absorption. The 'game' was too well under way for anything to stop its relentless progress. They made time for each other, often at Ladye's expense; and it was not long before 'the three of us were beset by conflicting emotions and loyalties.'[13]

Una was torn between loyalty to her cousin, friend, and confidante on the one hand, and her feelings for John, to which every other consideration had become subject. John, never one to curb a new erotic interest, was torn between the excitement of the new and fidelity to the old. Ladye herself, sensing in Una 'an awful threat'[14] began to feel jealous of her, and neglected by John.

Yet despite Una's emotional involvement with John she was not mentally submerged or uncritical; and characteristically records, against herself, that: 'John was in her thirties when I got to know her . . . and I in my twenties, sufficiently callous easily to lose patience and to say to her on one occasion: "The trouble with you is that you've got protection mania . . ."' and again: 'I remember once to my shame saying angrily: "You spoil everything! We can never go anywhere that you don't see some animal that makes you unhappy . . ."'

She also maintained her independence of thought against John's forcefully expressed views: 'She was at that time not only devout but, to my mind, bigoted in the extreme, and young as I was, and also devout, I rebelled at her militant theories. I remember saying to her, "I believe you would be prepared to torture heretics . . . in another age you would have been a Torquemada . . ."'[15]

For Una and John there was never enough time to be alone together, but the selling of The White Cottage gave them an excuse to go to Malvern for a few days at the end of November, leaving Ladye, whose health prevented her from making the journey, alone in London. Beforehand, John had intimated to Una that she wanted 'just to have you with me for a few days and nights . . . to sleep with you in my arms . . . to feel you beside me when I wake up in the morning . . . as though we belonged to each other . . .' and after four months of intense interest and accelerating affection, in Una also 'the body knew only the urge towards a complete fulfilment.'[16]

Yet John also wanted Una to have full knowledge of the possible consequences, and not to give herself 'until she had counted the cost of that gift'. We may safely surmise that John forewarned her that: 'If you come to me . . . the world will abhor you, will persecute you, will call you unclean . . .' since we have it on Una's authority that she was nothing if not honest; and concluded: 'have you understood? Do you realise now what it's going to mean if you give yourself to me?'

We may also confidently assume that Una's answer was as unhesitating as Mary Llewelyn's in *The Well of Loneliness*: 'What do I care for all you've told me? What do I care for the world's opinion? What do I care for anything but you, and you as you are – as you are, I love you!'

Una, fully in love for the first time, joyfully gave herself to John on their first night together, November 29th. There is absolutely no doubt about this, although her diaries for 1915 and 1916 were subsequently destroyed: precisely because they would have shown dates and places of their lovemaking before Ladye's death. November 29th, like August 1st, was always subsequently circled in Una's diaries as a special day; and in 1931 she noted, '16 years since John and I went to Malvern,' and more explicitly still in 1932: '17 years . . . She bought me yellow roses to commemorate our anniversary . . .'

On the subsequent anniversaries of their first meeting and first lovemaking they were often to attend a Mass of thanksgiving together.

This consummation on November 29th, 1915 was an 'infidelity' on John's part, and Ladye must have had a shrewd suspicion of what was going on at Malvern while she was left alone in London. On Una's part it was morally – though not legally as John was a woman – adultery: a breaking of her marriage vows, vows which had become a mockery in an increasingly unhappy marriage, and which Troubridge had already broken, perhaps more than once. Symbolically it marked the real end of her marriage, a point of no return. Her life could never be the same again: she had committed herself body, mind, and spirit. From that time onwards she began to redefine herself as an 'invert', closing the door for ever on her previous bisexuality.

After this decisive step she felt it impossible to go to Belgrade to rejoin Troubridge, and stayed in London. Fortunately, in wartime sound practical reasons could be given for not going, though she must have known that he would not accept excuses indefinitely, and would from time to time be home on leave.

Shortly after this visit to Malvern Wells, using the excuse of watering places and the beneficial effects of 'taking the waters', Una and John went for a few days to Tunbridge Wells, staying at the Wellington Hotel, overlooking the town on Mount Ephraim. They again left Ladye in London, and she realized that they were more interested in each other than in the Chalybeate Spring in the Pantiles. Una was eager to reaffirm and continue their now complete relationship, and put aside thoughts of their respective obligations to Troubridge and Ladye, grasping at even temporary happiness.

On their return to London John became keen to do some form of useful work for the war effort, partly perhaps because it would have provided ostensibly good reasons for being apart from Ladye, and therefore more accessible to Una. Ladye, becoming increasingly jealous, was understandably 'insistent that she would not be left alone', especially at night and during air-raids. She and John, still living at the Vernon Court Hotel, viewed, then bought the lease for, a flat at 22 Cadogan Court, Draycott Avenue, in January 1916, intending to furnish then move into it. John became ill for a short time, then recovered and 'confined her war work activities to visiting the wounded in St Thomas's Hospital and serving in a canteen.'[17] As soon as John had recovered, Una herself went down with pneumonic tonsilitis through which, doubtless to Una's deep delight, John nursed her.

Whatever frictions divided Una, Ladye and John, they transcended them that Easter and went all three together to visit the seven churches on Maunday Thursday, in keeping with Roman Catholic practice; then on to Westminster Cathedral to the ceremony of the Washing of the Feet, by Cardinal Bourne. Una had become so close a part of John's and Ladye's life together that they were all but *à trois* although not living under the same roof. Ladye's health and age were extenuating circumstances as she fully realized; and as she was anxious not to lose John totally, she compromised as far as she was able, despite her natural jealousy. She probably thought that although this 'lapse' with Una was more serious than John's other, earlier one had been, it too would pass, especially when Troubridge returned from the war. There were now no denials as to the nature of Una's and John's relationship, and Ladye was fully cognisant of the facts. She and John had always believed in frank and open speech, and had from the beginning 'made a kind of pact never to keep things from each other' since 'they both believed that perfect frankness was the only sound foundation upon which to build a very close intimacy.'[18]

In early spring Una and John went off together to Malvern for the second time, officially to supervise the handing over of The White Cottage to its new owners. They stayed at an inn, the Hornyold Arms, for a few precious days before returning to London. Shortly after her return a shock awaited Una, the thing she had tried not to think about, and dreaded most: the sudden and unexpected return of Troubridge. She had not seen him for over eighteen months, and her emotions were entirely orientated towards John; any resumption of marital relations was unthinkable to her. Troubridge was not a happy man, still smarting from Churchill's snub and its consequences: he had been deprived of a high position and had been occupying an inferior one. His pride had been wounded, and he had found his situation unpalatable. A retreat had been ordered and he had organized the evacuation of the Serbian army and refugees; and on arrival at the coast the Serbs had given him command of their own forces in addition to his own. He arrived back in London between naval appointments, his future plans very uncertain. Una seemed to him unresponsive, preoccupied, with her 'nerves' apparently no better. From her point of view he was a demanding, dissident element, and she was relieved when he left. She busied herself, taught John Neapolitan folk-songs on the mandoline, looked after Cubby and tried not to think too much.

On May 14th, John suggested a day at Maidenhead and Una agreed readily. They were going to look at a bulldog puppy which John wanted to give her. Ladye, though left alone, was quite happy preparing for a musical party at which she was to sing that afternoon. Though not in the best of health she did not feel or seem to be ill; but she was overweight, with a blood pressure of over 200, and had been seeing, as she noted in her diary for 1916, 'floating chenille worms' in front of her left eye. Unknown to them all at the time, this was symptomatic of an impending cerebral haemorrhage. She had never really recovered from the shock of a motor accident which had occurred nearly two years earlier, on September 22nd, 1914, when the car in which she and John were being driven was rammed in the side by a driver (female) who had accelerated instead of braking. Ladye had sustained several severe scalp wounds, and chipping of the cervical vertebrae. She had been taken to a nearby house and a doctor was called, but it had been several weeks before she could be moved. John had escaped with minor bruises.

Una and John dined at Skindles Hotel, Maidenhead, saw the puppy, which they thought unsuitable, and 'debated remaining for the night'[19] there, but at the last minute decided against it, feeling guilty at leaving Ladye to face night air-raids alone. They reluctantly went back to London, arriving late and parting at the station. When Una arrived home Ladye rang to ask whether John was on her way home as it was so late, and Una answered in the affirmative. It seems that over dinner Ladye and John quarrelled about Una, and John's seeing so much of her. Ladye was jealous and angry, and John hard and recalcitrant. Ladye, intending to make a dignified exit to show her disapproval, rose from the table and suffered an apoplectic seizure. John did what she could then rang Una to ask for the name of her doctor as theirs was away. Una quickly gave it, then took a taxi to their hotel. She and the doctor arrived together, to find Ladye unconscious. They put her to bed, but there was nothing which could be done as 'there was cerebral haemorrhage which formed a clot on the brain, and this led to progressive paralysis . . . with only occasional flashes of semi-consciousness . . .' Ladye 'lost all power of coherent speech almost immediately after her seizure,' but 'occasionally she used to make inarticulate sounds, as though trying to speak . . .'[20]

John sat by Ladye's bed night and day, prostrate with shock, until she died eleven days later, on May 25th, without regaining consciousness. Although she had been assured by the attending doctor that Ladye must have been suffering for several years from arterial sclerosis, and that the seizure would have happened sooner or later, John's remorse and guilt, as well as her grief, were terrible. 'She blamed herself bitterly and uncompromisingly that she had allowed her affection for me to trespass upon her exclusive devotion to Ladye, that she had brought me so closely into their home life . . .' Una remembered later.[21] All John's recalcitrance, wilfulness, selfish pursuit of passion, longing for freedom, were swept away by a flood of antithetical, penitential feeling: in a different age she would have taken to sackcloth and ashes. Ladye's death, removing a major impediment to the development of their love, precipitated John in almost the opposite direction; but it is hard to see what would have happened had Ladye lived on for years, rather than weeks or months. It is unlikely that John would ever have made a complete break with her for Una, which would have made Una's life very unsettled and precarious. Death, by removing one of the players, altered the possibilities of the 'game'.

A brief obituary appeared in *The Times* on May 26th, and a Requiem Mass was said for her in Westminster Cathedral a few days later. Ladye was embalmed, as Una told her via the medium: 'Tell her that after embalming she looked young and quite lovely – we both saw her.' (Psychic Records, October 1916.) John, determined that no ordinary grave was good enough for Ladye, purchased a catacomb chamber 'as a gift to her'[22] in Highgate Cemetery. Ladye's name was put over the entrance as the owner of the catacomb, and not John's. At the same time John added to her current Will her own desire to be buried there with Ladye in due course. John kept all Ladye's things, packing her clothes away carefully in trunks; had special Masses said for the repose of her soul; took wreaths to Highgate; and tried to have a memorial plaque put up in the church at Malvern. When the priest refused, saying that he was against the idea of personal plaques in church, John was very angry.

Una was more deeply concerned about the extremity of John's reactions, and their possible consequences, than about Ladye's death as such, though she must have felt some natural grief. She saw that Ladye's demise opened up for her the possibility of a permanent and central place in John's affections, so long as remorse did not win the day and Una find herself 'put . . . out of her [John's] life and offered . . . up as a sacrifice to loyalty.' That was her great fear.

John felt unable to remain in the hotel where Ladye had died, and did not want to move into 22 Cadogan Court, which had been intended for them both. Una urged her to share her house in Bryanston Street, but John declined and sought relatively neutral ground as a paying guest in the home of her American cousin Dorothy Clarke[23] at 1 Swan Walk, Chelsea. It was a long way from where Una lived, so she moved down to Royal Hospital Road, and took a furnished house just round the corner from Swan Walk, in order to be near John. They spent a few hours together 'almost every day', but whilst many of these were 'hours of mutual sympathy and understanding', there were 'quite as many . . . at first, when we frayed each other's nerves,' Una admitted later. There were unspoken thoughts and tensions, Una often wanting to comfort more tangibly than John would permit, being 'too numb with grief to feel any personal reaction'. Una believed that John would have given her up at this time had she not selflessly realized how important she had become to Una; and therefore continued the relationship chiefly for Una's sake. This shifts the onus on to Una, and seems to exonerate John, until we remember how keen she was to be 'unfaithful' to Ladye during her lifetime. It is more likely that John wanted Una, but also wanted her to share a portion of her own guilt and remorse. Altogether it was a very unhappy time for them both 'and there seemed no light ahead'. John 'was submerged by an all-pervading sorrow', and Una 'torn by sympathy and by anxiety on her behalf and also desperately miserable' at what 'looked like an almost total shipwreck' of their 'happy relationship'.[24]

In addition, and true to her pattern of response, Una was not well as 'an old heart affection had recurred under the stress of anxiety.' Only later was Una able to see that 'what seemed at the time a mere vortex of impulses and coincidence and tragedy . . . had its definite purposes.'[25]

Probate of Ladye's Will was granted on June 27th, to her only daughter and executrix, Cara Harris. Ladye 'made rather an unusual Will . . . she wrote it all out on foolscap paper and her style was not at all legal, it was a long and conversational document, and . . . portions of it appeared in the papers and this annoyed us all very much as we had particularly tried to keep it out of the press,'[26] John wrote later. Ladye had made her Will on April

1st, 1915 at The White Cottage, Malvern, using her gardener and cook as witnesses, and 'took a great deal of trouble to ensure for John certain privileges . . . with regard to burial etc. that would not have been accorded . . . in the ordinary way.'[27]

Ladye asked that John 'would help my daughter to carry out my wishes and give [her] . . . the benefit of her assistance and advice . . . in consideration of our long friendship and affection for which I am deeply . . . grateful,' adding, 'I further beg both my daughter and [John] R-Hall to bear in mind that it would grieve me greatly should they grow less friendly or lose sight of each other when I am no longer on this earth . . .'

'Grow less friendly' they certainly did, since 'certain affectionate wording regarding [John] had aroused the very devil of jealousy in her daughter Mrs. Harris . . .' John had certainly been given the pick of 'Gifts and letters from His late Majesty King Edward VIIth', 'all or any of my books', and 'gifts left me by the late Count de Mirafiore', and portraits by Sargent. Incongruously perhaps, she also wanted John to 'choose some lace and a fan'.

Cara Harris had long been jealous of John's place in her mother's affections, and finally declared her outright hostility after the Will. She joined forces with Dorothy Clarke, who was jealous of Una's place in John's life, and together they proceeded to make mischief between John and Una when they could, or between them and their other friends or relations, and later at the Society for Psychical Research.[28] Cara Harris and John fell out about who had the right to Ladye's last diaries; then John caught measles, and on this pretext was promptly ejected from Swan Walk. As 22 Cadogan Court was being temporarily let furnished, John went to stay with and be looked after by Una at her house in Royal Hospital Road. This was just what Una wanted, the chance to lavish love and attention on John; but on her recovery, the let of number 22 having expired, John went to live there by herself. For John, at this juncture, there was no question of life together, symbolized by a shared home; it was very much life apart, symbolized by living alone. Una understandably found this very depressing. It was ironical how they had longed – and plotted – to be together when Ladye was alive, and how separated they had become after, and by, her death.

Troubridge was promoted to Vice-Admiral on June 9th, 1916, with a salary of £1,460, and in September, to Una's relief, was appointed to the personal staff of the Crown Prince (later King Alexander) of Serbia, returning there to command a naval contingent which was to be successful in preventing Belgrade from being bombarded and the Serbian troops harassed. With Troubridge safely abroad again, Una could relax and even feel mildly fond of him from a distance.

In an attempt to relax more together, and hoping that a change of air would do them both good, John took Una to stay at a hotel in Llanberis. John's collie, Rufus, accompanied them. Una remembered: 'It was lovely and beautiful and we went to the top of Snowdon and trailed round Carnarvon Castle, with John nobly trying to be cheerful for my sake . . . but it was not a success.'[29]

During August and September Una and John developed an interest in Psychical Research (dealt with fully in chapter 7, Psychic Phenomena), attending sittings with a medium, and using Una's dining-room as an office. Between 3.00 and 6.30 p.m. each day they annotated their sittings, and Una happily acted as typist-secretary, glad to be of use to John. There had been times when they met only once within a fortnight,[30] and this new joint work provided a convenient motive for more frequent meetings. Some of the early sittings are revealing of John's and Una's feelings and states of mind. On October 2nd John hesitantly asks: 'Tell her [i.e. Ladye] Una will look after me – ask her if Una may look after me?'

The answer (strangely true!) was: 'She says yes, she is very glad if she will, that is, if you will let her; she says she [i.e. Una] has got a very difficult task.'

On October 13th Una says: 'Tell Ladye she's got to help me to take care of Twonnie [John]' and the answer, no doubt gratifying to Una: 'She says yes, she wants that, she puts her [i.e. John] in your charge.'

Una replies: 'Tell her I will do my best.'

The reply is humorous but prophetic: 'She says she's afraid you hardly appreciate the magnitude of your task. It will be perfectly awful sometimes, terrible!'

On October 20th Ladye gives Una some post-mortem advice,

via the medium: 'I have told you you must be firm enough with her [i.e. John] – perhaps if I ask her to be more tractable she will give you a better chance.'

Inevitably, the topic of Troubridge crops up in these sittings, as it was in Una's mind. Una says revealingly on October 20th: 'I hope T[roubridge] won't mind, I'm as nice as I can be to him, but I can't help who I'm fondest of [i.e. John]' and the tactful answer is: 'She says: "I don't want you to pretend, that wouldn't be nice, not to pretend that you aren't fond of Twonnie . . . but when he [Troubridge] is there she wants you not to show it so very very much – she's afraid you might be inclined to show it too much. She says to be careful about this is the kindest way to be."'

The following dialogue on November 15th shows John's insistent disregard for Una's feelings, but the communicator's high regard for Una, which must have pleased her as she listened:

John (to medium): Tell her [Ladye] that her influence over me was very great.
Medium: She [Ladye] thinks Una's influence was and is good and she likes to think that Una is with you.
John: Tell her I meant her, not Una.
Medium: But she means Una, and she says again that her influence is good . . .

The notes to these sittings also reveal that John had already started calling Una by the pet-name 'Squig' or 'Squiggie' (presumably because of Una's tendency to doodles or 'squiggles'), which endearment was to last for many years, so that she hardly ever called her Una.

The year 1916 ended as it had begun for Una, paradoxically both certain and uncertain: certain in feelings, uncertain in circumstances. John was living by herself at Cadogan Court, and Una by herself in Royal Hospital Road. Their relationship fluctuated, and nothing was settled between them. Ladye's unexpected death had divided rather than united them; and John's ardour had been cooled by grief, although towards the end of the year she had begun spending the odd night with Una. This in turn led to innuendo and speculation, and perhaps due to the machinations of Dorothy Clarke and Cara Harris, Una's landlady, Mrs Gregory, came to hear of it in Ireland, and Una received a letter from her, 'making the unusual suggestion that she should cancel her present agreement and allow [the landlady] to take immediate re-possession . . .'[31] This was nothing short of eviction, and plunged Una into despair, but it was to prove a blessing in disguise.

Una had known John for only seventeen months but they had been crucial and decisive ones. Nothing comparable had ever happened to her before, her life had completely altered as though an invisible line had been drawn across it. Loving a masculine woman at once freed her from her unresolved 'Electra complex', and satisfied her innate attraction towards the masculine principle; for she was feminine herself and needed her counterpart. John was masculine enough in both attitudes and looks, with her slim boyish figure and handsome features, without being male. John was tailor-made for Una's particular psychosexual needs.

Let us take a longer and closer look at this woman who, in such a short time, had become, 'the be-all and end-all of my [Una's] life'.[32]

# II

# Life Together: the First Years (1917–26)

# 6

# *My John*

Marguerite Antonia Radclyffe-Hall, known in childhood as 'Peter', but more permanently and universally after her majority as 'John', was born on August 12th, 1880 at Bournemouth. She derived from an English upper-middle-class father, Radclyffe Radclyffe-Hall (nicknamed 'Rat') and an American mother, Marie Diehl, who had already been married once and was destined to marry again. Her parents became separated when she was a year old, and divorced when she was three. In her own words, written in the third person in the notes to the Psychic Records[1] many years later, she recalls this time poignantly: although she never knew them to share a home she had 'recollections of one or two occasions upon which her Father visited her Mother, when scenes of a rather violent nature took place between them. These scenes affected her very much and greatly saddened her early childhood . . . It is not an exaggeration to say that the domestic upheaval was a very saddening factor in her childhood . . .' producing later 'an unhappy and questioning frame of mind regarding parental disagreement . . . from the moment she began to realize the ordinary facts of life . . . at about the age of ten or eleven . . .'

After the divorce she '. . . was only permitted to see him at rare intervals, in fact she cannot remember having seen her father more than a dozen times . . . during her childhood he evinced not the slightest interest in her . . .' When she was a very little girl he had called her 'Daisy'! What seems to have made the greatest impression on her was when at about seventeen

> . . . she saw her Father for the last time. On this occasion he was coughing violently, and he had some difficulty in breathing. He evinced much interest in . . . and for the first time a certain amount of affection towards her . . . she well remembers his saying to her . . . 'Be warned by me; decide what you want to do and stick to it. Never be a Jack-of-all-trades and master of none, as I have been'. . . . She felt greatly drawn to her Father on this occasion, and was deeply distressed when, not many weeks later, she heard that he was dead.

He died of pulmonary tuberculosis in his fifties. He had been an only son, educated at Eton and St John's College, Oxford; and before his marriage had wanted to be an actor, and 'to the immense chagrin of his family had toured the provinces in a theatrical company . . .' After his marriage 'he had discovered a talent for painting,' but 'he only painted by fits and starts . . . becoming a fair amateur but never sticking to it.' In addition, 'He was very devoted to both hunting and yachting, but in sport, as in more serious matters, he could never quite make up his mind what he wanted to do.' She knew 'from her Mother and also . . . heard . . . from her Father's old tutor, the Rev. Walter Begley . . . that her Father could never settle down to any one hobby or pursuit . . .' After the divorce he 'led a most unsatisfactory life, wandering about the world and having no sort of settled abode.' Nevertheless, according to a cousin, who was devoted to him, he was also 'a man full of good impulses and given to sudden fits of deep religious feeling.'

John inherited not only his fair colouring and facial features, especially the eyes, but much of his artistic and flamboyant nature. Ladye had observed a 'strong link' between John and her father, 'a stronger link than there was between her and any other member of her family'; and her own mother, Marie Visetti, exclaimed bitterly, after John's death, 'she had not an ounce of my blood in her. She was Radclyffe through and through . . .'[2]

Despite her obvious affection, John makes various frank and amusing comments about him, and indirectly perhaps about herself: in the notes to the sitting of October 26th, 1918, she observes: 'MRH's father was a typical "Squire of Dames" and found the opposite sex a very absorbing pursuit'; and on October 30th, 1918: 'he was very wilful and pig-headed, being determined to have his own way in everything . . .'

She did not seem to get on too well with Alberto Visetti,[3] her mother's third husband; and her relationship with her mother seems never to have been either warm or happy. Something of her mother's callousness and emotional distance is portrayed in Lady Anna Gordon in *The Well of Loneliness*. Indeed, this relationship was so poor that it led Una to say in her *Life* of John many years later that in her opinion John's father, though absent, was 'one hundred per cent the better parent,' and to describe Marie Visetti as 'a brainless, vain, selfish woman.' John recorded on March 20th, 1918 that her 'mother is not happy . . . suffers terribly from her nerves, and has an unhappy disposition . . .' Very mild words, all things considered!

So deep an impression did this childhood (which we would now call 'emotionally deprived') leave on John that her very first, but unfinished, novel ('After Many Days'),[4] started when she was still living with Ladye, '. . . dealt with just such a childhood as her own had been.'

John's early education, like Stephen's in *The Well*, came from governesses; one of whom, Miss Knott, affectionately known as 'Knotty', became 'her confidant and sympathizer', as was also her maternal grandmother, Mrs Diehl. Later she spent a year at King's College, London, then a year in Germany, which must have been a welcome relief from home as well as affording an opportunity for freedom and amorous adventures.

She was her father's sole heir and inherited her fortune in two phases, at the ages of eighteen and twenty-one. Sir Arthur Sullivan, one of her trustees, became a close personal friend. On her majority she and her grandmother left the Visetti household. Her early and middle twenties were spent in extensive foreign travel, particularly in America; in hunting, and generally enjoying herself: in her own words, 'Drinking deep the wine of pleasure'.[5]

'Throughout her adolescence and her maturity until the age of thirty-four', Una tells us, 'she was idle, bone idle . . .' However, she showed an early and apparently rare talent for musical composition, though she refused to have this faculty trained; and wrote poetry, publishing five volumes between 1906 and 1915.[6] Much of this poetry was about 'That potent passion, that divine desire', which she had felt from the age of seventeen onwards, for various women, principally the singer Agnes Nichols, the two American cousins Dorothy Diehl (later Clarke) and Jane Randolph (later Caruth), both of whom she brought back to England with her, at different times.

'I was love's prisoner'[7] she declared in one of her poems, and it seems to have been true of her all her life. She was, at this time, Una recorded later, 'exceedingly handsome' with 'plenty of charm, plenty of intelligence, plenty of money, no education to speak of', and was 'out exclusively to enjoy herself and to give others a good time'. However, she was no reckless libertine, and generously supported Dorothy Diehl both before and after her marriage to Conningsby Clarke, and Jane Randolph and her three children by her first marriage; for 'she inevitably developed a measure of affection for, and a protective sense towards, those with whom she fell in love . . .'

Her natural erotic and poetic propensities were expressed in a lyrical verse which, at its best, is faintly reminiscent of Shelley and Browning:

> When thy hands touch me, all the world is compassed
> Within the limits of their slender whiteness . . .[8]
>
> We were complete, a glorious, living whole,
> A perfect cadence of supreme delight –
> I think eternity was ours that night.[9]

Flirting and philandering seem to have been basic to her nature, which in this respect approximated to most men's. She exercised a fascination over women all her life, and had sown many wild oats by the time she was twenty-seven, when she met Ladye, then aged fifty, who had been a society beauty, and was cultured, talented and still very attractive. John seems to have been captivated by her from the beginning, and to have gone out of her way to woo and win her, by making herself more culturally acceptable to such a discerning patron of the arts, who was herself widely read and musically accomplished. As Una was to state later, 'in her immense desire to make herself worthy of someone she loved, John's real education began.'

This was John's first fully reciprocal, long-lasting emotional attachment. John records in the notes to March 27th, 1918: 'About a year before they became close friends MRH [John] and MVB [Ladye] met by accident at the North British Hotel, Edinburgh . . . in Sept. 1906 . . .' John was living in a flat in Albert Gate Court when she first 'became personally acquainted with MVB during a summer holiday' at a German watering place; and 'later on . . . visited MVB for the first time, at the latter's own house, going there to a luncheon party with her step-father.'

Ladye's husband, George Batten, was, like Una's, twenty-five years her senior; but unlike Troubridge, 'my old George' as Ladye called him, had long been 'like an indulgent father' to her. He seemed to take to John, rather than to resent her, and they all three went to Sidmouth, and 'lived in a furnished house that they had taken for some months, one summer . . .' After George died, John and Ladye lived together, and travelled extensively in Europe, the Canaries, Tenerife, Morocco and Corsica. They spent several months in Rome in 1912, where they were received by the Pope in a private audience; and during this visit John caught Roman Fever and nearly died.

Ladye encouraged John's poetry and music, and when she sang and played her Spanish guitar, John would often accompany her on the mandoline. John also composed songs at the piano, and later played the treble virginal. Ladye, like Una, was a Roman Catholic, and John also became a convert and 'was received into the Catholic Church, MVB acting as her God-mother' at Brompton Oratory in 1908.

Ladye was physically indolent, pettish, and liked to be spoiled;

she coined expressions of her own, such as 'sporkish' (a term of mild disapproval for things or people she did not like), and had recurrent bouts of 'Monte Carlo fever'.[10] John was devoted to her, and was faithful to her for seven years, apart from 'a trivial, passing lapse' which 'broke no bones and left no aftermath' (Una's *Life*). She often called John 'Johnnie' and her own special name, which no one else ever used before or afterwards, 'Jonathan'.

'There was an idyllic, peaceful happiness in those years that was all their own,' Una recorded later; adding, with typical generosity, 'and how glad I am to think that she had them . . . They were amongst the happiest of her life, for they were shared with a most delightful, sympathetic and versatile companion.' Ladye's effect on John was decisive and long-term; most particularly that she altered the emphasis in John's life from physical sports to mental pursuits, and encouraged the spiritual dimension. In many ways Ladye laid the foundations on which Una subsequently built; for with her, John was to find her most totally fulfilling relationship. Yet without Ladye's groundwork, John would not have been ready for this vital, crucial union with Una.

John had, to use Una's apt phrase, a 'complex nature': in some ways a typical ectomorph, she was energetic, intense, highly-sexed, quick-tempered, but also, at times, prone to depression and nervous agitation. She was a sensitive, emotional person, who worried easily especially about people or projects that were dear to her. When she refers in *The Well* to 'the terrible nerves of the invert' this is no doubt self-projection as well as observation of others. The subjective–objective, emotional–intellectual aspects of her nature coexisted congruously to form a very stable character basis. This is shown very clearly in the psychic research work, which will be covered in the next chapter. She was able to be detached and to adopt a scrutinizing, scientific methodology in what had begun as an intensely personal quest; and was self-critical, as is shown, often humorously, by the comments made in the third person in the notes to the sittings.

It is often said that she lacked a sense of humour in her life and in her writing. Neither is true: many of their friends, when recalling her after her death, remembered her laughter as one of her most prominent characteristics. 'How John laughed!' Micki

Jacob[11] recalled in her essay in 'Me and the Swans'. Behind the apparently deadpan seriousness of some of her photographs, and her books, there lies a distinct vein of humour. Even in a predominantly sad book like *The Well* (which will also be covered more fully elsewhere) there is a versatile humour at work.

She was assertive, dominant, decisive (usually), outspoken, often flamboyant (not just as a stance in defence of 'inversion', but by nature, like her father), and, Una tells us, deeply honest. She expected to be in command and usually made sure that she was. Whatever she did was done with great vigour, whether it was hunting (in the early days), lovemaking, or writing novels; she governed her life by principles, and pursued her chosen work or cause with unremitting conviction. As Una said, she was 'a born fanatic . . . one who, if the need arose, would go to the pillory or the stake for her convictions, one who would go through fire and water, would never accept defeat . . .'

Like Natalie Clifford Barney[12] (with whom, ironically, she never felt much rapport) she was 'the lover of women and the friend of men'. Her semi-formal correspondence with men such as Jonathan Cape shows a man-to-man directness, and is on a 'My dear Jonathan'/'Dear John' basis. She always apparently disliked doing business with women, except with her literary agent and friend Audrey Heath, sometimes greeted as 'Darling Robin'.

She made many lasting friendships with fellow artists, other 'inverts', psychic investigators, publishers, solicitors, as well as ordinary family and social friendships. 'I am convinced', Una tells us later, 'that there does not live, and never has lived, anyone who can truthfully say that Radclyffe Hall failed them, or ever let them down.' She confided to her diary, and later repeated to Lovat Dickson, her executor and literary heir, that John was 'the best friend a woman ever had'. No small tribute! If she could be a hard task-master to typists, secretaries and servants, she could also be very generous.

As well as friends, of course, she made enemies: personal, such as Fox-Pitt, Troubridge and Romaine Brooks; and public, such as James Douglas and Chartres Biron. Friends like Cara Harris, Ladye's daughter, and Dorothy Clarke, motivated by petty jealousies, succeeded in making mischief where they could, and stretched John's forbearance to its limits. When it ran out, she took a very firm, formal line. Her brusque manner was often misunderstood: it was partly defensive, as she was in some ways a shy person. She offended against the mores of the times, and her heterodoxy discomfited many smaller, less free spirits, and invited both censure and caricature.

John was a generous provider (to the several cousins already mentioned, to Una and Andrea, and later Souline)[13] and had a strong protective instinct towards animals, and those whom she loved. It is also quite clear that she felt a keen, specifically paternal frustration in being unable to give the woman she loved a child. When she and Una thought seriously of settling in Fiesole they negotiated to 'buy' a baby to bring up as 'theirs'; and she wrote to Souline much later, 'Had I been a man, I would have given you a child,' and 'I much long for an impudent Chink-faced brat.' (Souline had Mongolian features.) She was always painfully conscious of the bond which was 'so fruitful of passion yet so bitterly sterile'.[14] Perhaps writing was a psychological substitute for frustrated paternity, and more widely, an ultimately frustrated masculinity.

Reading between the lines of Una's *Life, The Well*, and John's letters and character, one may deduce that she was by nature a leader, not one of the led; a protagonist, rather than a sidesman; and that in sexual matters she was usually the initiator, being an active, tribadic lover, who was able to arouse and satisfy the deepest passions in her partners. Una told Lovat Dickson, after John's death, that she had known 'sexual rapture' for the first time with John; and Souline, despite her initial resistance, became 'the most passionate of women' with John (to whom she lost her virginity) for nearly nine years.

In her personal habits her one major excess was smoking: 'She systematically over-smoked, anything and everything, including green cigars . . .' Una said of her early life, but heavy smoking continued all her life despite several attempted 'cures', and may have eventually damaged her lungs. There is an amusing reference in January 1921 to John's having 'suffered lately from a soreness of her mouth and tongue owing to pipe smoking'! In contrast to her smoking she drank very moderately; but was given to swearing when crossed or annoyed. In the notes to the sitting of October 10th, 1917, John admits, with an edge of humour, 'It is true that MRH is in the habit of swearing occasionally (UVT says very freely and to a quite disgraceful extent) when she is irritated or angry.'

Her appearance, Una said, 'was calculated to arouse interest', but it also aroused antagonism. She seems to have become more heavily masculine with the years: she was forty before she cut off the nearly knee-length ash-blond hair, which she 'ruthlessly disposed of. . . in tight plaits twisted round her. . . head'.[15] This was partly due to Ladye's deep abhorrence at the very idea: she exercised a restraining influence on John's appearance during her lifetime, and for several years afterwards. The Buchel portrait of 1918 is a masterpiece of ambiguity and sensitivity; and there is much more facial femininity in the 1928 photograph showing the flamboyant Spanish hat and the pearl earrings, than in the photograph of 1938 taken in Rye and showing the rather more subdued French beret, the heavier, more masculine features. Perhaps the gypsy earrings in the later photos (for example, the 1935 photo taken by Una, showing John in pin-stripe suit and bow-tie) contrasting so much with the otherwise conventional masculinity, highlights the ambiguity, or duality, of John's nature.[16]

As well as references to silk ties and tweed skirts, breeches and men's stockings, there are also references to far more feminine clothes in the notes to the Psychic Records, between 1916 and 1921. In the notes to the sitting of May 9th, 1918 there is a reference to a recent discussion 'regarding some evening shoes of MRH's, as to whether or no these could be worn with a dinner gown, which MRH was about to put on . . .' In addition there are references to her wearing 'several kinds of scent' and using 'bath crystals . . . scented with Verbena' during this time. Later letters refer to her fondness for knitting and crocheting, rather traditional feminine activities for so ostensibly masculine a woman. Small things are often as revealing of gender behaviour as more important ones, and John's is certainly a curious mixture!

She was thus well into her maturity and the first years of her life with Una before she finally discarded, along with her long hair and stays, the trappings of an ambiguous, quasi-conventional image, becoming more outspoken in appearance, stance and attitude, and more purposeful than ever before.

She was always meticulously neat in appearance, and cut an elegant, memorable figure. Female observers in particular took in every detail, as did Ethel Mannin[17] in 1929, when John visited her:

> Her masculinity, sartorially, is of the exquisitely tailor-made kind, and she is one of the handsomest women I have ever met . . . She has a beautiful head, and sleek close-cropped fair hair with a slight wave; keen, steel-grey eyes, a small, sensitive mouth, a delicately aquiline nose, and a charming boyish smile, which lights up the pale gravity of her face remarkably, dispelling that faint suggestion of severity, which it has in repose. She has slender ankles and wrists, and beautiful, sensitive fingers, and she is slightly built without giving an impression of smallness; there is about her, generally, a curious mingling of sensitiveness and strength, a sort of clean-cut hardness . . .

This description is not merely factual, it is evaluative, appreciative, and is rather typical, in this respect, of other descriptions which have been given to the present writer, and which will be quoted later.

Appearance, like handwriting, evolves out of the personality, and may be 'read' or interpreted by observers as an index of this. The conscious choice of image is a self-statement made to the world, but also reveals unconscious factors. John's later clothes consisted of tailored suits, some with skirts, others with trousers; silk shirts and ties; dinner jackets, frilled shirts and bow ties; panama, homburg and trilby hats. In addition there are references to slacks, woollen sweaters, raincoats and overcoats. These, like her diamond cuff-links and shirt studs, watch, cigarette case and lighter, are all masculine. More intimately, she wore men's *crêpe de Chine* pyjamas, and the 'heavy silk masculine underwear' attributed to Stephen.[18] Their old housekeeper, Miss Mabel Bourne, volunteered this latter fact, as she used to do the washing!

She also suggested that 'Miss Hall' shaved, though this would seem rather less likely.

Certainly John showed 'all the outward stigmata of the abnormal'[19] in her appearance and masculine gender behaviour. Her self-attitude is also revealing: we may deduce that unlike Lady Anna, but like Stephen, John too had 'shrunk back resentful, protesting, when the seal of her womanhood had been stamped upon her'; and that, in the process of self-awareness she had 'felt appalled at the realisation of her own grotesqueness,' seeing herself as 'nothing but a freak abandoned on a kind of no-man's-land . . .'[20] This transitional view did not last long and she came to view herself as 'a woman who is a born invert',[21] seeing 'inversion' itself as 'a fact in nature'; and never seems to have suffered any guilt or qualms of conscience (despite the views of her Church) in the matter, and to have been, in the circumstances, remarkably well-adjusted.

Una makes some very significant observations in her *Life* of John: she remembers seeing 'a photograph done in infancy of a sturdy-looking baby with silky fair down on its well-shaped head, propped upon a fur rug. Its fists are clenched and its expression fierce . . . No one would doubt for a moment that this was a male child . . .' and also that 'throughout her infancy strangers always mistook her for a boy.'

Of her early childhood Una says: 'She hated dolls, loved drums and noisy toys, but such tastes are common to many girl children and might seem to have had little significance had not the future confirmed the fact of her sexual inversion.' Curiously Una chooses not to state what its significance was: that it revealed a very early masculine gender identity of the classic sort. Una draws no conclusions, merely recording 'the fact', though she obviously understood intimately the essential dynamics of John's nature.

Una seems to perceive John on several levels concurrently: the rational, on which she realizes John as ostensibly a woman; and the emotional and instinctual, on which she responds as a feminine partner to a masculine one. Perhaps this is best illustrated by the nomenclature 'my John', or, less frequently, 'Johnnie', combined with the use of the feminine pronoun: she uses these together quite happily, without seeing any discrepancy. This seems all the more strange since several of their more masculine women-friends, such as 'Brother' (Toupie Lowther), are referred to in Una's diary by the masculine pronouns. But never John.

John, who called herself 'a congenital invert' (in the terminology of her day, emanating from Havelock Ellis), would now be more correctly recognized (in the terminology of today) as a female-to-male 'transsexual' (a term first coined by Dr Harry Benjamin in 1949,[22] six years after her death): that is, as a genetic female (XX chromatin) with a psychosexual male identity, with some secondary physical androgyny. As I have already suggested, her self-image was largely masculine ('I can't feel that I am a woman')[23] and was mirrored in her appearance, behaviour and life-long adoption of the name John.

'Transsexuality' is a post-war phenomenon in terms of research and resources, largely due to the invention of synthetic sex-hormones and advances in plastic and reconstructive surgery. In addition, research into endocrinology and psychology by such pioneers as C. N. Armstrong of Newcastle,[24] now postulates that where there is any disharmony between the four primary criteria of sex-determination (chromosomal, gonadal, hormonal and psychological) there is, in effect, a state of 'intersex'. Thus the old idea of there being a 100 per cent female and a 100 per cent male is altered to the concept of a spectrum of sexuality between these two poles.

There was no choice for the Stephen Gordons of this world in 1928 but to live with the discrepancies of their natures as best they could. Science had no answer, and surgery no alternative to offer. It is tempting to wonder whether John, had she lived now, would have undergone sexual reassignment surgery with hormone treatment to produce secondary male characteristics, to enable her to live as a man. She already had a predisposing deep voice, only slight feminine contours, and a phallic sexuality, all of which would have made it a very short step to take. If it had been available to her as an option, would she have sought the expedient of the surgeon's knife to bring body more into harmony with mind and spirit, her nature with her possibilities? Could she indeed have said no to the possibility, in relative terms, of the healing of her, as she saw it, 'maimed and insufferable body'?[25] The drive towards individual wholeness, like species survival, is very strong, and there is ample evidence that she felt keenly the frustrations of her predicament, although she necessarily defined this in different terms, at that time, from those which I have suggested.

In the notes to the sitting of January 2nd, 1918, it is stated that 'MRH is not at all bad at weathering big catastrophes, but . . . small annoyances . . . occasionally irritate her beyond endurance.' Her gender dichotomy (the sense of having 'a man's mind in a woman's body') and its attendant angst was perhaps neither a big catastrophe nor a small annoyance but somewhere between the two; and her power of endurance was at times positively heroic, particularly in the last three years of her life.

She was a tempestuous, passionate being, whose various frustrations exploded in 'moods' and in fiery temper which was quickly spent and forgotten. Perhaps these were part of the release mechanism necessary to a nature locked in the dynamics of antithesis: at once so masculine yet so androgynous, so virile yet so impotent, so fulfilled yet so thwarted.

# 7

# *Psychic Phenomena (1917–21)*

Within three months of Ladye's death John was consulting mediums in the attempt to establish post-mortem communication with her. The sacraments and the communion of saints, which should perhaps have been enough for a devout Roman Catholic faced with bereavement, were not sufficient for John. (By contrast, when John's own death was imminent Una told her that spiritual consolation would be enough to sustain *her* during their 'temporary separation'.)

In the middle of 'the war to end all wars' there was naturally a growing interest in spiritualism; as Una recorded later, 'it was inevitable that someone should propose to John that a visit to a medium might result in consolation.'[1] It was not just consolation she wanted, but *forgiveness*: not via a priest in sacramental Confession, but from Ladye direct. The recommended medium was visited 'with disconcerting and, since the medium in question was mentally unstable, most unpleasant results,' Una wrote.[2]

This medium was a Mrs Scales, who was subsequently referred to in a sitting with Mrs Leonard in 1918 in scathing and unconsciously humorous terms as 'a hysterical medium with *errotic* [erratic?] tendencies . . .' Perhaps both terms were appropriate, as it was explained by Feda (Mrs Leonard's spirit guide, or 'Control') that 'abnormally large families were bad for mediums,' and that she attributed Mrs Scales's downfall to this cause, Mrs Scales being 'a phenomenal case, having produced triplets twice, and twins three times.' What Mrs Scales had 'proposed . . . in the first instance was sheer, uncritical, credulous spiritualism.'[3] Despite the initial emotional motivation this was clearly *not* what they wanted. They were both far too intelligent and inquiring to be taken in in this way; and neither 'was sufficiently unbalanced or uncritical to accept such phenomena as genuine . . .'[4]

Less determined or more easily disillusioned people might have left the matter there, 'but by that time John had read quite a lot on the subject and . . . was still anxious to pursue her investigations in some more reliable manner.' This word became crucial in all that followed. If John was 'anxious' so was Una, but the nature of their anxiety was different: Una was anxious for John, and anxious that their relationship should continue. She made herself the confidante of John's 'sorrow and . . . remorse'[5] and her chief supporter, and threw herself wholeheartedly into this pertinent new interest, which would serve not only to unite them at this dark and difficult time, but would guarantee much time together. As is made quite clear in the notes to the sitting of March 27th, 1918: 'MRH [John] took up Psychical Research to obtain hope of MVB's [Ladye's] survival. UVT [Una] took it up in order to help MRH.'

Putting her own role in perspective nearly thirty years later, Una said, 'In that investigation I was to make the more important moves . . . was to work with her as her lieutenant in closest co-operation and was, for my part, to develop the qualities that would enable me to give her the service she would require when she settled down to her real purpose in life.'[6]

Two of these 'more important moves' occurred early on. They read Sir Oliver Lodge's *Raymond* (1916), an account of communication with his dead son through a medium, and Una took the helm (as she was so often to do later) and wrote to him 'on John's behalf' for advice. He recommended the professional medium he had used himself, Mrs Osborne Leonard. This was to be a long and fruitful association leaving an extraordinary body of evidence covering over twenty years of sittings, averaging two a

week of two hours each for the first six years, and more intermittently afterwards due to foreign travel and the exigencies of a
literary life.

The other move Una made was even more pressing, since 'as
Catholics, we were faced very early on in our venture with the
Church's veto upon all spiritualistic practices . . .'[7] This was a
major hurdle which had to be surmounted for John's sake. Always
a regular penitent, and 'knowing that the Church disapproved of
Psychic Research she felt it her duty to mention her investigations
whenever she went to Confession', John said of herself in the third
person (sitting of October 12th, 1918). Consequently she 'came
for the first time into direct collision with the Priests of her Church
. . . and it is no exaggeration to say that . . . the Father Confessor
became a veritable torment.' (Curiously perhaps, she felt no
similar obligation to mention homosexuality in the confessional,
despite the Church's 'veto' on its practice, or she would certainly
have come into collision on this score long before. Her sense of
'duty' was obviously very selective, so one wonders why she chose
to put herself through this particular 'torment' rather than leaving
it, like homosexuality, between her conscience and God.) She
even contemplated a break with the Church but this prospect
'preyed upon MRH's mind, and greatly added to her grief'.[8] She
was appalled at 'the ignorance and cruelty of many Confessors in
the Church where this subject is concerned'. Una, knowing
'better than anyone else' how this affected John, 'spent the whole
of one day going from Priest to Priest in order to try and find a
sympathetic and understanding Confessor . . . unfortunately her
errand of mercy was rewarded by complete failure.'[9] But Una was
not to be deterred. Some articles in a magazine by Father Thurston, a Jesuit, who had written a book on the subject (and later
himself joined the Society for Psychical Research) led to a letter of
inquiry which produced a sympathetic reply. Serious research for
the purposes of scientific investigation *was* permissible, it seemed.

In the first instance John went anonymously (and alone) to Mrs
Leonard for a table sitting. The name 'Mabel Veronica Batten' was
obtained, and Ladye 'said' through the table, 'I have been with you
so much, especially at night. Been so anxious about you. Am
lonely, so miss you . . .' Towards the end this was said:

MRH: Have you any more to say, my dear?

Table: Heaps. You were so good to me I didn't like it just at first here.

MRH: Can you give the name you always called me by?

Table: Yes. John.

Mrs Leonard: No, no, you must be wrong, John is a man's name.

MRH: It is correct. (August 16th, 1916)

What the naturally surprised Mrs Leonard thought goes un-recorded; and fortunately things which would certainly have surprised her even more later were not 'heard' by her conscious self at all as she was in deep trance.

The first joint sitting (with Una) took place on October 2nd, 1916. With the medium in trance, one 'took' the session while the other 'recorded' it, transcribing all that was said. Usually Una did the recording. If one was ill, or otherwise absent, the other would both take and record the session. Feda, Mrs Leonard's Control, was said to have been a young Indian woman who had died in childbirth; and spoke in a rather childish pidgin-English, pronouncing 'r's as 'l's (for example, 'intelesting'). She could never say 'Johnnie' so always called John 'Mrs Twonnie' and Una 'Mrs Una'.

In this first joint sitting the following occurs:

MRH: Did she ever doubt my devotion?

Feda: She says 'No, I never, never doubted it . . .'

MRH: Does she love me more than anyone else?

Feda: She says, 'Silly question, more than anyone – there is more in our love than there has ever been between two women before . . . I am sure we feel more like married people do to each other.'

What Una felt (being so in love with John herself) hearing both John's questions and the 'answers', one can only imagine. Normally it would be impossible to be 'jealous' of the dead, but when they purport to communicate with the living fondly affirming their relationship, it may be a different matter! What *is* obvious is that

John is still possessive and does not want to be supplanted in the discarnate Ladye's affections (even by her equally discarnate husband, George!)

On October 9th, 1916 John asks the crucial question that had haunted her since May 25th:

> MRH: Something happened before she went over between us that made her unhappy . . . Has she forgiven me?
> Feda: She says, 'I've both forgotten and forgiven. You were not responsible . . . if you had known it would hurt me it would have been different . . .'
> MRH: Tell her I didn't know she was ill, her passing was the shock of my life . . .

Although this was the reassurance she had craved, the guilt still lingers, as it did, to some extent, for the rest of her life; perhaps precisely because she *was* responsible, and *had known* how much it had hurt Ladye. On November 15th she says:

> MRH: Tell her I think I was very selfish before she died.
> Feda: She says that at the time she sometimes wondered but now she knows that you couldn't know she was ill.
> MRH: That was no excuse for many of the things I did.

Reading between the lines, what seems to be on her mind is her 'infidelity' with Una; but she is more concerned with her own conscience than with Una's feelings listening to, and recording, this 'dialogue'.

One thing which must have upset Una at this time was Ladye's often expressed belief that John's own demise was imminent, and that she would shortly be joining her, leaving Una alone. Una obviously took this prognosis seriously and was feeling left out of things; and perhaps realized too that her real life, so centred in John, would be meaningless without her. Almost as a defence and to make sure that she was included Una evolved a convenient theory. 'UVT', John states, 'has recently evolved a theory that several people might form part of the same ego, which would account for the occasionally strong ties that sometimes seem inexplicable.' 'Ladye' takes up this idea later: 'You and I and John are bound up together . . . and it isn't only for the [psychical research] work, it's more than that . . .'[10] Indeed it was! This idea of the combined ego is probably the origin of the dedication in many of John's later novels, 'To our three selves'.

The prediction of John's death becomes a masterpiece of poignant understatement on October 26th, 1918, when John remarks in the notes: 'Undoubtedly UVT, who does not make many intimate friends, would feel MRH's death, which would leave her very lonely.' If Una, with her talent for friendship, made few 'intimate friends', she had even fewer passionate attachments; and of these her *grande passion* was a category of one: John.

They maintained contact with Sir Oliver Lodge ('Soliver' to Feda) and 'before very long her [John's] intelligent and cautious reports and comments had so impressed Sir Oliver that he asked for more and proceeded to train us relentlessly . . .' Una characteristically gives the credit to John, but it was certainly a joint effort. As well as often recording the sessions Una edited them afterwards and typed the notes. One of her rooms at 13 Royal Hospital Road – then later in several houses in Datchet – became their work room. It was not until they lived at Chip Chase in 1919 that one room was set aside exclusively as an office and a full-time typist employed.

'John, with myself as collaborator and second in command, was launched upon an existence of regular and painstaking industry . . . The idle apprentice was metamorphosed by sorrow into someone who would work from morning to night and from night til morning, or travel half across England and back again to verify the most trifling detail.'[11] What was true of John was true of Una also. She brought all her energy and intelligence to bear upon matters in hand, mobilized not by sorrow but by love.

They joined the Society for Psychical Research at Sir Oliver's suggestion, and carried out their 'investigations' under its auspices. Set up thirty-four years earlier, the Society was not trying to prove or disprove the existence of psychic phenomena, but simply to investigate the evidence as scientifically as possible. Amongst its Council and members were many eminent scientists and academics of the day, a high proportion of them Fellows of the

Royal Society. People associated with the Society included Gladstone, Balfour, Ruskin, Bergson, the Curies, Freud and Jung. Its bona fides were impeccable and John and Una were pleased to be associated with it. As well as their own work they 'undertook on Sir Oliver's behalf a special form of "war work". We dealt with a large proportion of the people who . . . wrote to him for information and assistance . . . and when we thought it advisable escorted them to sittings and acted as note-takers for them . . .'[12]

Given the very personal basis on which their activities began, it is remarkable that they came to have a genuine interest in this work for its own evidential value and to devote themselves to it with such vigour. The help and support they gave to other sitters was quite selfless as they themselves derived no personal benefit from it.

A note of tiredness and understated irritation creeps in occasionally, as on January 2nd, 1918: 'In addition to this [i.e. 'work largely among bereaved people'] there are not a few personal friends and relations who persist in thinking that . . . the Psychical Research work is all nonsense, that it is merely a fad on MRH's part, and that she neglects her social duties . . . These people have added not a little to the burden of existence.'

If John experienced family criticism, Una did even more so, both from her own family and Troubridge's. There were already difficulties and criticisms enough about her whole association with John.

They made both friends – Sir Oliver, the Balfours, Mrs Salter, Miss Newton and Mrs Sidgwick (widow of one of the founders) – and enemies – Fox Pitt – at the Society but were generally held in good esteem. As a measure of this John was co-opted on to the Council (the S.P.R.'s governing body) in 1921, 1922, 1923 and again in 1924, when she finally wrote a letter of resignation due to 'lack of time to participate fully in the Society due to the demands of professional writing.'

On Friday April 11th, 1919 they were invited for the first time to a Council dinner, and John recorded (in the third person as usual) that 'As recent workers for the Society they were extremely pleased and flattered at being asked to the dinner, and they had a very interesting and enjoyable evening.' Una recorded in her diary

102

of the same day that it was 'all too interesting'; so much so that they took three of the members on to the American Bar afterwards, and one, Dr T. W. Mitchell (later President of the S.P.R.), went back with them to the Savoy, where they were staying, until 11 p.m.

Dr E. J. Dingwall, now over ninety, who was a member of the Society at this time, and knew them quite well (he is mentioned in Una's diary of January 11th, 1921) remembers: 'Radclyffe Hall was extremely aggressive in manner, and always had an eye for the ladies! Lady Troubridge was passive and always wore feminine clothes.' There was, he says, a fair amount of gossip about them at the Society from time to time; and he thinks they 'loved shocking people and advertised the fact of their relationship.' Certainly they would not have been hypocritical or attempted to hide it; and close friends in the Society, such as Mrs Salter who visited them often, were perfectly well aware of the situation. To such friends they were 'John and Una' not 'Miss Hall and Lady Troubridge'.

Once when dreams were being discussed at the Society ('the psychology of dreams has always been a branch of the Society's work in which serious students were greatly interested,' John wrote in March 1918), Dr Dingwall remembers with amusement seeing the Chairman's face with his mouth dropped open as Lady Troubridge recounted a dream of hers, beginning, 'Last night I had a most strange dream so I turned to John and said, "Darling, I've just had such a dream . . ."'

Both John and the discarnate 'Ladye' make frequent references to Una's 'patient and conscientious work', and it seems that quite apart from supporting John she became genuinely interested in it for its own sake. She took some sittings by herself, often discussing her health or family problems with 'Ladye'. On July 6th, 1918, when by herself, she said: 'UVT to Feda: Tell her I feel that it [i.e. Psychical Research] is my work in this life and after.'

This is further supported by John's comments in the Notes to January 15th, 1919: 'Since she took up Psychical Research . . . UVT no longer cares to become intimate with people whose interests are widely divergent from her own . . . It may truthfully be said that UVT finds very little time in her life for Society people, or in fact for anyone except her immediate family, and those with whom her Psychical Research work brings her into contact.' To add further weight to this comment John adds: 'Mrs Salter also was struck with the idea that the tendency to ignore people whom she finds uncongenial might be characteristic of UVT.'

What these statements confirm about Una is a certain single-minded exclusiveness of interest in things or people; the ability to give herself wholly to the object of her interest at the time.

Compared to John Una frequently shows herself remarkably quick-witted, apt, and observant in following or connecting points during sittings, e.g. (a reference to Hurstmonceaux, May 14th, 1919):

MRH to MVB: I can't remember what we've been doing lately that made you think of it.
UVT: I do.
MRH: I don't.
UVT: About a week ago you mentioned it to me.

Una often corrects John, especially if she sees that John has inadvertently given away an evidential point: she will often say, 'Don't interrupt', 'Don't ask direct questions', or even exclaim, 'Shut up!' or 'Be quiet!' John takes these rebukes well, usually just saying, 'All right', but she has her own grumbles: 'UVT remarked to MRH that being very tired she had found it very difficult to keep up with her notes . . . MRH said peevishly to UVT that it was unfortunate that UVT should always feel tired at *her* sittings.' But John adds characteristically, against herself, 'This statement was both unjust and untrue . . .' (April 10th, 1918).

A measure of Una's real interest in the subject is the fact that she spent nearly two years (1919–21) researching and writing a paper of her own entitled 'The Modus Operandi in so-called Mediumistic Trance' (published in the *Proceedings* of the Society in January 1922). This, despite its title, is a fascinating and well-written document, showing a lucid, logical approach, much evidence of study of other cases, and the ability to assimilate, organize and manipulate ideas. She takes a critical, analytical approach and considers hypotheses. She makes it quite clear that it is the *processes* of mediumistic trance in which she is interested, and she considers mediumistic trance in relation to: various hypnotic levels (her interest in hypnotism goes back to Crichton-Miller in 1913); abnormal psychology; and telepathy. Una says that Mrs Leonard

> who alternates between a very normal 'normal consciousness'; a slight drowsiness or haziness productive of automatic script; a partially analgesic trance followed by almost total amnesia on waking, in which she shows the characteristics of a personality quite foreign to her waking self (i.e. Feda); and yet a fourth, also apparently a trance condition, in which she reproduces with more or less success, the vocal characteristics and mannerisms of deceased persons of both sexes, who were never known to her during their lives, is certainly a case of abnormal psychology.

Having established this so well, she continues: 'And from this fact comes my postulated ray of light. The abnormal psychology of Mrs Leonard . . . abounds in features common to many pronounced examples of what is known as Multiple Personality . . .' Reviewing a number of cases, she proceeds to compare mediumistic and non-mediumistic examples of 'multiple personality' in order to isolate the mediumistic differences. Though serious and demanding concentration, this paper is far from dry, and Una manifests a ready humour, as when she speaks of 'the normal Mrs Leonard and her various psychic lodgers'.

John wrote, just after the publication of this article, 'We are always finding ourselves confronted with something which would appear to disprove a hypothesis once we have evolved one.' One of their hypotheses was telepathy: 'We are justified in assuming . . . that if the dead communicate at all they do so by telepathy, and that a closer study of *telepathy between the living* . . . will help us considerably.'

As if to aid this study, John wrote a short paper called, 'Some Instances of Spontaneous Telepathy between MRH and UVT' (unpublished), which tells us quite a lot about their harmony and disharmony, independence and inter-dependence:

> spontaneous telepathy . . . exists between us . . . but it must not be thought that our minds are always in entire agreement, this is not the case. At times we have arguments amounting to disputes . . . we are not in the habit of slavishly following each other, and that while being very devoted and mutually sympathetic friends, we consider that we have each maintained our independence of view . . . When UVT and I are together . . . it will frequently occur that she will begin singing a tune aloud which I have been singing mentally to myself or vice versa . . . this musical telepathy occurs at all sorts of times and in all sorts of places, when we are dressing, UVT in her dressing room and I in my bedroom with the door open between; when we are gardening; when we are sitting together in a room or in a motor car . . . There are hundreds of occasions when precisely the same idea has occurred to us both with regard to a variety of subjects, when one or other of us have exclaimed, 'You took the words out of my mouth . . .'

Quite apart from any other interest this may have, it does illustrate rather well the mental and physical closeness of their relationship at this time.

The information given through the purporting communicator, 'Ladye' (known by her initials MVB in the transcripts), represents a formidable body of evidence either for the survival of human personality and memory after death, or for a very remarkable form of telepathy with precognitive features. Initially all information is given through Feda (arguably a secondary personality of Mrs Leonard), but later, the ostensible communicator controls the medium directly, without the intervention of Feda. It is in these 'direct controls' (the medium's deepest level of trance) that the personality of 'Ladye' is most manifest: her speech patterns, voice, laugh being identical to their memories of her in life. She gives much evidence of memory of her own life, people and places, some of this being known only to John and herself; in addition she shows knowledge of events since her death, gives details of the interiors of houses lived in by John and Una, and apparently 'overhears' their conversations! They discuss with her their current problems, for example, with the S.P.R. during the Fox-Pitt dispute; with Troubridge and other relations; their health, plans, and so on; and receive characteristic comments and advice! Often they are 'told' beforehand of something unpredictable which is about to happen, and several days later it does. If this is precognition, it is certainly an extraordinary form of it. 'Ladye' is often prophetic about health. For example, on October 20th, 1916 Una has been 'talking' to her (alone) about a recurrent lower abdominal ailment (probably salpingitis, a residual effect of the earlier ectopic pregnancy) and says:

> UVT: Tell her that she said my trouble would get well, and that now the doctor says it won't.
> Feda: She says . . . she is sure that in the near future it will be much better. She says something about fibroids – ask your doctor if there is any sign of fibroids.

This is significant because it *was* fibroids which necessitated Una's emergency hysterectomy many years later in 1932.

The other example concerns Andrea's health. In the sitting of December 27th, 1917 'Ladye' spoke of Andrea's health (which was good) giving an 'actual diagnosis of the exact place in which she is convinced that there is in the child a delicate or . . . a weak spot, which if care is not taken, may cause trouble . . . MVB . . . suggested the need of care . . . at the back, at the extreme base of the left lung,' but 'emphatically asserts that there is *no germ there whatever*, that she is speaking *before* . . . any possible future trouble . . . [John's italics]. UVT left Mrs Leonard's flat . . . in a very perturbed frame of mind . . . MRH was quite genuinely inclined to reassure UVT . . . that an unreasonable tendency on her part to morbid anxiety where the child was concerned had affected the medium's sensitive and receptive condition . . .' John's choice of adjectives implies criticism here and shows an ambivalent attitude on her part. She continues: 'MRH . . . agreed with UVT that the suggestion having . . . been made, only a careful . . . examination by a competent medical man would restore perfect peace of mind . . . UVT therefore made an appointment with Dr Birt [John's own doctor] for the following day . . .' One senses John exercising tolerance here, especially as she is probably paying the bill! After the examination, 'The doctor . . . told UVT that the child was splendid in every way . . . but he added, "There is just a little roughness of the breathing in one spot *at the base of the left lung* [John's italics]. It is nothing at all . . . but I can hear it in that one spot." UVT . . . said that if he had the slightest doubt . . . she was ready to employ every specialist in London.' Later Una read Dr Birt the extract from the sitting, and 'Dr Birt expressed himself much astonished.' He duly put this and his findings in a signed statement, which is still in the Psychic Records.

'Ladye' also 'foresaw' the legal separation from Troubridge before it was contemplated: in the sitting of September 12th, 1917, Feda says, 'she says . . . there will be a sort of arrangement that will have to be come to . . . things are not settled as they are now.'

To Una's amusement or possibly annoyance, 'Ladye' was still very possessive about John, calling her 'my Jonathan' as late as 1936; and she intruded her presence into their lives to the extent of calling Chip Chase '*our* house' and insisting on certain things being in certain rooms. Also, as she could retail their conversations in sittings, privacy must have seemed impossible at times!

The most interesting parts of these transcripts are John's extensive notes at the end of each sitting, which qualify or explain evidential points made. In a way that they could never have dreamed at the time, these notes are a biographer's gold-mine of personal and domestic information, at least as fruitful as Una's own diaries: although they have their tantalizing moments, when a revealing passage is suddenly punctuated by a row of crosses and the words 'private family matter omitted' or 'details of too private a nature omitted'.

They were invited by the Society to give a Paper on their work with Mrs Leonard, but during its preparation felt some misgiving: 'MRH has felt for some time that certain relations of MVB's [i.e. her daughter Cara Harris] and a particular relation of her own [i.e. her cousin Dorothy Clarke] may endeavour to make themselves unpleasant regarding the evidence to be read before the S.P.R.'[13] In the event John was correct, and wrote afterwards that 'trouble had broken out regarding the evidence presented to the S.P.R. by MRH and UVT . . . caused by C [Cara] . . . saying that the evidence was false.'[14]

The Paper was so long that its reading had to be divided into two parts. The first part was read by John at 4.30 p.m. on January 31st, 1918, at the Society's rooms. They recorded later, 'After the Paper a member got up and asked some ridiculous and most inappropriate questions. The member is known to be quite mad. . .' This may well have been Fox-Pitt, whose later comments about them and their Paper led John to sue him for slander. Mrs Leonard, of course, knew nothing of the contents of her sittings or of this Paper, but John observed drily, 'Undoubtedly imbecile Sitters, some of whom may have been present, have furnished Mrs Leonard with a three volume novel on the subject of that Paper . . .'[15] Such knowledge on the part of Mrs Leonard could invalidate evidential material subsequently obtained; but this remark also reveals John's attitudes to some of her fellow-members!

The second part of the Paper was read on March 22nd, 1918. Una recorded in her diary on that date: 'Our Paper 4.30. A big success. Sir Oliver in chair. In the audience John's mother and mine, Emy Campbell, Cara, Dolly and Honey, Iris, Buchel and his wife. . . John read *beautifully* and was heard perfectly . . . Miss Newton said the audience was saying it was a flawless Paper. After it much talk . . .' Not unnaturally perhaps, a little self-praise also creeps in: 'J. Balfour said I was the finest recorder he had ever known.'

Laura Hope (Troubridge's sister, wife of Adrian Hope and mother of Jacqueline Hope, Una's life-long friend) wrote in *her* diary of that date: 'To Steinway Hall to hear Una and JRH's paper on spooks read out – it was so dreary that the three great ones on the platform, Sir Oliver and Lady Lodge and Mr Gerald Balfour were all asleep!'

It is difficult to reconcile such diverse accounts of the same event, but what *is* certain is that before publication in the Society's *Proceedings* Sir Oliver Lodge 'complained to them in a letter that no one would read the Paper except possibly the Committee of the S.P.R. as it was too dull and technical.' (John's Notes, June 18th, 1919.) When it *was* finally published the communicator's initials were changed from MVB to AVB to disguise her identity, at Cara Harris's request.

As well as during sittings, Ladye manifested herself, they believed, in loud raps on the furniture and in little blue or white lights, both usually at night. 'Both UVT and MRH thought they saw 'hallucinatory lights' on several occasions, and a record of any such experience is kept in their diary.' (August 24th, 1918.) This reference to the diary implies that although Una wrote it, it was *theirs* rather than just *hers*.

This sort of thing happened very frequently: 'There is an entry in the diary on August 6th to the effect that UVT saw a globe of whitey yellow light above the foot of MRH's bed, which remained visible for from 10–15 seconds, and that UVT was too much surprised to speak until it went out, when she told MRH who had been nearly asleep and had seen nothing.' (John's Notes, August 24th, 1918.) And again: 'When MRH and UVT, who are sharing a bedroom, had turned out the light, they thought they heard two distinct little raps . . . they discussed this and wondered whether they had imagined it. They had not been long in bed . . . when they both simultaneously heard the raps . . .' (August 1918.)

There was obviously no privacy anywhere! Whether these occurrences were natural or supernatural, they often tied up with 'Ladye's' subsequent claims during sittings.

The S.P.R. work had its lighter side, as the following incident shows. Desiring to sit with a new medium, a Miss Ortner, on September 16th, 1918, they called on her on the 8th, a Sunday evening, to make the appointment. They presented a letter of recommendation from Sir Oliver Lodge, which said only that the lady presenting it could be trusted as a sitter, with any friend, and had lost someone. John explains:

Bearing in mind the fact that Miss Ortner might have received some description of their personal appearance, either from some Leonard sitter or from someone who had been present at recent S.P.R. meetings, MRH and UVT determined, both when making their appointment and taking this first sitting, to make an attempt to alter their normal appearance in a manner which would strengthen their anonymity. UVT therefore wore a close fitting toque which entirely concealed the fact that her hair is worn short, and a silk blouse with a ribbon tie after a fashion quite new to her. MRH dressed her hair on top of her head in a totally different way to her normal style, she wore a party gown of soft material, with open neck and a pearl necklace, a trimmed garden hat of UVT's, carried a vanity bag, a very ornamental umbrella borrowed from her cook, and left off all distinctive rings, etc. Although, of course, none of this constituted a disguise, they felt that it would effectively baffle anyone who had been told of two female sitters, habitually wearing tailor-made clothes of a severe cut, one of them with short hair [Una, surprisingly perhaps] the other with long fair plaits worn round the head . . . MRH and UVT laughed more than they have done for many months . . . their merriment was caused by the fact that . . . MRH looked particularly funny. They were still laughing when they arrived at the medium's house, and had some difficulty in pulling themselves together in order to make the appointment . . .

Another humorous incident reveals something of the nature of their domestic life at Datchet, and certainly shows John as 'master of the house':

On 12 Feb. (1918) MRH had discovered that a large piece of ham, recently purchased from Fortnum & Mason, had not only gone mouldy, but that the meat had become green. This caused her real grief, as she was feeling greedy about the ham. UVT was appealed to, and much sniffing of the ham took place, it was finally condemned as being unfit to eat. MRH however was unwilling that the ham should be thrown away, and insisted that the local grocer should be consulted first . . . As a matter of fact the ham had become rather a joke in the family, as MRH . . . had forbidden anyone to carve it but herself. This incident

111

of the ham took place at lunch time, other people besides MRH and UVT being present, namely the child [Andrea], the governess and a servant.

It is characteristic of John that she can laugh at, or relate incidents against, herself.

The following piece of sartorial amusement occurs on July 9th, 1919 in an MVB Direct Control:

MVB: . . . darling, couldn't you keep your stockings up?
MRH: No, I couldn't a little while ago.
MVB: (Laughs) . . . do tell me *why* the stockings wouldn't keep up.
MRH: They were men's stockings with roll over tops!

In the Notes, John adds 'The men's stockings which were referred to, were worn by MRH with breeches and came down because her legs are very thin!'

Many of the happenings in these Notes which reveal Una's own character, attitudes, and history, are quoted elsewhere in this book; but upon occasion Una herself acts as a go-between from John to the discarnate Ladye, as in a sitting she took by herself on November 13th, 1918:

UVT to MVB: Ladye, Johnnie has asked me to ask you something, she wants to know whether you will let her cut her hair off. She gets so tired taking care of it . . .
Feda: Ladye doesn't like it.
UVT: I knew she wouldn't, but tell her it won't alter Mrs Twonnie's spirit body.
Feda: Ladye doesn't think she'd look nice with it short.
UVT: (Wilily): I can't make up my mind about that . . .

Una, diplomatic as ever, did not win the day on this occasion, as it took a further two years for 'Ladye' to consent to a measure she had so strongly opposed during life.

They became competent, trained investigators much valued by

the Society, though there is some evidence of contradiction between theory and practice, as the following shows:

> It is . . . brought home to us how more than unwise are novice investigators and credulous spiritualists when they expect unadulterated phenomena from even the best medium, and permit anything received through a medium to influence their lives . . . or fail to subject everything thus received to a rigid examination and criticism in the light of common sense. [May 12th, 1920.]

Their association with the Society, in some ways a stormy one, gave them in return for their time, money, and energies, a good training, bone fides, and some standing in the field. There was no sudden cessation of interest in psychical research, and they continued sittings intermittently for many years; but after 1921 there was a decrease in intensity of interest, and a re-direction of energies into other channels.

John told Ethel Mannin in 1930 that, 'her psychic research work years ago did more for her in the matter of straight thinking and intellectual accuracy than any amount of ordinary educational mind-training.[16]

Later still, looking back after John's death, Una commented drily on 'the uncertain and meagre personal harvest that we eventually reaped from all this arduous labour . . .' adding, 'I . . . feel that . . . it served its chief purpose in training John in that infinite capacity for taking pains that . . became so salient a characteristic of her methods . . . later . . .'[17]

This is true in as far as it goes, and with hindsight, but at the time the psychic research work gave them a full, demanding occupation; a sense of intellectual purpose and usefulness; provided a new set of jointly-made, intelligent, sympathetic friends, and a good social life; helped to assuage John's emotional remorse; and perhaps most important of all, united them in a common endeavour which helped to cement their relationship.

# 8

# Our Union
# (1917–21)

The years 1917–21, amongst the most exacting and difficult Una and John were to know, laid the foundations of all that was to come: 'a friendship . . . grew steadily and ripened between us until it became as precious, fulfilling and essential to her as ever it could be to me . . . until neither of us could have claimed to care more than the other . . .'[1] Una wrote later. They were to develop 'the perfect companionship and understanding that constitutes the great strength of such unions.'[2]

The psychic investigations contributed to this development during these years; as did their love of books and reading. Una, always an avid reader and collector of books (they acquired 4,000 over the years), read aloud to John during many thousands of hours, so that they shared and discussed literature and many other subjects and she, in effect, finished off John's education. Also 'Our common love of our Church, of its ritual, and of religious art and literature, was always a very strong bond between us,' Una stated. In addition to this 'marriage of true minds', 'they two were now one' physically, and Una knew for the first time 'sexual rapture'.[3] Bisexual women say that 'when their lover is a woman, the mutual pleasuring is slower, more innovative and lasts longer. They have a total body response rather than a genital one, and feel a warmer,

114

deeper, reaction to their lover, because each is more sensitive to the other's needs.'[4] In addition, 'higher frequency of orgasm in lesbian sexuality has . . . been remarked on by . . . researchers . . .'[5] because as 'women are aware of their own psychological make-up, orgasms between homosexual women are more easily wrought than in heterosexual intercourse'; and 'unactivated by preconceived notions, lesbians can exploit the genuine erotogenic zones, rather than the "accepted" ones . . .'[6]

After her marriage, this was a new, liberating experience. Una's passions, like her intelligence, were fully engaged and developed; and all her inner resources were to be used, and often heavily taxed, during her years with John: 'Life with John was by no means easy, but her variety was infinite and it was always interesting. If I knew discouragement, weariness and exasperation throughout the . . . years that we were together I never knew boredom . . .'[7] In a sense she changed one 'husband' for another, one way of life for another; but she spent eight years with Troubridge, and twenty-eight years with John. That speaks for itself. Una showed very early 'the impulse to give that is common to all lovers',[8] and her many presents to John included a gold crucifix, a reset sapphire ring, a stoned ring set in silver, a fine old Italian chest, a scarf pin 'large and valuable', and a statue of St Anthony in ivory which stood by John's bed.

The dynamics of their relationship are worth exploring. It was ostensibly 'homosexual' but this needs some clarification. 'Homo' means 'the same as', and in a true lesbian relationship both partners perceive themselves and each other as female, in what is a mirror-image situation, without roles. John preferred, and as far as possible took, the male gender role; and in part her psychosexual identity was masculine. They had complementary natures, and theirs was essentially an attraction of opposites in a spectrum of sexuality which labels them both biologically, but not psychologically, female. Masculine-feminine polarities were at work: Una was attracted to the masculine principle in John, and John to that aspect of the 'eternal feminine' which Una embodied. Una could not, in her nature, have been attracted to a feminine woman, since she represented the feminine principle herself; and no normal man had roused Una's passionate nature as John did.

*Life Together: the First Years (1917–26)*

Equally, John could no more have been attracted to a masculine woman (such as 'Micki' Jacob or 'Brother'[9]) than to a man, as she identified herself with the masculine principle. This was not a question of conventional role-playing, but of their basic response to each other. Relationships find their own 'norms' according to the natures and needs of the partners. Una, the receptive, feminine principle, devoted herself to the comfort, well-being, and support of 'my John'. She mostly made John's concerns her own, deriving both emotional satisfaction and a sense of purpose from so doing. Una, like Mary in *The Well*, was all – or 'pure' – woman, one whose nature is undivided by masculine-feminine conflicts: she was every inch a lady. To Una, John was lord and (usually benevolent) master, whose strength gave her a sense of safety and security. She was, in all senses, happily dependent; and for her, their relationship was exclusive and sacramental in nature, expressed as 'our union'.

As a 'husband' John was essentially an enlightened despot, but was always amenable to the kind of subtle feminine persuasion that was Una's forte. 'John was always indulgent to me,' she tells us, with evident satisfaction.[10] 'If I could have I'd have married her . . .' Stephen says in *The Well*, and there is no doubt that John *would* have married Una, as she was to make clear to Souline later;[11] although, unlike Gertrude Stein of Alice Toklas, she never referred to Una as 'my wife'.

They were so lucky to have found each other; and despite their previous (and in John's case, subsequent) relationships, this was, for them both, not just the longest, but the one true 'union' of their lives. It changed them both profoundly. Without Una's unfailing support and encouragement, and their stable emotional life, John might never have written her books. Without John, Una might have remained an 'unlit lamp'. Each of their lives would have been the less without the other. John gave Una a diary and wrote on its fly-leaf: 'Squig. Good Luck in 1917,' and not surprisingly it was to be filled largely with details of their shared activities. It was their first full year 'together' and was to establish the permanence of their relationship, despite many problems.

Their 'togetherness' was shown early in the year by their first joint invitation to the home of Sir Oliver and Lady Lodge in

116

Birmingham, from January 9th to the 13th. Andrea went to stay with her aunt Laura in Tite Street. It was to be a memorable visit which included much discussion, reading aloud, and several table sessions with wine glass and letters. 'Such delightful people, one could not long be shy,' Una noted in her diary. Sir Oliver's 'ulterior motive' was to off-load some of his work on to such able and willing helpers, who were 'hugely honoured and pleased' to be asked!

On their return to London they were depressed. 'Poor John cried nearly all afternoon, and so did I!' Una noted in her diary on January 14th. Her 'heart trouble' recurred, but a doctor reassured her that it was only 'influenza and indigestion'. Having to vacate 13 Royal Hospital Road, Una looked at other furnished houses, and on January 23rd saw and made an offer for 42 St Leonard's Terrace. It was accepted and on February 13th she went through the inventory with the landlady, and moved in on the 15th, when she noted sadly in her diary: 'I very much depressed at new start in another squalid little lonely abode but one must just do one's best and go on . . . I am very very tired . . .' It was a very emotional time, with frequent depressions, upsets and reconciliations with John, letters to and from Troubridge, Andrea to look after, and preoccupation with sittings and meetings of the S.P.R. On January 31st Una noted, 'we met George Fox-Pitt,' an association which was to have very serious and unforeseen consequences. They also became friendly with W. B. Yeats: 'Yeats came and talked all evening til 11 o'clock about the Psychic Telegraph.'[12]

Una was seeing her mother and Viola, Laura and Jacqueline Hope, and she and John were involved in uneasy friendships with Dorothy Clarke and Cara Harris. These meetings often precipitated personal upsets: 'Dolly [Clarke] came to dinner at 7.30 and staid till 11.15. John very depressed and in vile temper – not a nice evening and I cried much after I was left alone.'[13] However, after she had been in the new house little more than ten days, she records on February 27th, 'John staid the night.' Humorously, and discreetly, reference is made to this in the sitting of the next day, February 28th:

I had spent the previous night at UVT's house, and she had

come in herself to wake me in the morning. She did so by letting the blind go up with a bang, and a flood of light struck my eyes suddenly. I rolled over on to the other side of the bed, loudly voicing my indignation. The usual proceeding when I am in my own flat, is much less abrupt, I being . . . aroused by a servant with a cup of tea; there is no garish light let in upon me, so I have no occasion to expostulate . . .

Things were beginning to settle down again and they were resuming their physical relationship.

> I shall wake in the half light and I shall feel contented,
> I shall wake in the half light, content, and wonder why;
> Till drowsily and drowsily my hand shall go to seek you,
> And drowsily and drowsily shall touch where you lie . . .

John had written in a poem called 'Waking',[14] which certainly referred to Una. Sometimes Una felt the need to give a more ostensible reason for John's presence at night: 'John staid night as my heart was bad'[15] or 'John so tired she stayed night . . .'[16]

On May 1st they were unpacking at 22 Cadogan Court, where they 'made common cause',[17] living partly there and partly at Una's official residence, 42 St Leonard's Terrace. On the same day, Una went to view 6 Cheltenham Terrace, and made an offer for it on May 2nd. This was an unfurnished house on a lease, which she signed on Troubridge's behalf in his absence on May 21st. On May 10th Una stayed with John at Cadogan Court for the first time: 'While she lived there I would sleep there as often as not,' she recalled later.

They missed each other when they were apart. Una went alone to Edinburgh from March 10th to the 19th to stay with the Nevadas, Mignon and 'Papa', and to go to the operas: *Bohème*, *Aida*, *Butterfly* . . . They wrote to each other daily, sometimes twice, and sent frequent wires as well. Una broke the journey home at Birmingham where John met her and they went to the Lodges for the second time.

On Easter Sunday they took flowers to Ladye's tomb at Highgate, as they were to for many years; then on April 10th, went for a week's early holiday to Bournemouth, where they rested, took Turkish baths, read, walked, and went to bed early; the pattern of many of their later holidays.

Back in London they went to the Bath Club, lunched or dined often at the Queen's Restaurant, Sloane Square, the Rembrandt Hotel, or the Berkeley or Prince's Grills. Andrea, like Sidonia in *A Saturday Life*, went to dancing classes, and sang; and also spent much of her time at More House, Tite Street, especially when Una was away. When they went to sittings, she would usually be left at home with nurse or maid. Mrs Leonard was then living in a cottage belonging to a Mrs Bamber at Datchet-on-Thames, so Una and John commuted there once or twice a week.

Una and John also went for long weekends to Pittleworth Manor, a large old house in Buckinghamshire belonging to Austin Harris, Ladye's son-in-law. Austin and Cara's children, Peter, Karen and Honey, were there also, and things were usually quite amicable: 'Austin, Peter, John and I – shopping, seeing [Mottisfont] Abbey, later to river til 8 o'clock. Austin took photos. John smoked a big pipe and survived it! . . .'

On May 25th Una noted in her diary: '*This day last year Ladye went over*. 8.45 John fetched me in car [to] Mass in Cathedral crypt. Met Cara, Honey and Karen there and then to breakfast at Cara's . . .' Despite the solemnity of the anniversary, Una and John later took Cubby to Gamages where John bought her a tricycle; but they did not spend the night together: 'wrote letters . . . John rang up at 10 and I to bed . . .'

On May 28th Una 'receive[d] news of a startlingly unexpected nature, which caused her temporary anxiety . . .'[18] She had only written to him the day before, and nothing could have been further from her mind than 'the sudden and unexpected return of Admiral Troubridge.'[19] At 5.30 Olga the maid telephoned Una at John's flat to say that Troubridge was coming home the following day. In a panic they took a taxi to the Admiralty to try to find out about it, but with 'no result'. She went back to number 42, then in the morning John came to breakfast, and they looked to see if there was any mention of Troubridge's return in the daily papers. Una then went to Taylor's depository and took out Troubridge's civilian clothes. Later she dined with John, then met Troubridge at Victoria at 9 p.m. and took him to the Charing Cross Hotel, staying talking with him until 10.30. She went back to John to tell her all about it, and then home to bed. What she had said to Troubridge unfortunately remains unrecorded. He may well not have approved of her signing leases in his absence, or of the life she was leading, and he certainly disapproved of her absorption in Psychical Research. None of her frequent letters to him survive, but his sudden return may indicate alarm at their content.

The next day John went alone to Mrs Leonard, while Una went to meet Troubridge, and they went together to Tite Street to lunch. Troubridge then went to see Carson at the Admiralty and Una went back to John. That evening, and on many subsequent ones, Troubridge dined with John and Una at Cadogan Court. Some strange but amicable arrangements were arrived at: Troubridge stayed as a guest at 22 Cadogan Court, and Una went 'home' to 42 St Leonard's Terrace; but if she *did* stay at 22, she slept alone on a divan in the drawing-room. Una and Troubridge *dined* together at 42, but Troubridge never slept there: 'Over to 22, and we all, Troubridge, Cub, John and I and Olga to Mass at St. Mary's . . . back to 22, John, Troubridge and I dined Café Royal and afterwards back to 22 and talked til 12.30. So I staid night sleeping on the drawing room divan.'[20]

At night: 'to 22 where Troubridge joined us for dinner and I home in a taxi at 11 . . .'[21] and the next morning: 'Over to 22 at 9.30. Saw Troubridge who went off at 10 . . .'[22]

How Troubridge was induced to accept this situation is not known, but accept it he did. He and Una dined with members of his family, and with his friends at the Savoy or the Travellers' Club; but otherwise she continued her normal life with John, going to sittings as usual, shopping, and meeting their friends: 'Out with John to buy a refectory table – tried 10 shops in vain, and at the 11th she bought me the most beautiful one I've ever seen . . .'

Later John bought her 'two beautiful Cromwellian oak chairs,' and she wrote: 'I do love to feel that so many things I shall use in my house will have been given by and associated with her.'[23]

Troubridge was kept quite busy, which was convenient for Una. On June 18th Una, John and Cara went to 'Cobb's lecture at Lady

Glenconnor's 5 pm, saw Sir Oliver there, Emmie Clarendon and Emy Hack.' On the way back they drifted unintentionally towards Cara's house, and Una was 'in time to confine the housemaid and save and baptise "Joy".'[24] John elaborates further:

> Cara was met on the threshold by the housekeeper, who told her that one of the servants was very ill and . . . having a miscarriage. UVT, who afterwards said she did not know from what source the inspiration came, dashed upstairs saying: 'I am quite sure it's a baby!' On entering the room UVT found the mother and two or three of the servants. UVT discovered that her worst fears were realised and had considerable difficulty . . . to restore the child to a semblance of life . . . feeling sorry for . . . the apparently uncared for and unwanted infant . . .

As well as being a capable midwife, Una was also a good vet to her own dogs. After this incident they all stayed at Cara's for dinner, then went home to tell Troubridge all about the drama, after which Una herself felt 'very tired and rather sick now it was all over . . .' When they were back at Cadogan Court, Una 'staid [the] night in John's room she sleeping in drawing room.'

They were careful that Troubridge should not know that they ever slept *together*, although he may have had an inkling of the truth. If he did, he kept it to himself at that time.

Una accompanied him on duty or family visits, including to the wedding of his younger sister Helen and the reception at More House afterwards. On July 6th Cubby had her tonsils out in a nursing home, and Una and John, not Troubridge, were there to see that all was well; and on the 16th Una noted: 'early to no. 6 [Cheltenham Terrace] and the move all day. John helping . . .' The move took some time, but it must have depressed Una that it was her marital residence, emphasizing that she belonged officially to Troubridge and not to John. She continued to refer to 22 as 'home', and the division in her loyalties and activities is marked: 'Zyp [Troubridge] and I to no. 6 and lunched 42. John picked me up at 3 and we to Nevada's musical party. Home to 22 at 6.30 and dined and slept there.'

Troubridge presumably made allowances because of Una's 'health', to ascertain the precise nature of which he accompanied her, on July 25th, to Sir James Mackenzie, 'who said my heart trouble was just worry and unhappiness that had rendered it sensitive to every shock – and was and would be painful but no remedy except being perfectly happy and other still more impossible circumstances . . .'

Troubridge must have realized that the specialist, in eliminating any organic dysfunction, was tactfully saying that Una's 'illness' was in fact psychosomatic. After this Una went 'back to 6 Cheltenham Terrace where John awaiting me – Bless her – the best friend ever woman had. We lunched 22 and worked all afternoon . . . Dined and slept 22 . . .' The implication here is clearly that Una found John more sympathetic than Troubridge, who now probably thought, rightly, that there was nothing really 'wrong' with her.

John went alone to Pittleworth Manor for a few days, during which Una was left with Troubridge, and 'duty' entertaining of her sister-in-law Helen and step-son Thomas. She wrote daily to John, and recorded most days, 'Heart very painful all day.'

On August 1st, their anniversary, Una wrote *and* wired, and left with Cub, nurse and two dogs, for Bournemouth, seen off by Troubridge. John arrived there three days later from Pittleworth. They went together to Paignton, where Mrs Leonard was on holiday, for sittings. At the end of the day Una noted, 'then John and I to bed sharing a room . . .' They stayed at Paignton a few days then went back to Bournemouth, Una returning to London for the day on the 16th, the last time she was to see Troubridge before his departure. Back in Bournemouth she and John 'were very sad discussing all sorts of sad possibilities in the next state of existence till we hardly knew which was the most unhappy of the two . . .' Being wrenched apart either by circumstances or by death was obviously in their thoughts, particularly Una's. A little later, 'John promised I should if I died before her be buried at Highgate as near her as possible – and should she go before me I can see to it myself – so I am happier.'[25]

Then, 'John wrote and sent letter ref. Codicil [i.e. to her Will] anent my having her clothes and little personal things if I survive her . . .'[26] so that 'I can have and hoard the things really connected with her . . .'[27]

On August 26th, 'True [Troubridge] left at 1 p.m. for Greece
. . .' Una noted dispassionately, and no doubt with relief. Things
were not settled but conditions were 'so peculiar and so difficult'[28]
that it was hard to see a solution, and Una admitted that 'I don't
quite know what I ought to do,' as 'the difficulties and complications seem never ending.'[29] Two days after Troubridge's departure, a 'batch of disturbing letters'[30] arrived from him, but 'by
work we became more peaceful.'[31] Una had declared earlier, 'I am
quite ready to meet any trouble that comes, trusting that it will
be all right in the end,'[32] but it was not always easy, and Una
was, like John, a worrier.

The external tensions affected the equilibrium of their relationship, and there were frequent upsets: '. . . cried most of the
morning . . . then we made it up and worked til lunch . . .';[33]
'the alarm clock . . . didn't go off . . . John furious! . . . made it up
at breakfast I being by then too miserable to bear it.'[34] More
seriously: 'I feeling mortally sad and discouraged – it all seems very
uphill and hopeless today – neither past present nor future bear
looking at and I feel almost too desolate sometimes to go on . . .'[35]
Sometimes she blamed herself: 'Before dinner I said something
about a photo that made John furious and we both said very hurtful
things – but made it up before bedtime – though I remained
miserable and wild with myself that my provocation should make
me unkind to John . . .'[36]

In October they went for the first of many much-needed and
happy holidays to Lynton in Devon, staying at the Cottage Hotel:
'lovely rooms – we felt cheered . . . John very dear and sweet and
kind . . .'[37] While there they viewed houses, and talked about the
future. The main fly in the ointment was Troubridge: 'Talked
much to John anent Troubridge . . . To sleep late after much
uneasy, sad thinking and to uneasy, troubled dreams . . .'[38] Una
wrote.

The anxiety was that, as John said in the Psychic Records:
'When UVT's husband returns from the War it will not be
possible for UVT to look upon herself as a free agent, and that
under those circumstances she would find it difficult to be at
MRH's beck and call . . .'[39]

Troubridge had written to Una, 'Owing to this interest [i.e.

psychical research], you have completely dropped your relations and mine . . .'[40] 'Some interfering relations' of Troubridge's (presumably his sisters) suggested that she was neglecting Andrea, and Una remarked indignantly, 'I mind their saying I don't care for the child.'[41]

To escape proximity to such relations, and the London air-raids, and to be nearer Mrs Leonard, Una decided to move out of London to Datchet-on-Thames, and took a furnished villa, 'Grimston', rented from a Miss Turner. Cubby and her nurse, Carrie Dillon, were to go there to live, while John and Una would commute between this house and Cadogan Court, leaving 6 Cheltenham Terrace unlived in. They and the Cub moved in on December 1st, Una carefully clearing silver and other valuables out of number 6. She must have known that she would never live there, although it would remain Troubridge's London home.

Before this move, on November 25th, Una was operated on by Mr Dudley Wright for haemorrhoids. John was much in attendance and ordered Una a sapphire ring which she had admired, to cheer and distract her from 'feeling rotten'. Una confessed to her diary: 'I was very tiresome all evening til finally John took the dressings out and got me opium injection.'

On the 29th they went to a special Mass of thanksgiving, and John gave Una a dog called Baby; but later Una was: 'In pain and felt very low. Cried a lot in afternoon, could not help it – felt very lonely and sad. Wondered would there ever be an end to loneliness – here or beyond . . .' Later still things improved: 'we talked til 12 with peace at last.'

They were busily commuting between London and Datchet, and their three residences; attending sittings; having very late nights, and eating much Grill Room food, all of which served to add stress, and fray Una's nerves and John's temper. She would flare up frequently over little things, often reducing Una to tears: 'Our notes left in Mrs Leonard's room and John was very cross about it . . . lunched Prince's Grill and made it up . . .'[42] 'John and I quarrelled most of the night' on December 16th about domestic matters such as the boiler and servants. Una added to the deficiencies of servants by not 'bringing them to book', John argued, and Una promised to amend. The truth was that she disliked having to be firm with servants; and wanted to leave hiring and firing to John: 'Wheeler so tiresome John gave her notice . . .'[43]

At Datchet they got to know Ida Temple, a jovial Irish woman, widowed with three children, and for six years beginning in 1917, they and Cub were to spend Christmas at her house, all going to Midnight Mass at a tiny village chapel, followed by days of jollity which included singing, dancing and playing the piano.

Although technically Grimston was Una's abode, it was the first place she and John took together as a joint base, albeit far from ideal. It was too small for them, Cub, servants, and three dogs! On December 29th: 'John awoke frightfully angry about the dogs. I wish they could all go, as their misdeeds seem to make her dwell on the other discomforts here which I *cannot* help: Cub and her toys at close quarters, difficulties of food, warmth, and service. I am in despair . . . every morning now I get up and help to do breakfast and clean up myself any mess the dogs make . . . I know we are all uncomfortable but *cannot* do more . . .'

John could be 'impatient and over-exacting',[44] and Una was desperate to please her in every way. Things were not to improve much domestically until they moved to 'Swanmead', another, slight larger furnished house in Datchet, the following year.

Una heard later that Lanteri had died from influenza on December 18th, 1917, and wrote with a sense of clear regret at her own frustrated hopes and ambitions, and a hint of guilt: 'He lived long enough for me to disappoint him . . . to see me throw overboard with complete indifference the talent he had nurtured and on which he had built such high and unselfish hopes . . .'[45]

Her absorption in John and the psychic records, even more than in her marriage earlier, had brought this situation about, and she did little real sculpture after 1915, apart from a bust of John in October 1917. She put the claims of her emotional life before those of her mind, without counting the cost of this sacrifice at the time.

By 1918 John was beginning to realize that, 'She must put away all these thoughts of the past and compel herself to think of the future. This brooding over things that were past was all wrong . . .'[46] and she started to think seriously of buying a house and settling with Una just outside Datchet. Troubridge was abroad and would, they hoped, remain so; and John knew for a certainty that Una's affections were all directed towards herself.

Una tried not to feel that she was living with Ladye's ghost, or to worry unduly about the still uncertain future. She threw herself vigorously into the psychical research, writing to Jacqueline: 'Work is very strenuous just now, generally into the small hours and Johnnie and I are part of a small Investigation Committee including Gerald Balfour and his sister, and that means a lot of extra work.'[47]

The year began with domestic troubles, but Una treats them humorously. On January 1st: 'the boiler burst during breakfast!' and on the 4th: 'To Fortnum and Mason where NO MORE SWEETS! Then home and found Baby [dog] had had more hysterics and seemingly potty so we sent for Vet . . .'; and synoptically on the 5th: 'So here we are – no boiler – no cook – no typist – no house parlour maid – puppy sick – I with piles.'

They set to, to 'do' for themselves, with burlesque results: 'John up early to do breakfast and help me – a real help in time of trouble. I cooked and she did housework all morning. In afternoon we agreed the stew had been a failure and I wept in John's arms!' Cooking was not Una's strong point, as John was soon to realize; and they went servant-hunting the next day.

Their episodic rows no longer had the depth of despair evident in the previous year: 'After lunch a violent row with John which lasted all afternoon til we more than made it up after tea. Bless her, she is so dear when the storm has blown over . . . and I just love her anyway.'[48]

Una recorded in thinly-veiled code John's declarations to her: 'J. s. I've m.L. and I've m.y.'[49] The 'm' here must mean 'married', thus 'John said I've "married" Ladye and I've "married" you,' which Una obviously wanted to remember.

Her health was not perfect, although she always dramatized it: 'heart attack' meant an attack of her nervous 'heart trouble'; 'colitis' meant bowel upset, which had been defined by one doctor as 'intestinal indigestion', but she *did* have recurrent salpingitis and haemorrhoids. Inexplicably, and certainly less than truthfully, she wrote to Lady Denbigh: 'I am a partial invalid and have lived for some years quietly in the country . . .' She recorded on February 5th: 'Attack of colitis – longed to die except for leaving John and Cub. Sick of an inefficient body.' Her 'inefficient body' was to last for another forty-five years; but the order in which John and Cub appear is significant. It is *John*, first and foremost, whom she does not want to leave; her child comes second, and Troubridge nowhere at all.

It was said by her critics that she abdicated from full maternal responsibility, and neglected Andrea; and that the child was always made to feel unwanted, or in the way, as Una was so preoccupied with John; but this seems rather unfair. Una worried about the child's health and welfare, and took stringent steps to ensure that she was well cared for and looked after, although she 'brought up her child in a very hardy, if not Spartan way'.[50] Andrea spent quite a lot of time visiting her Troubridge relations when Una was away, or with her nurse even when Una was at home, but middle-class children did in those days. Parents paid a professional child-minder to mind their children. A degree of consternation could therefore be caused when this minder had a rare day off: 'Cub very good but on our hands!' Una exclaimed in her diary at the end of 1917. Certainly she was not 'child-centred' in the modern sense, and was a woman first and a mother second; and being a woman first meant, for her, being John-centred.

John's attitude to Andrea was ambiguous. She was generous, buying her a bicycle, a watch, toys, and taking her out: 'John took Cub a walk in the meadows.' (February 28th.) And also, 'John taught Cub to bicycle in one lesson.' (February 25th.) She acted in a quasi-paternal role towards the child, and even on one occasion 'made up her mind that if the child showed any signs of having a good brain, the child must be sent to a University later on, and given a thorough scientific education, in order that she might become a useful investigator in Psychical Research.'[51]

At the same time, John wanted to give Una 'such a love as would be complete in itself without children,' so that she 'would have no room in her heart, in her life, for a child . . .'[52] and John certainly resented Andrea's claims on Una's time and attention, and Una's maternal anxieties. More deeply, the presence of

Andrea touched the springs of John's 'masculine' pride and frustration, emphasizing the sterility of her own sexual life: that she could not give Una a child herself.

Settled in Datchet, Una and John took to bicycling in the village, into Windsor or Slough, and to their sittings with Mrs Leonard. John bought Una 'a beautiful Sparkbrook bicycle' (which she promptly christened 'Clara') as a birthday present, and Una was 'unusually particular when selecting her bell. She insisted on a . . . very loud and aggressive' one and soon 'acquired a habit of ringing this bell furiously on all occasions,' so that John eventually 'besought her to ring her bell a little less frequently for the sake of the neighbours.'[53] What this tells one about Una's character is perhaps debatable but it is certainly amusing. Occasionally, all this exercise had unforeseen consequences: 'Palm Sunday. John and I bicycled to Slough for Mass. I turned faint at the Gospel, had to lie down in the Padre's house.'[54]

There were still periods of gloom: 'Deadly depression over us both . . .'[55] and disagreements: 'John and I both had dinner in bed and were very quarrelsome in evening and into night – making it up in the early morning.'

Simple cause and effect played its part: 'Carrie [Dillon, Cub's nurse] gave notice. I a violent attack of the usual.'

At times John took a 'chauvinist' attitude, expecting Una to do two jobs whilst she herself did only one: 'A turn up [i.e. row] because I got fussed anent the fact that household matters all behind and neglected and John thought I wouldn't help her with the work,' i.e. the S.P.R. work.[56] John's attitude to servants was not dissimilar: 'Confound them! I can't get my orders carried out!'[57]

Nevertheless Una, not satisfied with sculpting John herself, with photographs, or just with her in the flesh, insisted that she have her portrait painted. Una selected, from among the artists she knew, Charles Buchel, with whom she had become familiar years earlier, through Sir Herbert Tree. Sittings were arranged at his studio in Acacia Road, and Una settled with him that he should paint John for £35, which she herself paid. They were pleased with the finished product which hung in John's study; and was to be left to the National Portrait Gallery many years later, in Una's Will.

Una was still writing long letters to Troubridge and he sent them 'a parcel of butter etc.' from Serbia. When she wrote telling him of a house in Datchet called 'White Cottage' to which she wished him to move from Cheltenham Terrace he dug his heels in and declared his antagonism both to psychical research and to living in Datchet. He may even have declared his growing antagonism towards John; and wrote letters to them separately to make his points. 'True wrote to John he wouldn't move to Datchet,' and the next day Una received 'two letters from True refusing to move . . .'[58] If the light had not fully dawned on Troubridge before, it certainly did now. John, mindful of the value of written evidence, kept some of Troubridge's letters. The extraordinary thing is that he wrote to John at all, in the circumstances. Una's response to this frustration of her plans was to retreat to bed with 'ovarian pains and chill' followed by violent 'raging' headaches. John often joined her there: 'John and I in bed til noon . . .'

By the time they had returned from their annual holiday at Lynton – where they rested, read, and rode ponies – in mid-June, relations with Troubridge had deteriorated further: 'Unpleasant letter from True, as usual,' Una noted.[59]

Other troubles were also brewing at the S.P.R. where Dolly Clarke and Cara Harris were casting aspersions upon their veracity. John was adamant: 'Our word has been denied and our character taken away, to the S.P.R. . . . I can't let that pass . . . Una and I may be crushed out of the Society; we can't let people tell lies about us and not tell our side of the story,'[60] and went as far as consulting Messrs Hastie, her solicitors. Cara bypassed John and 'Wrote me [Una] in the morning asking me to use my "tact, good help" to assist her against John!'[61] She should have known better, and that Una's loyalty to John was unwavering.

In July Andrea went off to Runcton, and Una and John returned to the peace of Emmie Hole's Cottage Hotel at Lynton, 'a very comfortable "country house" type hotel with food fresh and plentiful,' with 'lovely, lovely country, few people, a golf course . . .' as Una wrote to Mrs Sidgwick[62] ecstatically. But all was not peaceful even there and rows left Una 'feeling rotten and utterly discouraged'[63] at times.

On their return to Datchet they lunched with the Temples spending the afternoon singing and playing the piano, which made Una 'sad over my lost voice which I still sometimes regret poignantly.'[64] They frequently went to London to see Minna and Viola, John's mother, and other friends; and Una resumed her visits to Crichton-Miller who hypnotized her. They made new friends through old ones: at a musical afternoon they met Lady Kimberley, who subsequently: 'asked us both to dine so we went . . . and a very nice evening. John played her own songs and they loved them – and her.'

Her pride in John is evident, and it must also have pleased her that they were invited together, treated socially as a pair. They certainly thought of themselves as such, and were treated as such by Una's old friend Jacqueline, now married to Hedley Nicholson:

> Dearest Jacqueline,
>
> I wanted to get you and Hedley to lunch with me and John somewhere . . . we must try and meet the next week. I am hard at work re-reading all the Bronte novels – I do adore them, don't you? . . . Fancy the Cub being 8 years old tomorrow it doesn't seem very long since she was born . . .
>
> Much love dearest Jacqueline,
>
> > Your loving Una

They frequently went to London for shopping as well as social purposes: 'To London – for parrots . . . to Harrods where we bought George Robey's parrot on one month's approval – we took him home to tea and he was very talkative –' As they had recently been reading world religions they christened him Karma, and added him to their menagerie of four dogs, various other birds, hamsters and fish. A little later Ellen Wilder, the house parlour-maid, had to be dismissed for stealing not only John's cigarettes but also 'a considerable quantity of parrot food'!

There was a temporary lull in hostilities with Troubridge, since Una was arranging in October to send 'a quantity of sweets out to her husband'[65] in Serbia; and noted in her diary in November, without any apparent alarm: 'Long letter from True who may come home for [a] few days.'

In December they moved to 'Swanmead' and Una arranged for Andrea to take lessons with the Temple children; and signed an agreement letting 6 Cheltenham Terrace on a short-term tenancy. She and John were still looking at houses with a view to John buying one for them both: 'To new hideous houses at Twickenham, Richmond, and Sheen – God forbid! – p.m. to see houses in Mulberry Walk . . .'[66] Despite Troubridge, and his eventual return, they were thinking in terms of a shared future – a real house of their own. Whether they were thinking in terms of an *à trois* situation or a complete break is uncertain, but the latter is more likely.

At last, at the very end of December, they found Chip Chase, a large secluded house with mock battlements at Hadley Wood, talked it over, and made their plans. In the mean time Una received a 'wire from Troubridge asking for great coat to be sent to Paris, dated Salonika, December 7th.' He was obviously on his way home.

Just before the end of 1918, after a joint bout of severe influenza, various specimens were taken from them both by a Dr Sachs, in conjunction with a pathologist colleague, Dr Teale. John's specimens were satisfactory, but, Una recorded: 'Doctor came and said my specimen very odd!'[67] and two days later, 'Doctor came – he doesn't seem to know a bit what bug he is likely to find.' A little later still, 'Doctor came and said . . . so far analysis not complete. I think he fears the other thing and wants to prepare us!' The 'other thing' they feared was gonorrhoea, which they must have suspected themselves; but it seemed a false alarm as the next day 'Doctor arrived to say no bugs in my specimen! Only post-flu troubles – John very relieved.' No doubt Una was also, but it was to prove a false comfort.

Matters with Troubridge were gathering momentum and coming rapidly to a head. He was promoted to full Admiral with seniority on January 9th, 1919, and wrote to Una from Paris on the 21st, and in response to his request she went to Cheltenham Terrace and fetched and packed his clothes. She spent five days in bed, her usual response to worrying situations, being visited by

Minna, Viola and Crichton-Miller, who was 'very kind and sympathetic'.

Concurrently with these events, John and Una decided on Chip Chase for themselves, and on Hampworth Cottage at Oakleigh Park for Mrs Leonard, in order to have her near them for sittings. After her husband had viewed it, Mrs Leonard accepted it, as a gift from John, who agreed to buy both properties. Una went to Maples to choose her curtains, and she and John talked over details of furnishing. John's solicitor, Messrs Hastie, acted on her behalf about title deeds; and after talking 'much anent Troubridge' with John, Una consulted Hastie herself on January 27th. His advice seemed 'very satisfactory'. She went to him again on February 3rd, and arrived home 'finding Troubridge there, whom I saw in John's presence – he left then I wrote to Hastie and John and I dined quietly and talked.' There is no record of exactly what was said on this momentous occasion but there was 'an unpleasant scene',[68] which obviously amounted to an ultimatum.

On the 4th, 5th and 6th, Una went to Hastie, who 'said he thought he could settle things for me.' On the 6th she went by taxi to Harrow to ask Crichton-Miller's advice about the proposed Deed of Separation, then went home and rang up Hastie to say that she agreed. The next day, the 7th, Hastie's clerk brought her the draft of the Deed at 3 p.m. and explained it. That same evening at 6 p.m. Aubrey Birch Reynardson, a solicitor, accepted the Trusteeship under the Deed.

On the following day, February 8th, at 11 a.m. Troubridge signed the Deed of Separation; and unbeknown to either Una or John, made his Will on the same day, in which he stated categorically:

> In the event of my wife Una Vincenzo Troubridge formerly known as Margot Elena Troubridge predeceasing me I appoint my sisters Laura Hope and Violet Gurney to be the Guardians of my infant daughter Andrea Theodosia Troubridge during such period or periods as I shall be on foreign service and I direct that my said daughter shall under no circumstances be left under the guardianship or care of Marguerite Radclyffe-Hall.

Una noted in her diary on the 8th: 'John and I . . . talked late – a great peace and relief upon me.'

She signed the Deed herself on the 10th, then collected the Cub from Minna's where she had been staying and 'talked over various matters with her', presumably explaining about the separation. Contrary to other, later accounts [69] John stated firmly: 'On February 8th 1919 Admiral Troubridge . . . found himself compelled to sign a deed at the request of his wife, consenting to a separation between them and giving her the sole custody of their child . . . it goes without saying that he had only consented to sign this deed in the full understanding that should he refuse to do so, the scandal would be made public . . .' and Una would 'sue publicly for a judicial separation.'[70]

On March 11th Una was

> summoned to London by letter to receive grave news that her husband had written threatening to break the terms of the deed so recently signed by him, and intended trying to obtain custody of the child. After an interview with her husband's solicitor Una consulted expert opinion and according to this very high legal authority [i.e. Sir George Lewis] the deed signed by the Admiral was binding, he could not take the child, and his letter was a mere subterfuge written with a view to intimidating Una into making certain statements to his advantage.[71]

Troubridge showed himself to have a sting in his tail, but its thrashing was futile. He obviously felt bitter and resentful; but must have realized that any attempt to prove Una an 'unfit mother' would involve exposing himself to ridicule.

After these stressful events they relaxed, went to London to buy furniture and fittings for Chip Chase, to restaurants and theatres, and stayed at the Savoy, and for one night at the Royal Court Hotel where Minna dined with them, then: 'John and I and Laryngitis shared narrow bed!!!'[72] During their shopping they 'hankered for a beautiful Elizabethan bed' (presumably a four-poster) which they had seen; but later 'decided we couldn't have Elizabethan bed', and Una, falling back on her feminine wiles, added: 'so I will fuss about the other one.'[73]

Chip Chase, John wrote, 'is very luxurious, unusually so for a country house, having a really over-powering gorgeous bathroom, central heating . . . a wide and rather handsome oak staircase which runs up . . . the . . . side of the dining hall.' They took possession on April 17th of this their 'first real home', staffed by five indoor servants and two gardeners, on a ninety-nine-year lease. Having her finances now settled under the Deed of Separation, Una instructed her bank 'to pay so much a month into John's bank, as her part towards the upkeep of the house.'[74] They completed the move out of Cadogan Court, and took Una's furniture out of Taylor's Depository; and by the end of April most things were moved into Chip Chase. Una had an archway cut between two bedrooms, using the smaller as her dressing room, which in turn connected to John's bedroom. They all, John, Una, and the servants, 'worked at getting order out of chaos,' arranging furniture, cleaning and polishing; and in the garden cutting down large trees and putting in new smaller ones. Between these tasks they took Cub for walks in the nearby Hadley Woods. The house looked romantic at night: 'Home by lovely moonlight – we saw the little castle for first time by it –' Una wrote in her diary on May 10th.

On one afternoon 'John did gardening – I lay on a rug and looked on'. John noted an interesting contrast between Ladye and Una when it came to moving house:

> . . . nobody really enjoys the discomfort of a move-in, but some people, Una for instance, are rather amused by the excitement of seeing where things will go. This would never have amused Ladye who loathed discomfort in any form. It would have been quite unthinkable to suggest that Ladye should be sleeping in the house during the move-in, she would have been comfortably installed in some hotel and have come in when everything was in order as she did in the past.[75]

Una quickly discovered in the garden several white lilac bushes, and 'made these her special care in memory of her Father, whose favourite flower white lilac was.'[76] Among their earliest visitors were both families: Minna and Viola, and the Visettis. They also dined with J. L. Garvin and Viola at the Savoy, and Viola filed a divorce petition against Maurice Woods shortly afterwards.

Strange that their two marriages, Una's and Viola's, begun in the same year, should end in the same year, and that they should dine together each with her new partner.

John's and Una's households now finally became one, symbolized by the mingling of their furniture and effects: *their* home, fully shared at last. Una, 'dowered with a desire for a real home . . . with the talent for making one' was feeling much happier and more secure.

On March 7th Crichton-Miller had diagnosed Una as having nervous exhaustion, and had ordered six weeks' complete rest. They had delayed this until they were moved in; but Una eventually, and reluctantly, went on June 2nd to Bowden House, Harrow. John continued the psychic work alone, and Mrs Harold Austin, 'Peggy', came to look after her domestic needs. John took Una to Harrow by car, and commented, 'Squig's room very nice – she put to bed at once and left her somewhat depressed – but the flowers we took from Chip made the room look home-like.'[77] John rang up every day for a progress report, wrote frequently and sent baskets of flowers and grapes. Una quickly became discontented because her room was near the nurses' pantry and very noisy. She also slept badly. On June 4th she was asked by Miller temporarily to write only postcards, upon which she was not to discuss psychic matters; and was only allowed to resume writing letters on June 19th. Her mind was still dwelling on the subject, despite Miller's injunctions, as she was recording nocturnal tappings and hallucinatory lights in her diary. During this time she wrote begging John to arrange to hire ponies from a nearby livery stable, so they could ride once a week; but when John told her that the Jobmaster was giving up business, Una 'began to feel that her only desire in life was to ride, especially as the possibility appeared to be receding from her grasp.' In addition she 'threatened to ride a donkey if she may not ride a horse . . .'[78] This shows the obsessional aspects of Una's character. As she appeared to be making little progress, Crichton-Miller suggested 'a new form of treatment' on June 20th: psycho-analysis. Una was outraged at the suggestion, and went home to John the next day, the 21st, three weeks earlier than had been expected.

Whilst she was away, Minna had rung John to say that Una was now a 'Lady', and John commented sardonically in the diary: 'She [Minna] meant that Troubridge has had K added to his threadbare CMS(G).' Una's attitude to this social rise was twofold: she claimed, perhaps for John's sake, to be indifferent to it, explaining to Feda during a sitting, 'It's a title, and it's rather a bore';[79] but she realized that it gave her added prestige, could command better service and open doors, and put her on a par with some, and above many, of her friends. She was not above using it to her own and John's advantage; and with her well-developed social senses often positively enjoyed it. After the separation she became 'unmentioned' and unmentionable to most of the Troubridges, who resented the fact that she used his title.

Although under the terms of the separation Troubridge had agreed to make 'adequate provision' for Una and Andrea, John discovered on June 5th, in Una's absence, that only £45 instead of £65 had been paid into Una's bank. She immediately asked Sir George Lewis to look into it; and wrote to Minna, who was looking after the Cub, sending a cheque herself to cover expenses. John also paid Miller's bills in full, and later Andrea's school fees.

Una was almost ecstatic on her return to Chip Chase, and she and John amused themselves about the house and garden, in a holiday mood; but 'they soon settled down . . . very much as quite ordinary people will do,'[80] into a pattern of life together, in a well-run home. The office adjoined the study downstairs, where they worked 'office hours' at the Psychic Records; they entertained family and friends, including Toupie Lowther and others of 'les girls'; went frequently to London for restaurants, theatres and medical appointments; joined the Kennel Club and took to dog-breeding. Their domestic habits were exemplary middle-class: they bathed every day; took the *Daily Mail* and *Daily Telegraph* newspapers; liked their maids to wear small toques; and dressed for dinner.

Amidst Troubridge family criticisms (including from her stepdaughter, Mary, then married to Robin Otter) that Una did not give up enough of her time to the child, Una was discussing with John the advisability of sending Andrea to boarding school. This suggests that it was very much a joint decision. Of the expected opposition to this move, Una declared resolutely, 'I shall not be influenced by what people say . . . if some people misunderstand there will always be those who don't.'[81] John maintained that the child 'ought' to go, and that 'whether she'd like it' or not was not a pertinent consideration, since in life 'one has to do lots of things one doesn't like.'[82]

They visited a convent school at Mayfield in Sussex to inspect it for suitability, and agreed to send Andrea there that September, aged nearly nine, and duly delivered her into the care of Mother Mary St Joseph.

As well as making decisions about Andrea jointly with John, Una regarded her as an ultimate authority in the home, much as a father would normally be: 'John had Cub in after lunch and lectured her – I do hope with effect,' Una commented in her diary (August 24th). Her own role she saw rather differently: 'I talked to Cub anent the snares of life . . .'[83] though precisely which ones, she does not say! Andrea went fairly frequently to Runcton with Laura Hope, to the Temples at Datchet, and for periodic visits to her father, under the terms of the separation.

Their many visitors to Chip Chase included the Lodges, Helen Salter (editor of the *Proceedings* of the S.P.R.), Everard Feilding, the son of Lady Denbigh, and his unhappy fiancée Stasia Tomczyk (the Polish medium with multiple personality), Buchel, the Visettis, and Father Thurston whom they proposed as an associate of the S.P.R.

They were busy and often overwrought, and on one occasion thought seriously of parting: 'John and I talked all afternoon from 3.30 to 6.30 and decided I should set up on my own. But an hour later we changed our minds and had a peaceful happy evening.'[84] It was the nearest they ever came to parting.

John could be strangely moody and unpredictable: 'John was perfectly miserable before breakfast and wept and would not eat anything!'[85] but Una was becoming more able to deal with these upsets; and John, ever repentant, reassured Una in large things and in small: 'She told me she has left me the vault and permission to be buried with her. I feel I can never be *really* unhappy again and thank God's mercy.'[86]

Throughout 1919 Una was being treated by Alfred Sachs and a Dr May. Her blood test had proved positively that venereal disease was present, and the treatment was local and 'painful', and she suffered greatly from 'inflammation'. On November 17th she recorded in her diary: 'May came and treated me – said innards would always be sensitive but 3 years extreme care might make me relatively sound. I think it so damnably hard on John and an uphill lookout!' This was a source of great difficulty and misery to them both, and explains why they had separate bedrooms at Chip Chase. It undoubtedly added another strain to their lives, and fuel to their disputes.

On October 7th Mrs Sidgwick told John and Una that she had proposed one of them for the Council of the S.P.R. and they were to decide which of them would stand for election. Una wrote: 'I persuaded John to accept – I should have been miserable otherwise attending meetings from which she was excluded – as it is I am happy we were both *asked* and she gets it.' This was to have unforeseen consequences, as they had unwittingly made an enemy of George Fox-Pitt who disliked their published Papers.

On December 17th Una saw in *The Times* that Troubridge had arrived back in England. He was to meet Fox-Pitt at The Travellers' Club, in early January, 1920. Troubridge told Fox-Pitt that Radclyffe Hall was a 'vulgar climber' and 'a grossly immoral woman', that she had 'come between him and his wife and . . . wrecked his home.' Fox-Pitt went to the S.P.R. and saw Miss Newton, the Secretary, and reiterating these statements, said he would strongly oppose Radclyffe Hall's election to the Council. Mrs Sidgwick was informed of these accusations, and told John, who immediately went to consult Sir George Lewis, who issued a writ against Fox-Pitt for slander.

The case came to trial ten months later before the Lord Chief Justice and a Special Jury. The case was written up in *The Times* and given wide publicity. Sir Ellis Hume-Williams, K.C. appeared for John (the plaintiff) whilst Fox-Pitt chose, unwisely, to conduct his own defence. The two slanders complained of were, 1) That Radclyffe Hall was a thoroughly immoral woman; 2) That she was consequently quite an unfit person to be on the Council. The first slander 'could only mean that the plaintiff was an unchaste and immoral woman who was addicted to unnatural vice', it was alleged by John's counsel. The phrase 'unnatural offences' was to be heard again even louder in the trials of *The Well* eight years later.

'Unfortunately, they could not leave out the names of Admiral Sir Ernest and Lady Troubridge because the defendant said that he had made the statements complained of because of a communication made to him by the Admiral . . .' Hume-Williams said at the outset, and proceeded to chronicle the 'friendship' of John and Una, the estrangement from Troubridge, and their psychical research work. Troubridge's statements loomed large in the proceedings, and despite Fox-Pitt's confident assertion that 'Admiral Troubridge is not afraid of anything. He would not mind its all coming out . . . he does not fear publicity,' this was far from the case. This was the last thing Troubridge wanted; and he became subsequently, according to certain members of his family, 'the laughing-stock of Europe'. The Troubridge name in the public eye was an 'unending source of embarrassment' to the family; and Una's photographs were cut out of all the Runcton albums.

Una was called to give evidence, answering very discreetly, but trying on one occasion to use social prestige as an index of morality:

Counsel: Who was A.V.B.?
Witness (Una): A lady who is now dead; she was my cousin. If his Lordship would allow me I should like to say that in life she occupied a high social position and lived in perfect amity with her husband.
His Lordship: How does this affect the case?

Fox-Pitt's self-defence was inept, and his cross-examination often irrelevant, proving no points in his favour. He chose to deny having made the statements attributed to him; or if he did make them, he denied that he had used 'moral' in a sexual sense. He was eccentric, eventually accusing the court of conspiracy against him. If he had been defended by a good counsel instead of defending himself, or if he had attempted to prove instead of to deny that John was 'immoral' he would probably have won his case. John was very lucky, but must have known that she was taking a great risk in bringing the case at all. If she had been asked point-blank whether she was having a sexual relationship with Una, or had done so with Ladye, she would presumably have had to answer honestly in the affirmative, thus substantiating the charge; or lie outright and deny it. In view of her courage eight years later, it is unlikely that she would have taken the latter course.

John won her case, and was awarded damages of £500. However, Fox-Pitt appealed and a fresh trial was ordered. At that point, very sensibly, John, on the advice of Lewis, dropped the matter.

Earlier in the year, while the court case was pending, Andrea became ill, and had to undergo a double-mastoid operation, which caused 'grave anxiety'. On top of this she caught chicken pox. Una and John visited her daily, and John sold a picture to defray the expenses of the nursing home. After her illness, they removed her from Mayfield and sent her to the convent school at St Leonard's.

Una's own health problems were far from solved: blood tests and swabs confirmed the earlier diagnosis, and a course of vaccinations, twice a week, was begun by Dr Sachs and Dr Teale. Courses of various vaccines were tried without success for over two years; and there were often signs of false comfort: 'Cheered when Sachs rang up to say culture had produced nothing . . .' which later proved erroneous. There were periods of waiting and hoping between vaccines, followed by intense disappointment. John was patient and supportive: 'Oh! John is good to me – where should I be in this terrible trouble without her devotion and friendship?' Una asks her diary rhetorically.[87] John remarked in the Psychic Records at this time 'that it was to be hoped there was much fulfillment and consolation in the next world to compensate for the extraordinary unpleasantness of this one.' Late in the year Una wrote: 'To Sachs – cried all evening about being still ill! John an angel to me . . .'

On their anniversary on August 1st they were 'both depressed and sad, but we can at least be so together. We talked of where we should live if we ever left Chip. John very anxious not to distress me about it, but I don't care where it is as long as we are together,' Una declared. In lighter vein, on December 17th, 'after tea I cut off John's hair and we washed it.' John was in her fortieth year at the time.

Due to the expenses of the slander case, John found herself for the first time financially embarrassed; and she had been feeling for some months that the house had many 'worrying features', and that 'the move to the country had not been completely successful after all.' Consequently, they put Chip Chase on the market and determined on a smaller house in London. After several disappointments with potential buyers, the house was sold to a Mr Thomas early in 1921. On February 14th, they moved to a furnished house, 7 Trevor Square, Knightsbridge, and felt 'much freer, lighter and happier,'[88] although it was only a temporary arrangement. In the mean time they looked around for a more permanent abode. Una even 'wrote for particulars of a lighthouse.'

Once back in London they began to enjoy their friends and go out more, and there was less intense concentration on the Psychic Records after nearly six years' very demanding work; but they still had their mutual medical problems: John was diagnosed as having 'nervous exhaustion' in March, and Una was told to give her 'port, oysters, champagne, beef tea, ovaltine, and turtle soup'! Ironically, the day after this diagnosis they went to 'Brother's' Fancy Dress Ball until 2 a.m.

Of Una, John wrote, 'We are hoping that treatment may shortly stop altogether . . . at a recent test of blood . . . nothing was found . . .'[89] but it was a forlorn hope. 'I had hoped it might be all right,' Una noted painfully; and again several months later, 'We went to Sachs and he told us test was positive and we were very depressed.'[90]

On August 31st they left Trevor Square, having earlier seen and bought a small town house just opposite Harrods and off Montpelier Square (a few hundred yards from Una's childhood home) – number 9 Sterling Street. They had had six hectic months of socializing: parties, fancy-dress balls, clubs, theatres, restaurants and dog shows, often with other inverts: Toupie Lowther, Romaine Brooks (over from Paris), Susan and Honey, Gabrielle, 'Teddie' Gerrard, Violet Hunt; keeping very late hours and eating rich foods.

Before settling into Sterling Street they decided to have a long holiday in Italy, and having despatched Andrea back to St Leonard's, they left England on September 1st.

# 9

# *The Marriage of Pen and Paper (1921–5)*

Una had been to Cook's to make their travel arrangements, booked their hotels, seen to the passports, and supervised the packing of their large, joint trunk, proving herself an efficient organizer as she was so often to do. She had tried to persuade John to fly with her to France, but John, less adventurous, had resisted, so it was to be train and boat after all. Una had also been to Dr Sachs to obtain a plentiful supply of vaccine as she was still not cured, and also had 'the rather unpleasant and exhausting results of the treatment already undergone.'

It was their first journey abroad together, the war and their commitment to psychical research having precluded their going before. Una was excited at the prospect, and it was to prove very memorable. They left their cares at home, and Una was glad to be relieved of 'a characteristic habit' of John's of 'waking in the early morning . . . and thinking out duties for me.'[1]

She was anxious to get John abroad as she had been ill in August, and also 'fretting and worrying and very much distressed.'[2] Una was concerned about her in more ways than one, and had been 'lecturing' her (John's word), fearing that 'because of a series of misfortunes [she] might easily become bitter.' Una thought, and said, that this attitude of mind was extremely harmful, and that 'she had noticed an undesirable tendency in John's attitude towards people and things.'[3] John must have taken this to heart as 'Una is the most strictly truthful person I have ever known . . .'[4] Romaine Brooks had written from Capri in August that she was 'distressed to hear of Johnnie's illness', and asking them to her villa there. Evidently they did not want to go, as Romaine wrote again several weeks later, 'Toupie writes me that you are better and leaving for Italy . . . Do send me news . . . my plans depend somewhat on yours . . .' At the end of October she wrote again, lamenting, 'I am indeed sorry you never got here after all . . .'

While Unà and John were away Viola was finally to marry Garvin, a widower many years her senior, with six adult children, whose eldest daughter, by a strange coincidence, was also called Viola. Sterling Street was ready for occupation on their return. Andrea, during the holidays, had a governess, Miss Lynn, and went to stay with the Troubridges or Minna. Her visits to her father were rarely happy: she went reluctantly, and returned gladly. Troubridge, although remaining President of the International Danube Commission, officially retired in August 1921 after forty-six years' service, with a drop in his annual income from £2,555 to £1,275, which also affected Una's and Andrea's allowances. During the previous year Una had been trying to sell some of her jewellery, and was relying economically more and more on John, who paid the bills and bought most of Una's clothes.

But this was all left behind as they set off on their 'great experience'. They went to Paris, stopping at Dover and Calais on the way, shopping, eating out, and ordering Masses to be said for Ladye at Notre-Dame. Then they went by 'de luxe' train to Geneva, Una being 'dug out onto [the] platform at 1 a.m.' because the Customs found 'a new lace gabot' on top of the trunk! Una had to be treated by a Dr Faraggione for prolapsed haemorrhoids and spent several days in bed on their arrival at Levanto on September 10th. She had not been there since her unhappy visit in 1914 and was keen to introduce John to her old friends the Massolas. They stayed at the Hotel Stella, where 'May [Massola] came round almost at once – just the same perfectly darling creature . . .' Una recorded. When they had settled in they spent their days relaxing on the beach, reading in the evenings, and often going to bed early. Una's old friends the Rigolettis were there with the 'many divine children they have had since I was here!' They saw much of a man called Price and a Miss Richter, a German; and went almost daily to Santa Caterina, the Massolas' home, for lunch, tea or drinks. If Una was indisposed she 'insisted on John leaving me and lunching at Santa Caterina as I want her to know May better.' Few such enforced friendships flourish, and it is not known what John and May thought of each other; but Una's and John's stay at Levanto was amicable enough, with many invitations received and given. 'Various folk came to talk – evidently to *call* on them all is the right thing . . .' Una commented, unconsciously echoing the social pattern of her mother and of her own youth as accomplice in the hired carriage.

Una was taking her vaccinces every ten days or so, and John had a recurrence of her old 'hunting vein' (the result of a severe hunting accident) which made her leg ache badly. Nevertheless they socialized a good deal, and went to the Casino where Una's losses were less than a quarter of John's! Cencio Massola had taken himself off in his yacht *Artica* as if to leave the women to it – but all seemed friendly on his return.

Their hotel left much to be desired: '. . . a starvation dinner and to bed angry and hungry – John ate a stale rusk at 1 a.m.!'[5] so Una wrote to the Hotel Albion in Florence, and booked rooms for November 6th, and wrote also to her cousins the Tealdis of their forthcoming visit. Things with the Massolas were becoming a little strained, and Una notes almost petulantly: 'May came out with us and was peevish and took [the] part of a beastly man in a shop who let his dog snap at me!'[6] but even Cencio turned up at the station to see them off on the 6th.

'Firenze with John,' Una noted rapturously in her diary, praising their 'lovely room' with its balcony on to the Arno and Ponte Vecchio, and the 'nice hotel, good food'. They each loved Florence, and were quickly 'out to see the beloved city' together and to share it for the first time. John had been there with Ladye and they had thought of buying a villa in the foothills outside the town; and Una must have remembered the other Marguerite, so different from yet so strangely like this one, her John. Between the two had come her marriage, but she must have seen a certain continuity. Marguerite Michel would certainly have been in Una's thoughts because she and John intended, whilst in Florence, to verify certain parts of the Psychic Records pertaining to her.

It had been cold with gale-force winds in Levanto, but on arrival in Florence Una and John immediately bought hats, knitted knickers, and overcoats. They went to see all the churches, particularly Una's favourite, Or San Michele, which she was delighted that 'John adored' also; and walked 'the divine streets' of 'our beloved Florence'. They went often to Santa Maria Novella to see Brunelleschi's crucifix; to Santa Trinita, 'pure Gothic – so wonderful'; to the Medici Chapel, the Pitti Palace, the Uffizi, the Piazza, and to see the Dante Celebration decorations. They made many friends, and visited or were visited by old ones: 'Nino [Tealdi] dined and stayed til nearly midnight – . . . He was very amusing and a darling and John loved him.'[7]

They stayed at the Hotel Albion on the Lung Arno Acciaiuoli all that winter and into the spring of 1922, before returning to England. Their families and friends kept in touch by letter, and Una received a 'good report of Cub from Convent' in November, and Andrea went to her father at Cheltenham Terrace for Christmas, then to stay with the Nevadas before returning to school. At eleven she was perhaps passed round like the parcel at a Christmas party; but as Una remarked in another context, 'Children and young people are marvellously uncomplaining. They accept philosophically such treatment as is meted out to them. . .'[8] and Andrea does not seem to have suffered unduly from this long separation from her mother, according to Jacqueline Hope's children, Andrea's second cousins, who knew her well.

Una bought John expensive jewelled cuff-links from Settepassi on the Ponte Vecchio as a Christmas present, and John in turn gave Una a large sapphire ring from the same jeweller's, which Una was always to wear.

That was not the only thing John contemplated 'buying' for Una: they visited an orphanage where, Una later remarked laconically in her diary, 'John sorely tempted to buy a baby!' John the frustrated 'father' would have wanted to bring up the child as 'theirs'; it was Una who was not so keen, and presumably dissuaded John from so rash an act!

Another incident Una always remembered seeing but not hearing (as John forbade her to go out) was the young Mussolini arriving to address a Fascisti demonstration.

John's poems and songs had been quite successful. In 1920 her song 'The Cuckoo' was 'advertised, sung, and reviewed in the press'.[9] Their friend Mignon Nevada sang some of John's songs at her concerts; and in late 1920 John was trying 'to publish an album of songs written and composed by herself', but this was rejected by the publishers in 1921. Perhaps because of this, John began to work very seriously on a novel, initially called *Octopi* and begun on December 26th, 1919. In her *Life* of John, Una gives the genesis of this book as an incident which took place in the dining-room of the Cottage Hotel at Lynton.[10] The theme was of parental predatoriness, the old sucking the life out of the young like octopi. John was so struck by the two embodied examples in the dining-room that she determined to write it as a novel. Una, there at the inception of the idea, later isolated this moment as a changing point in John's life. What Una did not know was that the genesis of this book was twofold; and John herself may have forgotten that in 1910 she and Ladye had read a book called *The Devourers*, in which a brilliant woman is preyed upon by her daughter, so that gradually the mother's mentality is swamped and absorbed by that of the child. This is the reverse of *Octopi* (*The Unlit Lamp*) where the brilliant daughter is sacrificed to the selfish, absorbing mother, missing life's chances, but the theme is identical. John had been so impressed by this book at the time that she gave Ladye a copy inscribed, 'To Ladye from John. How we loved this book when we read it together at Sidmouth!'

John had worked on the idea intermittently, but in Florence she took it up in earnest, writing often till midnight or later; and Una, although pleased, was vigilant for the sake of John's health: 'we had a lengthy discussion re. her overworking during the holiday . . . she is better but still tired and easily done up . . .' Una had started her life as watchdog to John's health and habits, little knowing that it would become almost a full-time occupation, incorporating critic, reader, secretary, editor, proof-checker – and sometimes whipping-post as well.

Early in 1922, before returning to England, they made a long sojourn in Paris, where they socialized avidly with both old and new friends. The post-war need for distraction and excitement meant that Paris, like London, was buzzing with activity: cafés, clubs, shows, soirées. On their arrival, Romaine, in no way snubbed by their failure to turn up at Capri earlier, collected them from their hotel in an open car and carried them off to lunch. She had written to them in Florence: 'I do so want you to meet my great friend here, Natalie Barney . . . she has an unusual mind of the best quality . . .'

Natalie was a rich American who had made her home in Paris since the earliest years of the century, and was to become infamous for her homosexual love affairs (at least one woman, Renée Vivien, committed suicide for her), and famous for her salon at 20 Rue Jacob, held on Fridays between 4.30 and 8 p.m. for over half a century. No alcohol was served, and the guests were of both sexes and orientations, many of them rich, titled, or distinguished in their fields. Her soirées were well-attended, the celebrities over the years including: Rémy de Gourmont, Apollinaire, Isadora Duncan, Tagore, Paul Valéry, Gertrude Stein and Alice B. Toklas, Ezra Pound and James Joyce. This was Una's and John's first introduction to the 'gay' Paris set, which apart from Romaine and Natalie, included Colette and Dolly Wilde (Oscar's niece). Like their London gay friends, who included actresses, musicians and artists, they were 'people with whom one got intimate quickly and was thus saved a lot of unnecessary trouble'.[11]

As well as Natalie Barney's salon, Una and John were to become familiar over the years with the clubs and bars of Paris, some of which were to be reflected in *The Well* later. After the relative isolation of Chip Chase, the constraints of the psychic investigations, and their legal and family troubles, they must have felt newly liberated, free to enjoy themselves and new experiences.

When they returned to England in the late spring of 1922, it was not to a cloistered life, but to a continuation of the liberated one.

They settled into Sterling Street with a domestic staff of three, quickly finding the house very cramped after Chip Chase, although easier to run. They shopped at Harrods, walked the dogs in the park, ate out at their favourite restaurants, entertained at home and accepted invitations in return, paid 'duty' visits to Minna and the Visettis, and started sittings again with Mrs Leonard but without taking exhaustive notes. John worked on and finished *Octopi*, then took up again the first novel she had ever attempted (whilst living with Ladye), 'After Many Days', and finished this towards the end of 1922. Early in 1923 she started a third novel, called *Chains*, which was finished in four and a half months, then corrected and retitled *The Forge*. Within a month of this she began *A Saturday Life*; then, six weeks later, started a saga novel, 'The Cunningham Family', which, like 'After Many Days', was destined never to appear in print.

It is amazing how prolific John was in these early days, as though an inner spring had been released; the more so as, almost in proportion, their social lives became more full of frantic activity. Several examples from the 1923 diary are illustrative and typical:

*26 April* . . . John wrote 'Chains' all day. At 6 we dressed for Toupie's (Fancy Dress Ball). Honey and Diana dined and went on with us. Home by 4.30!

*27 April* John and I up at 6.30 – to Dog Show, where we did splendidly . . . John had her dinner in bed and I ditto, both with headaches!

*2 June* . . . afternoon matinee . . . Guy dined – then we all went to Romaine's and to Cave of Harmony 11 p.m. and danced til 4.30.

*3 June* John and I up to breakfast after 2 hours in bed! and in car to Brighton where we lunched Princes Hotel and exercised the dogs. Home via Eastbourne where we had tea – back by 9 o'clock to late dinner . . .

This pace of life, though exhausting, seems to have suited them. An artist friend with a studio, Guy Allan, gave Una dancing lessons, so that she and John could foxtrot together at appropriate

Una, aged seventeen

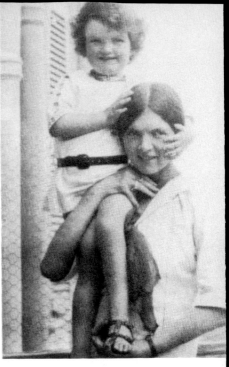

Una and Troubridge on the
bridge of H.M.S. *Defence*, 1914

Una with her daughter Andrea,
Malta, 1914

Una pictured in the *Tatler* of September 30th, 1914, at the time of
Troubridge's recall to England for the *Goeben* inquiry

John and Una at the Ladies' Kennel Club Dog Show at Ranelagh,
May 1920

*top*     Una at her desk, *c.* 1930
*above*    A rare picture of John smiling, February 1932

Una and John at the Lyric Theatre for the first night of *When Ladies Meet*, 1933

Una in Levanto, after John's death

Studio portrait of John, February 1932

*left*     Ladye's tomb in Highgate Cemetery, bought by John, where John herself is buried

*top right*     Una's grave in the Anglo-American Cemetery (section D), Rome

*right*     Commemorative plaque for John placed by Una, 1943

clubs and parties. Fancy dress balls were popular, and they spent much time fitting costumes and wigs at theatrical costumiers. As their house was so small, they hired Guy's studio to give a party themselves:

> *2 July*. John and I up and out early and all day at studio preparing [for] dance . . . we lunched there and worked til we dressed. Guy utterly useless. Dance a huge success and ended with bacon eggs and coffee at 5.30. I a harlequin, John an Indian chief.

Upon occasion, when things clashed, they went their separate ways socially.

> *2 Oct.* – I to Dachshund Club meeting and Dinner 7 pm Connaught Rooms – John to Pen Club with Vere[12] – we met at home about 10.30.

There were times when their patience with 'the girls' and their *affaires* wore thin:

> *30 Oct.* . . . Teddie [Gerard, the actress] and Jo Carstairs arrived at 11.30 [p.m.] – without Etheline [Teddie's 'girlfriend'] and stayed til 1.30 when we were glad to see the last of them.

They often got up late after these nocturnal excesses:

> *28 Nov.* . . . Got up for lunch and blew up the new cook.

Due to lack of supervision things got (often humorously) out of hand:

> *2 Dec.* John and I up after breakfast and had to turn out the cook for insolence and drinking all our brandy.

*The Unlit Lamp* was difficult to place with a publisher, and *The Forge* was accepted first, a contract with Arrowsmith being signed in September 1923, and during November and December Una and John were correcting proofs, and reading extracts to some of their friends:

*Life Together: the First Years (1917–26)*

> *1 Dec . . .* Vere and Budge dined and heard a lot . . . of 'The
> Forge' and howled with joy over it til past midnight.

Una spoke of the 'relentless perseverance' of John's working
habits, and it is clear that, as time passed, she drove herself very
hard, often going to bed grey with tiredness towards dawn. The
ceaseless social round had to give way to more 'quietness and
seclusion' to facilitate 'inspiration' and to ensure that sudden
interruptions did not 'frustrate the output of many hours.'[13]

As John developed her literary habits and Una realized that
they had come to stay, and that John had at last found her life's
work, she began to redefine her role in John's life. No longer just
lover and companion, she came to see herself as an essential part of
the creative process: providing and maintaining an emotionally
and domestically stable and harmonious home in which John
could work with a free mind. The life that 'proudly and joyfully'
was to be hers for so many years was 'a life of watching, serving,
and subordinating everything in existence to the requirements
of an overwhelming literary inspiration and industry', and of
'guarding and sustaining a physique that was never equal to
John's relentless perseverance or to the strain she compelled it to
bear.'[14]

Writers all have their own rituals and habits of work. John was
never to work regular, fixed hours; and fluctuated between almost
manic activity at times and inarticulate stagnancy at others. She
always wrote in longhand, finding what she called 'the marriage of
pen and paper' essential to her inspiration. Her manuscripts, as
Una soon came to realize, were untidy and frequently malpunctu-
ated and misspelt (for example, 'failiour' for failure, 'pore' for
poor). Una spent much time correcting, taking John's dictation
and reading aloud to her what she had written. When the first
draft was written and corrected it would be dictated to a typist, or
in the early days to Una, and revised in the process. John never
learned to type herself. Una knew John's writing well and could
understand 'the wildest scrawl', and with her trained voice could
read aloud, if necessary, for hours. She would often have to read
aloud many versions of the same piece until John was satisfied with
one of them – sometimes far into the night. Reading aloud,

150

dictating alterations, and retyping would take place several times, and must have been wearing and even boring; but fortunately Una found that 'there was immense interest for me in my share of her labours.' She enjoyed being the first person to see what John had written, and offering her advice when asked. She would 'read the riot act' when she found that John had inadvertently destroyed an earlier and better draft of something than the one she had kept; and collude in John's games of bluff and counter-bluff by dutifully simulating 'approval and appreciation' of passages which they both knew were below par. Sometimes she would be told by John that she was 'reading abominably', or that she was a fool, or incapable of appreciating what she was reading. Una became a mistress of patience and forbearance; and, having a degree of natural masochism, enjoyed her role in this exhaustive process. She was always happy in a supportive role, being lieutenant to John's captain. Correcting, proof-reading, and negotiating with agents also came into Una's province; as did humbler tasks to ensure the author's comfort:

> . . . John, who had been resting in bed for several days, had a sudden inspiration just before dinner time, asked Una for pencil and paper and commenced writing . . . while she was engrossed . . . Una, there being no servant in the house, went downstairs to prepare John's dinner. Una's culinary efforts were however . . . disastrous. She produced with much good will and small skill a very large omelette which adhered closely to the floor of the frying pan and which by the time a portion of it was taken upstairs to the inspired authoress had assumed the consistency of a stale crumpet, and the appearance of a burnt india rubber tennis shoe sole. John [made] polite efforts to tackle this offering while continuing her composition between . . . mouthfuls . . .[15]

There is a humorous passage in *The Well* which is a fictional replica of Una's account of John's writing habits, which Una must have read with some amusement. Puddle represents Una, and Stephen, John:

Puddle looked up. 'You're smoking too much.'
'I dare say I am. I can't write any more.'
'Since when?'
'Ever since I began this new book.'
'Don't be such a fool!'
'But it's God's truth, I tell you – I feel flat, it's a kind of spiritual dryness. This new book is going to be a failure, sometimes I think I'd better destroy it.'
She began to pace up and down the room, dull-eyed yet tense as a tightly-drawn bowstring.
'This comes of working all night,' Puddle murmured.
'I must work when the spirit moves me,' snapped Stephen.
Puddle . . . was not much moved by this sudden depression, she had grown quite accustomed to these literary moods . . .

John's first published book, *The Forge*, came out on January 25th, 1924, dedicated 'To Una with love'. It is a comedy, with elements of caricature, and is obviously broadly based on themselves and aspects of their own lives. The Brents, Hilary and Susan, grow bored with each other and with marriage and split up (as John and Una nearly did at Chip Chase) for a year, before coming back together at the end.

Hilary is John: he wears 'heavy tweeds', has 'fair hair', and is thirty-nine years old in 1919, when the book begins (as was John). His 'nose was high-bridged and arrogant' and his eyes 'had a fierce, caged look'. He came into a fortune at twenty-one, had 'done very little' although 'a few slight books of poetry had been published and well reviewed . . .'

Susan is Una: 'not more than six years her husband's junior . . . her glossy brown hair was straight and bobbed . . . her large grey eyes . . . calm and innocent . . . she possessed a sense of humour and a strong will of her own . . . she had been an art student . . .'

Like John and Una, they had met at the house of mutual friends. Bambury Hall is a grander version of Chip Chase; even the dogs are theirs: 'Sieglinde' is Thora, Una's dachshund, 'Rueben' is Rufus, John's collie. The artist Venetia Ford is Romaine Brooks, who even paints the same picture, 'The Weeping Venus' (a portrait which was to annoy Romaine, and perhaps influence her painting of Una, of the same year). Curiously, it is *he* who is moody, whimsical, restless and dependent; and *she* who is calm, collected, logical, and depended upon. Does this amount, one wonders, to a deeper insight into John's and Una's relationship, or is it just a reversal of the expected pattern? At the end they are reconciled, and realize 'the divine necessity for chains', and that 'of all the chains in the world the heaviest chain is love . . . yet it's the easiest to carry . . .'

Una sent out postcards to all their friends giving details of the publication of *The Forge*, presumably to encourage sales as much as to inform anyone who had missed it in the press. She also kept regular checks on its sales at bookshops, and detailed records of sales received from the publishers; she made a press-cutting book in which she pasted reviews.

In April they sold 9 Sterling Street, having tired of its few charms and many inconveniences, and took a flat at Kensington Palace Mansions. No sooner had they moved in than they saw and negotiated for another house, larger than Sterling Street, at 37 Holland Street, W.8. On May 25th, after nine months, John completed *A Saturday Life* for Arrowsmith; and in June Cassells took *The Unlit Lamp*, but it had to be substantially cut. Una and John worked for many hours 'boiling' it down! Natalie and Romaine were in London, and when they were all together and Una reading passages from *The Forge* to Natalie, 'Romaine came in and made a hideous scene abusing *The Forge*, John, and Natalie like a fishwife!' She did *not* like herself portrayed as Venetia Ford, and was to remain an enemy of John's for ever after. Romaine had hired a studio in Cornwell Road and Una was having sittings for a portrait. When Natalie returned to Paris, Romaine wrote to her: 'Una is funny to paint. Her get-up is remarkable. She will live perhaps and cause future generations to smile . . .' Why Una chose to pose in such very masculine 'get-up' (black jacket, white starched shirt, monocle) is debatable, and it certainly leaves the viewer in little doubt as to her proclivities. Perhaps that was the point, a public statement of commitment to a cause. The portrait has been called 'a tour de force of ironic commentary'[16] and a 'caricature' and it is doubtful whether Una liked it. Toupie Lowther told Romaine that she did not; and John did not offer to buy it, as presumably Romaine had thought she might. However, it was shown in New York, Chicago, London and Paris the following year.

Una and John holidayed in Bagnoles for the waters; taking the last batch of proofs for *The Unlit Lamp* with them, which they corrected and despatched at intervals. Andrea went to her father. On their return to London they met Leonard and Molly Rees (of the *Sunday Times*), Violet Hunt, Michael Arlen and Margaret Irwin at a party; and Una recorded proudly in her diary: 'a great fuss made of John.' John was working on short stories, 'The Lover of Things', 'Two to One' (never published); and writing reviews for the *Sunday Times*, at Rees's suggestion. Una, herself, was working at a translation of *Le Grand Eunuque* from the French, which Audrey Heath, John's agent, showed to Cape.

They were as busy as ever: having weekly sittings with Mrs Leonard, visiting the Temples at Datchet, socializing with their gay friends Toupie, Gabrielle, Vere and Budge, and with their new literary friends, attending first nights, measuring up and buying things for 37 Holland Street.

*The Unlit Lamp*, dedicated to 'Mabel Veronica Batten, in deep affection, gratitude and respect', was published by Cassell on September 25th. Una again sent out postcards far and wide advertising it, and cut out reviews. She also went to The Times Bookshop and Harrods to check how sales were going, and was delighted to find that both were sold out. Minna liked it, and Una 'Heard Viola and Garvin are wildly enthusiastic about *The Unlit Lamp*.' Una took pride in John's achievement, and hoarded up other people's praise of her. She also enjoyed the fact that some of John's new prestige rubbed off on her too as *alter ego* at Pen Club dinners and literary parties, where they met May Sinclair, Rebecca West, Alec Waugh, E. V. Lucas and others.

*The Unlit Lamp* was very favourably received, and is arguably the best book John was ever to write. As a first novel it is an outstanding achievement, and it remains one of the unacknowledged minor masterpieces of English literature. It will bear comparison to anything written by her better-known contemporaries D. H. Lawrence, Virginia Woolf, and E. M. Forster. Its power is unremitting, its delineation of character masterly, its strengths

154

succinctness and understatement. The powerful dynamics of incest and homosexuality are covertly, never overtly, suggested; and the action rivets the reader from beginning to inevitably tragic end.

On December 4th they moved into 37 Holland Street, and Una noted in her diary: 'moved into our new home – with which we are enchanted.' Instead of the separate communicating bedrooms they had occupied at Chip Chase and Sterling Street, they were now sharing one room, 'our bedroom'. As Una had stopped her vaccines from Sachs she was obviously cured, and they had resumed their love-life, as the following entry implies: '. . . we early to bed ——— ———.'

The traumatic early years of their relationship were behind them: they were settled and happy and comparatively free, had many friends, and John was beginning to be known as a writer. Una had won a central, indispensable place in John's life, and felt secure in John's love. She had made John's concerns her own, and was reaping the rewards; she was still young, and was living a full and fulfilling life. Her personal ambitions had changed considerably and had become largely sublimated into John's; but she must have been disappointed to learn in early January 1925 that her French translation had been turned down by Cape. She corrected John's final copy and read to her what she had written. Using her artistic skills, she designed a book jacket for *A Saturday Life*, and later for *Adam's Breed*. She continued her translations nothing deterred; then wrote a series of autobiographical sketches at John's suggestion, which were to remain unpublished, but aspects of which were to appear in John's novels. Later Una was to read manuscripts for Audrey Heath, and for certain publishers, on a freelance basis; and to write the occasional review.

*A Saturday Life* was published on April 1st, 1925 and well reviewed by their friend Leonard Rees in the *Sunday Times* four days later. This curious book, based on the theme of reincarnation, was 'Dedicated to Myself' by John, who appeared in it as 'Frances Reide'. Frances's great friend Lady Shore, the vague widow of an archaeologist, is *not* Una; but many aspects of her daughter Sidonia are based on Una's autobiographical sketches. Sidonia, like Una, drew a remarkable Adam and Eve at the age of three, and took up successively drawing, morbid poetry, religion, sculpture and singing. In addition, Sidonia at fifteen was perhaps a reflection of Andrea who was fifteen that year: for a time Sidonia had a full, florid adolescent 'crush' on Frances, her mother's friend:

> Oh, you! You're all Mother's! Mother this, Mother that! God! I'm sick of it! Don't I count at all? . . . Why can't I have you? Aren't I younger than Mother? Aren't I attractive? Don't I interest you enough? . . . Frances, why won't you love me?

Later Sidonia says: 'I long, simply long to hate you. But you've always been there, you and Mother . . .' This was to be strangely prophetic of troubles with Andrea later.

Frances Reide was the prototype of the 'masculine' woman who started life as Joan Ogden in *The Unlit Lamp* and was to become Stephen Gordon in *The Well*, and Miss Ogilvy in the short story of that title. Such women, very much a twentieth-century phenomenon, were not really on the literary map before Radclyffe Hall, and perhaps this is her main contribution to literature as an extension of human understanding.

Thirteen days after the publication of *A Saturday Life* John began her fifth[17] novel, *Food*, later retitled *Adam's Breed*. Una was writing draft advertisements for *A Saturday Life* for Mr Cobb of Arrowsmith, and also having 'family troubles' with Minna, who was writing her memoirs: 'Mother dined and was very tiresome . . . talked [i.e. to John] all evening anent Viola, Minna and co . . .'[18]

Whatever this was it blew over, like the periodic problems with the Visettis, whom Una had never liked, describing Marie Visetti later as 'a brainless, vain, selfish woman'. Her demands for money, and frequent dramatic false alarms about her health, annoyed Una as she saw that John's sense of duty was often exploited.

Una collected reviews as usual, and read large chunks of the new book to Audrey Heath, who was impressed with it. When they went to Lynton in June Una, ever vigilant of John's health and working habits, complained in her diary: 'John wrote most of day . . . the hours worked have gradually increased to a full day, although this is a holiday!'[19]

156

Una herself renamed the book *Adam's Breed* from a Kipling quotation as Newman Flower of Cassells would not accept *Food* as the title, complaining that it would be mistaken for a cookery book! She was also working on the book's jacket which was to include a 'spine drawing'; then did John's income-tax accounts.

Both Minna and Audrey Heath were being read instalments of *Adam's Breed* by Una as it was written; Minna thought it 'a great book', and 'Audrey says she cried all the way home after . . . and can't bear to think how dull she will feel when it's finished.' Una's own admiration was, as usual, unbounded; though it is difficult to understand such unreserved enthusiasm for what would now be regarded as a tedious, long-winded and overwritten book. John finished it at Brighton on November 7th, and Una helped her to correct it, then they packed and delivered it to the publishers. Afterwards, in relief, Una commented in her diary: 'we are hugely enjoying our well-earned holiday . . .' and one day, 'we met Minna and Viola and brought them back with us to tea and dinner – in the evening we all attended the hotel dance and I danced with John and two unknown young men!' It is obvious from Una's amazement at herself that dancing with *any* men had become very strange to her!

Una spoke of John's 'natural genius', of her 'beautiful prose', and of what she had 'immortalised' in her various books: and it is clear that one of the greatest illusions of Una's life was her belief that John was a genius. Perhaps it was a 'saving' rather than a 'killing' illusion, since she subordinated her own time, energies and talents to support and encourage this presumed possession in John. No doubt many of John's moods and ways were attributed by Una to this cause. However, she was certainly aided and abetted in this belief by the acclaim of public and press alike, and by the honours and awards showered upon John, especially for *Adam's Breed*. Even at the trials of *The Well* later, John was described as 'one of the most distinguished novelists alive'. The judgments of contemporary literary history are notoriously unreliable, as they were of Una's grandfather; but of other contemporary writers of the 1920s – such as Berta Ruck, Stephen McKenna, Marie Corelli, Michael Arlen (whose *The Green Hat* was a bestseller in 1925), Philip

Lindsay, Elinor Glyn, Charlotte Yonge – John is remembered more than many, although none is regarded as mainstream English literature.

John certainly had talent, but remained essentially an inspired amateur, lacking the critical detachment of the professional. Each book is remarkably different stylistically, yet they share common weaknesses: a tendency to be platitudinous, pompous, to overstate, sentimentalize, and over-employ the pathetic fallacy. We can hardly blame Una for not being more accurate in her literary judgments than most of her contemporaries; and it is to her credit that her belief in John, like her love for her, never wavered.

# III

# The Well . . . and After (1926–34)

# 10

# The Palace of Truth: Stephen (1926–8)

On January 29th, 1926 Minna rang Una at 8.15 in the morning to tell her of Troubridge's sudden death in Biarritz the day before. She had read of it in the morning papers. Una spent most of the morning on the telephone to the Admiralty, and went to see the Accountant General in the afternoon, to discover to her dismay that her pension was to be only £225 per annum and Andrea's £24. It is pointless to pretend that she mourned him in any way, all fondness had ceased many years before; but she was concerned at the sudden change in her financial circumstances. Troubridge's total estate was only £452. 18s. 11d., even less than her father's had been.

Her step-daughter Mary, with whom she had had no recent contacts, rang her up several days later, and Troubridge's son Tom, sole executor, visited her for two hours to discuss matters, particularly the continuation of Andrea's schooling. She was then in her sixteenth year and at St George's, Harpenden, and hoped to go on to university.

When Una went to her mother's she found 'Viola very nice', but 'Minna intolerable'; then a second time, 'Viola again nice', and 'Minna more damnable than ever'. As a consequence, 'wrote my mind to Minna,' Una recorded. What this was all about is uncertain, but it may be that Minna had urged Una to consider remarriage for security reasons.

Troubridge's Requiem Mass was sung at Westminster Cathedral on Saturday February 13th, and in the press reports 'Lady Troubridge, widow' heads a long list of family and distinguished people attending. It was to be the last time she would attend such a gathering of the Troubridge clan. She was well aware of their feelings towards her, and may have felt hypocritical herself, but her attendance was obligatory. Andrea accompanied her, and John took the dog, 'Nut', for a walk!

Una was to spend much time going to the Ministry of Pensions, the Officers' Families Fund, and to Sir George Lewis, trying to sort out her financial affairs. Many months later she went to a Pensions Appeal Tribunal, and as a result her pension was increased. This was followed by 'much rejoicing'. Certain members of the Troubridge family were to resent the fact that Una drew this Widow's Pension until the day she died; but as she and Troubridge were never divorced, she was both legally and morally entitled to it.

On March 4th, whilst all this was going on, *Adam's Breed* was published by Cassell, and soon went into second, third and fourth impressions. It was quickly put up for the Femina Prize, and later for the James Tait Black Prize. When John was invited to the Women Writers' Lunch, Una took Audrey Heath out to lunch; but they went together to the Writers' Club, and to a Pen Club Dinner, 'at which', Una noted with pleasure, 'John was much lionised . . .' They also dined at the Society of Authors; and John spoke to the Writers' Club about *Adam's Breed*, Soho, and why she wrote the book, and Una noted that it was 'a great success'.

Una herself was reading manuscripts for Cassells, translating Colette into English, and writing occasional reviews. On April 11th they heard that *Adam's Breed* had been awarded the Femina Prize; congratulations poured in and John's photograph appeared in the papers. At the ceremony on May 16th Galsworthy presented the prize, and there were many other authors there 'praising John'. Later John and Una gave a tea to the Writers' Club themselves, which was attended by 'a big crowd'; and had a Negro concert at their Holland Street house attended by seventy people, including the Galsworthys and Sybil Thorndike.

The decision to write the book which started life as *Stephen* and was eventually renamed by Una *The Well of Loneliness* was not sudden: 'she had long wanted to write a book on sexual inversion, a novel that would be accessible to the general public who did not have access to technical treatises . . .'[1] She wanted to put the record straight and was convinced that 'such a book could only be written by a sexual invert . . . qualified by personal knowledge and experience . . .'[2] John realized that such a public statement would inevitably implicate Una; and Una remembered how, one day, 'John came to me . . . with unusual gravity and asked for my decision in a serious matter . . .' After explaining her intended subject, John, ever honest, 'pointed out that in view of our union and of all the years that we had shared a home, what affected her must also affect me and that I would be included in any condemnation.' She placed the onus of decision on Una as to whether she should 'write or refrain'.

Knowing Una after eleven years, John could hardly have been surprised by the characteristic and unhesitating answer: 'I told her to write what was in her heart, and that so far as any effect upon myself was concerned, I was sick to death of ambiguities, and only wished to be known for what I was and to dwell with her in the palace of truth.'[3] Brave words, which show both an impatience with pretences, and that she now regarded herself, like John, as an invert. She pinned her colours to the mast beside John's with that staunch loyalty which was her hallmark: 'I always replied that I would follow her anywhere . . .'[4]

John had delayed writing such a book 'until her name was made: until her unusual theme would get a hearing as . . . the work of an established writer.'[5] In mid-1926 she thought that the time was right, with four successful novels behind her, and a considerable literary reputation. She was prepared to put that career in jeopardy if necessary, to 'speak on behalf of a misunderstood and misjudged minority'.[6] It assumed the nature of a campaign even in the conceptual stages.

Later she wrote to J. L. Garvin,[7] Una's brother-in-law:[8] '*The*

*Well of Loneliness* treats of a subject that has not so far been written of frankly and openly by any English novelist, and it has seemed to me high time that the subject should be boldly tackled, not only for the sake of those of whom I have written but for the sake of society in general.' Una agreed.

Having been given the go-ahead by Una the book was begun in the summer of 1926, much of it being written at the Hotel Pont Royal, Rue du Bac, in Paris. Una mentions in her diary of July 20th, 1926: 'John began notes for *Stephen.*' It was to take nearly two years to complete and 'infinite pains'. There were few precedents and no real models, so it was to a large extent an original and missionary work, arising from the corpus of its author's experience and considered opinions. It was not an autobiography, as Una makes clear: 'many of Stephen Gordon's feelings and reactions, though practically none of her circumstances or experience, were her own . . .'[9]

John had dealt with the theme of 'inversion' before, in *The Unlit Lamp*, where it is a sub-plot or subservient theme to the main one of parental predatoriness and its tragic consequences. The theme was to emerge again, much more mildly and peripherally, in the persons of the two old men, Jumping Jimmie and Watercrease Bill, in her last novel *The Sixth Beatitude. The Unlit Lamp* will bear both comparison and contrast with *The Well.*

At twelve, Joan Ogden, the heroine, was 'never tearful, never violent, only coldly logical and self-assured and firm.' Physically she was 'large-boned and tall for her age, lanky as a boy, with pale face and short black hair.' As she grows older, she wears the collars and ties and cropped hair typical of Stephen, and fired by her tutor-friend, Elizabeth Rodney, reaches out towards higher education and a broader horizon than Seaborne offers. Elizabeth's attitude to Joan is ambiguous from the beginning:

> Elizabeth, tall and erect, was dressed in some soft green material . . . she suddenly . . . said: 'Joan, do you like my dress?'
>
> 'Like it?' Joan stammered, 'I think it's beautiful.'
>
> Elizabeth wanted to say, 'Do you think me at all beautiful, Joan?'

Years later Joan realizes that 'she did not want anyone to know Elizabeth better than she did. This discovery startled her . . .' More crucially perhaps, 'She became suddenly aware that she could make or mar not only herself but Elizabeth, that Elizabeth had taken root in her and would blossom or fade according to the sustenance she could provide.'

Elizabeth uses every pressure she can to make Joan break with her mother and Seaborne: it is *she* who is aware, knows what she wants, and plans their future: 'Are you serious, are you going to break away in the end, or is it – am I – going to be all wasted? . . . Haven't you any character? . . . No will to help yourself with?'

Things reach a head:

They stared at each other, wide-eyed at their own emotions. They realised that all in a moment they had turned a sharp corner and come face to face with a crisis, that there was no going back, that they must go forward together or each one alone . . .
She looked into Elizabeth's troubled eyes.
'What do you want of me?' she asked.
'If I told you, would you be afraid?'
'I want you to work as we are doing until you come of age, then I want you to go to Cambridge . . . but after that . . . I want you to come to London and live with me there . . . I'd get a job while you studied at the hospital; we'd have a little flat together, and be free and very happy. I've wanted to say this to you for some time and today somehow it's all come out; it had to get said sooner or later.'

She extracts a promise from Joan to this effect, which Joan twice breaks. When, after the first broken promise, Elizabeth returns to Seaborne after nearly a year's absence, there is a temporary renaissance of feelings: 'A deep sense of peace enveloped her; Elizabeth felt it too, and they sat very often with clasped hands without speaking, for now their silence drew them closer together than words would have done.'

On another occasion:

They walked home arm in arm through the twilight.

Joan said: 'Our life seems new, somehow, Elizabeth . . . We aren't doing anything very different – but it all seems so new; I feel new myself.'

Elizabeth pressed her arm very slightly. 'It's as old as the hills,' she said.

'What is?' asked Joan.

She asks because she does not fully grasp the situation, which is implicit and never explicit. It is not so much a passionate friendship as an unconsummated love affair. Because it remains unfulfilled it becomes destructive, reducing them both ultimately, in different ways: each becomes so much less alone than they might have been together.

There is no sense of passion or frustration in Joan, as there is in Stephen; she seems unaware of any physical attraction to Elizabeth, and Elizabeth herself, although aware, usually suppresses this, although it is there clearly in her verbal declarations: 'This part of me loves life . . . feels young . . . demands the pleasures of youth, cries out for them . . . all the more because it's been so long denied . . . it is jealous . . . of any affection that might rob me of even a hair's breadth of you . . . it wants to keep you all to itself, to have all your love . . .' Like Stephen she craves fulfilment, but unlike Stephen she never realizes it with the object of her desires.

Joan is also unfulfilled, collaborating with her mother and Seaborne, allowing herself to be well and truly 'bottled'. She realizes *some* of the dynamics of her own nature ('Well, I shall never marry!') but never confronts the ontological responsibility of such knowledge. She evades the issue.

With Stephen and Mary in *The Well* John allowed the relationship to fulfil its passionate potential, but to wreck itself against the 'iron flanks' of 'custom' and 'precedent', those rigid norms against which Stephen is powerless to protect Mary. *The Well* takes up and furthers many of the themes already suggested in *The Unlit Lamp*; and certainly at least one character from the latter would be equally at home in the former, the aptly but obviously named Beatrice Lesway, possibly a caricature of Toupie Lowther.

Just twelve days before she started work on *Stephen* John had finished a rather remarkable short story, 'Miss Ogilvy Finds Herself'. The 'self' which Miss Ogilvy finds is a previous, *male* incarnation of several thousand years earlier; but as John explained in her 'Author's Note' eight years later, it contained 'the nucleus of those sections of my novel which deal with Stephen Gordon's childhood and girlhood', and with work done by women at the Front in the Great War. Miss Ogilvy had been, like Stephen (and her creatoı), 'a queer little girl, aggressive and awkward . . .' and, like Stephen, had a 'tall, awkward body with its queer look of strength, its broad, flat bosom and thick legs and ankles . . .' Miss Ogilvy was therefore, like Joan Ogden, a preliminary study for Stephen Gordon.

*The Well* is worthy of consideration on many fronts: as literature; as psychology; as part of the history of censorship in our times; and from the biographer's point of view, as a rich source of information, inference, and perpetual questions. The central message is clear: She (i.e. Stephen but also John) 'must stand or fall by the courage of that love to proclaim its right to toleration.' The ultimate plea is not just to God but to society: 'Give us also the right to our existence!' It was not apologetic, made no excuses, pleaded no extenuating circumstances. She protested both the innate dignity and decency of inverted love.

It is a carefully constructed social critique of the attitudes of its time: Stephen has to fight against 'this world with its mighty self-satisfaction, with its smug rules of conduct . . . those who strutted and preened themselves as being what they considered normal . . .' 'Normal' vice is held up to less criticism than 'abnormal' virtue, since 'normality' itself is a protection: 'the vilest of them could point a finger of scorn at her, and be loudly applauded.' Perhaps this is most fully emphasized in the 'bitter truth' that Stephen rehearses earlier, but puts off telling Mary until the last possible moment.

That 'most pitiful bond, so strong yet so helpless' is contrasted with the sanctions of marriage and social approval accorded to 'normal' relationships. The inability of the invert lover to protect the beloved is early made clear in Angela's pointed comment, 'Could you marry me, Stephen?' and is doubly hammered home when Stephen remembers this just before the visit to Morton without Mary. The marriage of 'Adele and her Jean' from Stephen's house in Rue Jacob makes clear the contrast in social attitudes: there is joy, celebration, religious and civic approval in the coming together of the young couple; for Stephen and Mary there is nothing but rejection and hostility, although 'they craved a blessing on what . . . seemed sacred – a faithful and deeply devoted union. But the Church's blessing was not for them . . . her blessings were strictly reserved for the normal.' This rankled deeply with both John and Una, who regarded themselves as both Catholics and in every sense 'married' to each other.

Nature itself seems to combine with society against the invert: 'the splendid and purposeful meaning of their [i.e. Stephen's parents'] passion' and that of Adele and Jean, is contrasted with the love that is 'so productive of passion yet so bitterly sterile'; with 'our enduring passion/That yet remaineth barren!'[10]

Yet John is continually at pains to show the love of Stephen and Mary as both part of nature and like that of 'lovers throughout the ages'. Their lovemaking had 'something fine and urgent about it that lay almost beyond the range of their wills', so that 'Something primitive and age-old as Nature herself, did their love appear to Mary and Stephen.' Frank and forthright, yet poetically expressed, John depicts this relationship (to some extent a mirror of herself and Una) as *part* of nature, in harmony with it, rather than against it. This was her revolutionary contribution to sexual understanding. She sweeps away all arguments about 'perversion' and 'unnaturalness'. By aligning it with nature she points to a simple yet profound equation: if it occurs in and is part of nature, how can it be *un*natural? She is *not* a separatist, pleading a special case, so much as a radical rethinker acknowledging the essential synthesis of human emotions and experiences.

She also protests certain previously ignored truths about the nature of female sexuality. The suggestion that a woman's sexuality is autonomous and spontaneous, like a man's, must have seemed something of a heresy at the time. The prevailing belief was still that woman only became a sexual being when 'awakened' by a man with whom she was in love; to suggest that she experienced desire, and frustration, in itself, independent of anyone else, must have shocked those who still clung to the unrealistic sentiment that women (and children) were sexually innocent. It was not too many years earlier that the very suggestion of female orgasm had been regarded as either a slur against 'pure' womanhood, or a myth! That women's passions could be aroused and deeply satisfied by each other, with all the ardour and emotion of heterosexual lovers, must have been a shocking revelation to many at the time, especially when the author postulated and pleaded for parity and equality between these relationships.

As well as a radical view of female sexuality, John evolves a theory of types and roles in the book. This works largely by contrast: Stephen 'can't feel that [she is] a woman', whereas Mary is 'perfect woman'; Stephen is 'the lover', Mary 'the beloved' who 'gives herself' to Stephen. They represent opposite poles, the masculine and feminine principles, within one biological sex. Stephen was one of 'those who stand midway between the sexes', being composed of a 'sexual mixture' of both male and female: she has both a 'shy gentleness' and a 'strength which at moments could not be gentle'. At times 'all that was male in her make up' would predominate: at the outbreak of war, then later on when she takes up her writing again. 'A drop too little of the male in the lover, and mighty indeed will be the wastage,' John tells us, adding, 'And yet there are cases – and Stephen's was one – in which the male will emerge triumphant . . .' uniting love with purposeful endeavour. Jamie's is a similar nature to Stephen's, and Barbara's to Mary's. In both pairs the male-female polarities are in evidence.

John mentions the 'pitiful . . . lot of a girl who, herself being normal, gave her love to an invert', as Mary (and perhaps Una?) did. It is confusing here as to whether she means an 'invert' or a masculine-identified woman (i.e. a transsexual) who has the innate and/or overt masculinity to attract a 'normal' woman. The one thing her 'inverts' do *not* do is attract each other; it would be as impossible for Stephen and Jamie to be attracted to each other as for Mary and Barbara. These 'types' are psychological *and* physical: Stephen is portrayed as taller and stronger than Mary, with a fine athletic physique, and wears masculine outer and under clothes; Mary is slight, not strong, and wears dresses and other normal feminine clothes. (This 'typing' becomes positive androgyny in the case of Pat, whose 'ankles were too strong and too heavy for those of a female', although she is a woman.)

The implication of this theory of types is that there are only masculine 'inverts', who cannot love each other, and innately 'normal' women. This is not cognisant of the facts of homosexuality as we know them today, where masculine, feminine and neutral gender-types are found within one genetic sex and within one orientation.

The 'roles' evidenced fit in with the two basic types outlined: Stephen and Jamie naturally adopt the dominant, worker-provider, masculine roles, whilst Mary and Barbara fit into the feminine, dependent role of 'wife': 'They soon settled down to their more prosaic days, very much as quite ordinary people will do. Each of them now had her separate tasks – Stephen her writing and Mary the household, the paying of bills, the filing of receipts, the answering of unimportant letters . . .' There can be no doubt that this role-division is a fairly faithful representation of John's and Una's after the psychic research work was at an end and John settled down to being a novelist. There is little doubt too that as John shared the nocturnal writing habits she ascribes to Stephen, the following was autobiographical: 'Stephen would be torn by conflicting desires, by opposing mental and physical emotions. She would want to save herself for her work; she would want to give herself wholly to Mary.'

Mary 'belongs' to Stephen, and having given herself rests 'without thought . . . exultation . . . question . . .' in perfect trust. In the first flush of her love for Stephen she wanted to do 'womanly things' for her, such as sewing and looking after her clothes. Later, left alone in Paris while Stephen reluctantly goes on a duty visit to Morton: 'being a woman, she suddenly ached for the quiet, pleasant things that a home will stand for – security, peace, respect and honour, the kindness of parents, the goodwill of neighbours; happiness that can be shared with friends, love that is proud to proclaim its existence . . .' It is almost as though being an 'invert' and being a 'woman' are incompatible.

Perhaps Una also, 'being a woman', wanted these things; but she was certainly prepared to forgo some of them. They had the 'respect' of those people who mattered to them; certainly shared their happiness with their friends; and although they never proclaimed their love from the house-tops they never hid it either. Like the most positive of her inverts (only referred to, never depicted) John and Una 'did not . . . live out crucified lives, denying their bodies, stultifying their brains, becoming the victims of their own frustrations. On the contrary, they lived natural lives – lives that to them were perfectly natural. They had their passions like everyone else . . .'

Stephen, the central protagonist of the book, is an ambiguous creation. In some respects she is too much her creator not to be a fictionalized self-portrait; but also, clearly, she represents a type. The question is whether she is a typical 'invert' or really something quite different. As I have already said, no feminine, true 'invert' is presented to us; and Stephen, who has on her own admission (like John), 'never felt like a woman', would seem to have a gender problem. Is 'inversion' then a gender problem or, as John would appear to be arguing, a perfectly valid alternative life-style? It cannot be both. As a conscious artist, she seems to be arguing the latter; yet, perhaps unconsciously, she also suggests the former. Stephen knows that 'the loneliest place in this world is the no-man's land of sex . . .' This is the negotiable, indefinite area between male and female: and those who dwell there are *not* 'inverts' but transsexuals, who 'stand midway between the sexes.' This is the real 'loneliness' of the book; a point which does not seem to have sufficiently struck either the author or her readers! This makes the book doubly courageous, and with hindsight arguably the first transsexual testament.

John has a habit, probably common to many authors, of mentioning or setting scenes at places which have associations for her: Oratava, Tenerife, Watergate Bay, and even Skindles Hotel at Maidenhead in *Adam's Breed*. What she also does occasionally is to fictionalize an actual experience of her own. Thus Ladye's death, with all its anguish and deep guilt, becomes metamorphosed into Barbara's, and John's comments to Una become Jamie's to Stephen: 'Oh, my God – we quarrelled . . . last night . . . I was angry . . . I get like that . . . Oh, my

God . . . why did we quarrel?' . . . 'Just before her death she kissed Jamie's hand and tried to speak, but the words would not come – those words of forgiveness and love for Jamie . . .' What did Una feel reading this, one wonders?

Much may be said about the faults of *The Well* as a novel: it is overbalanced on the side of the early years (Mary does not enter the story until nearly two-thirds of the way through), it is too long, and the end is less than satisfactory. It has irritating stylistic features, such as the quasi-biblical language ('and so in these days . . .'); the direct authorial exclamations ('Oh, great and incomprehensible unreason!'); the faintly moralistic comments ('God alone knows who shall dare judge of such matters'); the continual rhetorical questions ('Who shall say?', 'and why not?'); and the extensive use of pathetic fallacy (particularly what birds or dogs 'say' or 'think').

The reader is continually reminded that 'passion' also means suffering: that 'the will to loving' and the capacity to suffer have a common origin; and that her tale is 'a hard and sad truth for the telling'. She resolutely loads the dice against her inverts: the world defeats them or they defeat themselves: Puddle, the repressed, who advocates sublimation and hard work, but who, in the final analysis, has no help or consolation to offer Stephen, and sees with shocked clarity the emptiness of her own life; Brockett, the effete cynic, who turns his malice into clever plays, and has no illusions about 'the normal' and their attitudes to inverts; Valerie Seymour, aloof like a magnificent lighthouse, indulging in multiple affairs, but ultimately hard and sterile. The couples fare no better: Barbara and Jamie are defeated not just by ill health and poverty but by ostracism and enforced exile. The double death (from tuberculosis and suicide) is a double negative harshly dealt in a world where positives are barely possible: a pointed vignette leaving a sense of tragic waste. Stephen and Mary, starting off so positively, are slowly, subtly changed: Mary becomes harder, embittered by the rejections of Morton and the Masseys, seeking escape in the cheap, sordid gaiety of Parisian bars, amongst the 'desolate . . . outcasts . . . despised of the world'. Stephen accompanies her reluctantly, secretly shocked by the changes in her face, habits and attitudes. When Martin reappears and mutual attraction between him and Mary develops (incredibly perhaps), the scene is set for sacrifice: the 'norm' wins out, aided by a selfless Stephen, ruthless to be kind. Mary is 'saved' from a life which Martin said she would not survive, for the norms of marriage, children, and social acceptance – all the things that Stephen, despite fame and money, could not, in the scheme of things, ever give her.

The ending is depressing, and the whole book presents a tragic vision, which did not accord much with her own experience. Why then did she do this? The answer is simply that, as a novelist, she knew that to make her plea forcibly she had to overstate her case. Besides, it must be admitted that tragic ends are common to most of her novels, as they are to Hardy's. *The Unlit Lamp* is so much finer a book than *The Well* because she was not consciously writing either a controversial book or a 'tract'. In *The Well* she was writing with as much conscious moral purpose as Bunyan, George Eliot or D. H. Lawrence.

*The Well* was a watershed in John's literary life, and brought with it a whole host of troubles, disruptions, defeats and triumphs. It affected their domestic lives, fortunes and plans. Una stood 'shoulder to shoulder'[11] with John, in full support, exposing herself fearlessly in the process; for she was made of sturdier stuff than Mary Llewelyn, and was 'strong enough to fight the whole world, to stand up against persecution and insult . . .' when necessary. She had long found her 'security, peace and love' with John, and had set up her abode with her in 'the palace of truth' and had no wish ever to leave it.

# 11

# Trials and Tribulations (1928–9)

While John still basked in the after-glow of the James Tait Black Prize and gave interviews to the press she was finishing the last chapters of *The Well*. The book had been read in instalments by Una to a very enthusiastic Audrey Heath, who as well as being John's literary agent had become one of their friends and regular diners. Una noted in her diary of January 5th, 1928: 'Carl [i.e. Brandt, Heath's American outlet] told Audrey it [*The Well*] was "great".' Three months later to the day, Una wrote: 'Audrey and I to first night. John working. Came home to find John had finished *The Well of Loneliness*.'

Then began the laborious process of final corrections. At last, on April 16th, they bound four final copies of the book, and the next day, the 17th, took three of these to Audrey. They must all three have realized that for such a book at such a time there would inevitably be problems ahead, but could hardly have anticipated the furore that lay just round the corner. On April 23rd they took the fourth copy to Havelock Ellis. While Una waited in the car outside 'John in to talk with him for over an hour. He promised to read *The Well of Loneliness* and to let his opinion be quoted if he approved. They called me in to tea . . .' Later, Jonathan Cape was dissatisfied with the first version of this Commentary, and John and Una went to see him again and he agreed to change it.

The first and most pressing problem was actually placing the book with a publisher. A number of reputable publishers, including Arrowsmith, Cassell, Heinemann and Martin Secker, turned it down because of its theme, often with profuse apologies and comments about its literary worth: 'Newman Flower wrote a wonderful letter about *The Well* but said he would not publish it,' Una noted in a typical entry at this time. While all this was going on John lectured on Animal Welfare at Westfield College, where she and Una dined; and they, together with Minna and Andrea, went to the Femina prize-giving. Finally, on May 7th: 'Cape telephoned he thought he could publish *The Well* and made an appointment for lunch tomorrow.' They, and Audrey, met him at the Berkeley Grill, 'and he arranged to publish *The Well of Loneliness* in the autumn – 1250 copies 1st ed. at 25/-.' Not surprisingly, Una adds: 'Home relieved and exhausted.' Three days later, on May 11th, after a last-minute hitch, the contract was signed; and towards the end of the month John and Una corrected the proofs within seven hectic days.

At the same time, Una herself was being pressed for translations, and agreed on May 18th to translate *La Chinoise Emancipée* by August 11th, which she did, and was then interviewed by the press herself! She arranged that they should give a tea to the Writers' Club; and kept up a lot of home entertaining. Her sister Viola proved troublesome ('Viola came and did it again – once too often,' she notes, without specifying the offence), and then suddenly, on July 10th, Visetti died and they were thrown into supervising burial arrangements. 'John went to see the body moved . . . and was abominably received,' she wrote with indignation. Yet despite all these tribulations she still finds time to note: 'a nightingale sang in the garden opposite our house . . .'

Cape seems to have been impressed by John's sincerity and moral courage in writing the book, and in support he determined that it should be 'soberly and carefully published' and 'produced in large format, in sombre black binding with plain wrapper, and priced at . . . twice the average price for a new novel.'[1] All these tactics were to ensure its reception as a serious, not a salacious or sensational book. John was pleased by this: 'Cape has certainly done more than most publishers would have done in the way of a beautiful and dignified production – thus presenting the book in the most favourable manner – I am very grateful to him.'[2]

Publication date was fixed for July 27th, before which the first impression was sold out and review copies had been sent to a selection of the better newspapers. Anxiety as to its fate must have been uppermost in John's and Una's minds at this time. John wrote to Garvin, the Editor of the *Observer*,[3] on July 15th, sending a copy of the book direct:

Dear Garvin,

You may have heard from others that my new novel was completed and was shortly going to be published. You may also have heard a certain amount of discussion regarding this particular book . . .

I realise that my subject, however seemly the treatment, may – in some cases – be met with prejudice. But whether it meets with your approval or disapproval, I do not feel that prejudice can enter into the judgement of a mind such as yours . . .

It would be childish for me to pretend that I do not know how much your support in *The Observer* would contribute from the first appearance of my book . . . towards its success – above all towards its reception in the proper spirit . . .

. . . Well Garvin, there it is, and now . . . you know my motives in taking this . . . step, I think I will let the book say the rest . . .

She is careful, however, to say that whatever his professional attitude may be, she would still be 'anxious as a writer' to have his 'personal reactions' to her 'two years of work'. She makes no personal family comments of any kind, though they had met socially at Minna's and he was married to Una's sister Viola. Whether he realized the true nature of John's relationship to Una is not clear, though Viola can have had little doubt.

On publication day 'wires and flowers came' and it was 'Dinner Here Everyone!'[4] The reviews were varied, though despite John's letter I have not been able to trace any review in the *Observer*. *The*

*Times Literary Supplement* called it, 'sincere, courageous, high-minded, and often beautifully written.' Vera Brittain, a young journalist at the time, reviewed it favourably but not uncritically, in *Time and Tide* on August 12th:

> Miss Radclyffe Hall's important, sincere and very moving study demands consideration from two different standpoints. In the first place it is presented as a novel . . . in the second place it is a plea, passionate yet admirably restrained, and never offensive, for the extension of social toleration, compassion and recogni-tion . . . it is the problem which it discusses, rather than its rank in fiction, which lends to Miss Hall's book its undoubted significance . . . 'The Well of Loneliness' can only strengthen the belief of all honest and courageous persons that there is no problem which is not better frankly stated than concealed . . .

Not everyone was to agree!

What really started the furore was James Douglas's (Editor of the *Sunday Express*) long, emotive, condemnatory review, pub-lished on August 19th. After dismissing both the publisher's and Havelock Ellis's defence of the book on the grounds of its 'perfect frankness and sincerity' and 'deep psychological insight', Douglas proceeded to describe the book as 'the first outrage of the kind in the annals of English fiction', which was 'not fit to be sold by any bookseller or to be borrowed from any library'. The tone was one of moral indignation and vituperation, and marshalling both Chris-tianity and civilization to his aid, he declared, 'I would rather give a healthy boy or a healthy girl a phial of prussic acid than this novel. Poison kills the body, but moral poison kills the soul.' It was a particularly nasty piece of cheap sensationalism calculated both to stir up a hornets' nest and increase sales of his paper. He used the imagery of disease throughout: 'contamination', 'pestilence', 'unutterable putrefaction', 'the leprosy of these lepers'; con-demning not just the book but inverts themselves, 'these moral derelicts'. 'This undiscussable subject' (about which he talked at great length) was an 'intolerable outrage' to 'literature as well as morality', he maintained; and the book itself 'a seductive and insidious piece of special pleading designed to display perverted decadence as a martyrdom inflicted on these outcasts by a cruel society'. He called on the author and publishers to withdraw the book, or if they did not, for 'the Home Secretary to set the law in motion' by instructing the Director of Public Prosecutions.

Jonathan Cape, who had been told by Douglas of his forthcoming review two days before, was, on reading it, so angered that 'that very morning he wrote to the Home Secretary, sending him a copy of the book and a selection of the serious reviews . . . and inviting his response to the sanctimonious hypocrisy of the article.'[5]

This ambiguous action on the part of the publisher is open to several interpretations, as is his later conduct. The one thing he had *not* done beforehand was to tell John, who was understandably 'at first much upset by his precipitate action.'[6] What anger or sense of insult she and Una felt at the tone of Douglas's review, and what anxiety at the ominous turn things were taking, can only be imagined; for although Una was busy making a press-cutting book for *The Well* she is surprisingly silent about their reactions in her diary entries.

The Home Secretary, Sir William Joynson-Hicks (unpopular, and satirized as 'Jix'), contrary to what Cape had no doubt hoped and expected, replied hastily that if the book was not withdrawn proceedings would be started. A second impression of 3,500 copies had been printed, making nearly 5,000 copies in circulation. Jonathan Cape, in his own interests (and perhaps to ensure the survival of the book), quickly leased his rights in *The Well* to the Pegasus Press in Paris, and ordered the printers to mould the type and send the moulds to Paris. He had, in effect, unwittingly hastened the prosecution of the book, but privately ensured its continued publication abroad. John Holroyd-Reece, who ran the Pegasus Press which specialized in producing English editions of books proscribed in Britain, was to figure importantly in Una's affairs later. At this time though, his main function was to prepare a Paris edition, which he instantly did, bringing it out within weeks, on September 28th. Circulars were sent out, and orders taken from British booksellers, but copies were seized by Customs on arrival, then briefly released before the trial and re-seizure.

The prosecution was set in motion under Lord Campbell's 1857 Act. The owners of the books, and the premises where they were found, were prosecuted, *not* the author, who could neither be directly represented nor summoned to give evidence. The verdict had to be given by the Bench, as publishers did not gain the right to jury trial, in such cases, until 1967. Jonathan Cape and Holroyd-Reece were summonsed 'to show cause why the articles seized should not be destroyed', so that the onus of proof lay on the defendants not on the Public Prosecutor. Holroyd-Reece engaged a keen young solicitor, Harold Rubinstein (of Rubinstein, Nash & Co.), to defend the Pegasus Press. He set about his task with great energy and enterprise. As well as briefing the young Norman Birkett as defence counsel, he sent out letters and forms (with space for full name and address with titles, qualifications, opinions of *The Well*, and other observations) to hundreds of potential witnesses in support of the book, from all walks of life: other writers, scientists, doctors, churchmen, members of Parliament, the distinguished and respected in various fields.

His son Michael Rubinstein, now senior partner in the firm, showed me one of his firm's most treasured possessions: a folder of letters to his father from many of these potential witnesses. They make interesting and revealing (and occasionally amusing) reading. Many of those approached declined as they had not read the book: the Bishop of Birmingham, Robert Baden-Powell, the Earl Beauchamp, Sir William Beverage, May Sinclair, Frank Swinnerton, Humbert Wolfe, The Archbishop of York. John Drinkwater declined on the grounds of 'practical difficulties'; H. G. Wells had 'gone abroad', and Arthur Conan-Doyle, his secretary said, had 'left for South Africa'.

Harley Granville-Barker said, 'No, I had better not give evidence. I don't like the book,' adding that it was 'not a fit subject for art; it belongs to sociology and pathology.' The same, of course, could be said for many of Shakespeare's themes, to those so minded!

Galsworthy replied, 'I much regret that I am not prepared to go into the witness box on behalf of Miss Radclyffe Hall's book . . . I am too busy a man and I am not sure the freedom of letters is in question . . .'

179

Nigel Playfair, of the Lyric Theatre (of which John and Una were frequent patrons), found it politic to agree with his colleagues: 'I have had a long talk with Mr. Galsworthy and Mr. Barker and I have decided that I think it would be inadvisable and unhelpful to give evidence.'

Arnold Bennett, in a letter to Mrs Williams-Ellis on the subject, said:

> Just before the summons was issued I had written an article for the *Evening Standard* tearing Jix to pieces; this article could not be printed . . . I feel it to be important that the witnesses should have a clear understanding with Mr. Rubinstein of what line of examination the counsel for the defence will take . . . If prosecuting counsel asks, e.g. 'Do you think this book is a proper one to put into the hands of young persons?' the witness should absolutely refuse to say either 'Yes' or 'No.' If he says 'No' he should add, 'And I say the same of the Bible and Shakespeare.'

J. A. C. Crew, of the Animal Breeding Research Dept, Edinburgh University, commented sardonically, 'I am quite prepared to support Miss Radclyffe Hall. I have not read her book but I am sure that if Mr. James Douglas condemns it, it must possess considerable merit.'

Charlotte Haldane replied on behalf of her husband, 'His scientific occupations do not permit him to take part in such controversies.'

Alfred Noyes (of *The Highwayman* fame) thought 'publication [of *The Well*] . . . quite unjustifiable'. An unexpected comment perhaps from a friend and frequent visitor.

Violet Markham of 8 Gower Street, Bloomsbury, declared ardently, 'I shall be glad to associate myself with the protest against the suppression of Miss Radclyffe Hall's "Well of Loneliness." I have read the book and think it a scandal that so fine and serious a work should be banned, especially in view of the amount of corrupt and degraded literature which circulates without hindrance.'

Lascelles Abercrombie declined due to health and commitments. He had not read it but believed 'the action taken against it . . . stupid and oppressive'.

Geoffrey Faber replied, 'I am on principle strongly opposed to the action taken by the authorities; and I have publicly expressed my dislike . . . of any interference with the liberty of the press and of literature. But my position as the Head of a Publishing House prevents me from exercising the same freedom of expression where a particular book is concerned.'

Dr R. Gruber of Harley Street (one of Una's doctors) said, 'I have not had a chance to read "The Well of Loneliness" but I have the pleasure of knowing Miss Radclyffe Hall personally and feel certain that nobody but a congenital idiot could think her capable of writing a book which a healthy minded person would call obscene.'

Gilbert Murray declared, 'I cannot say that it is a book of much artistic merit. It seems to me to have almost no attraction except that which comes from the curiosity aroused by the discussion of sexualities.'

Hugh Walpole, positive and to the point, replied, 'I am ready to go anywhere and protest against any censorship and if you want me at the court for that purpose I will gladly come.'

The Pen Club, of which John was a prominent member, and to whose dinners she and Una frequently went, explained that the Committee had turned down the suggestion that General Secretary Herman Ould should speak in its defence, as he had no authority to speak on behalf of *all* members. 'I am sorry. I think any opportunity to "make a stand" should be seized; but you will see how I am placed,' he apologized.

Others who agreed to support the defence as witnesses included Virginia and Leonard Woolf, E. M. Forster, A. P. Herbert, Vita Sackville-West, Laurence Housman, Julian Huxley, Lytton Strachey and Rudyard Kipling. Those who declined included Bernard Shaw.

The trial began at Bow Street Magistrates Court on November 9th, 1928, before Sir Chartres Biron, a man whom Harold Rubinstein later described as 'pathologically boorish'. John sat at the solicitor's table, and Una presumably in open court with the many witnesses: estimates of these vary; Michael Howard (the

Cape firm's own historian) says there were forty, but Una herself wrote later of 'our 57 witnesses in its favour'. No doubt their presence gave both John and Una a sense of moral support. Things began badly as Birkett arrived two hours late then proceeded to exceed his brief by suggesting that the book described only 'normal friendship' between women, a claim, in any case, impossible to substantiate! Biron promptly refused to hear any of the witnesses for the defence, which he was within his rights to do despite Birkett's contention that it was not for the magistrate to act upon his own personal view, but upon the views of reasonable people generally. No change in the law to allow witnesses to give evidence of a book's literary or scientific merit was made until the Obscene Publications Act of 1960, which was followed by the acquittal of *Lady Chatterley's Lover* on the testimony of expert witnesses.

'During the luncheon recess Radclyffe Hall, flushed and tearful, furiously attacked Birkett for his attempt to undermine the purpose of her book and the conviction with which she felt it ought to be defended. She insisted that in the afternoon he should retract his misrepresentation of its theme. In deference to his client's author he was obliged to do so,' Michael Howard recalled later. After this retraction Birkett said to Biron, 'Nowhere is there an obscene word or a lascivious passage. It is a sombre, sad, tragic, artistic revelation of that which is an undoubted fact in this world. It is the result of years of labour by one of the most distinguished novelists alive . . .'

Biron countered that certain passages appeared to him to be 'obscene', 'lascivious' and to contain 'lurid descriptions of unnatural vice'.

At the end of the day he adjourned the case for a week to consider it. John and Una, with Holroyd-Reece and Audrey, considered it themselves till 2 a.m. that morning after dining together at the Hyde Park Grill.

The case resumed on November 16th with Biron's lengthy summing-up in what one newspaper[7] described as 'quiet, conversational tones':

The mere fact that the book deals with unnatural offences between women does not make it obscene. It might even have a

182

strong moral influence. But in the present case there is not one word which suggests that anyone with the horrible tendencies described is in the least degree blameworthy . . .

He described one passage as 'the life of these two people living in filthy sin' and spoke also of 'moral and physical degradation'. What, one wonders, did Una feel as she sat listening, in effect, to her love for John, in all its aspects, so described? As she heard, 'The degrading of all that to them was sacred'? What *John* felt was soon made characteristically clear:

> 'I protest,' she exclaimed. 'I emphatically protest!'
> Sir Chartres rebuked her. 'I must ask you to be quiet.'
> 'I am the author of this book . . .' she began, but was not allowed to.finish.
> 'If you cannot behave yourself in court,' he asserted, 'I shall have to have you removed.'
> 'Shame!' she shouted from her seat at the solicitor's table.[8]

What apparently provoked this outburst was Biron's comment about 'suggestions' being made against a women's ambulance unit at the Front. John was adamant that she had shown utmost respect for such women in her book.

Biron, in what must have been a clearly inevitable conclusion, declared the book to be obscene and ordered it to be destroyed, with costs of forty guineas. Sir Archibald Bodkin, the Director of Public Prosecutions, who had been present during the summing-up, must have felt gratified.

Una contented herself with remarking caustically in her diary: 'Sir Chartres Biron lied solemnly for more than one hour and condemned *The Well of Loneliness* to be burnt as an obscene libel.'

On November 17th, the day after the summing-up, the *Daily Express* noted that 'Miss Radclyffe Hall, the writer of the novel . . . wore a sprig of white heather at the side of her sombrero.' She had obviously cut a colourful figure, which the press were quick to seize upon. On the same day, the *Daily Mirror* recorded that 'Miss Radclyffe Hall, interviewed after the case was ended, said: "Long passages in my book were misinterpreted in the most amazing and shocking manner."'

John, being 'an indomitable fighter', lodged an Appeal on November 22nd, an Appeal on which she 'insisted as a moral gesture though well aware that the outcome was a foregone conclusion,' as Una said later. On November 23rd at Bow Street, 'John, Stella Churchill, and the Woolfs went surety,' Una noted. The Appeal was heard on December 14th at the County of London Quarter Sessions, before 'Sir Robert Wallace and 11 magistrates who had not read the book,' Una said. The other eleven magistrates, presumably, had read the book! Sir Thomas Inskip, the Attorney General, said, 'It will not be disputed that the vice is an unnatural one, and that *The Well of Loneliness* was a picture of indulgence in it. Therefore I would suggest that the tendency of the book is to deprave and corrupt. . .' Their defence counsel, Mr J. B. Melville, argued that the treatment of the subject was 'decent'. One of their favourite writers, Rudyard Kipling, sat behind counsel, and others present included Dr Marie Stopes and Sir William Wilcox, the Home Office Pathologist.

The magistrates retired for approximately ten minutes to consider their verdict before dismissing the Appeal with costs.

Just as she had been mobbed at the theatre for her autograph after the publication but before the prosecutions, so now, after the Appeal, John was pressed and jostled by crowds of sympathizers as she left the court, and 'two young women pressed forward and raising her hand, kissed it,' the *Daily Express* reported next day.

To the same reporter John said, 'I would like to fight on, but I am advised that the question cannot be carried to another court. I was not exactly surprised at the decision after the way the case went before the Magistrate at Bow Street, but I do feel most strongly that I as a serious writer have not been fairly treated. Neither has my book.'

And that, as far as the British situation was concerned, was that. John, with an understandable edge of bitterness, wrote to Lytton Strachey, one of her supporters, on December 18th:

Dear Mr. Strachey,
    As you were not present at London Sessions on Friday last, December 14th, to hear how the Attorney General found it necessary to open his case for the prosecution of the publishers

of 'The Well of Loneliness' by narrating the entire story of the book, and detailing the names, functions, and actions of each separate character, to the bench of magistrates who presumably should have read the book before sitting in judgement upon it, you may find the enclosed letter from the Public Prosecutor Sir Archibald Bodkin interesting in throwing light upon the Government's legal (?) procedure in connection with the preparation of their case.

Yours sincerely,

Radclyffe Hall

PS. As you may know, the Chairman of the Court mentioned in Bodkin's letter is Sir Robert Wallace, whose judgement of my book you will have seen in the papers.

Unfortunately the letter from Bodkin is not with this letter, which resides alone in the British Museum.

In America the situation was reversed. After prosecution under Section 1141 early in 1929 *The Well* was triumphantly acquitted after being brilliantly defended. It was published there by Cape-Ballou, a subsidiary company of Jonathan Cape, which subsequently went bankrupt. Before the Official Receiver took over, Jonathan Cape himself insisted on paying John $1,900 outstanding royalties, as a matter of honour. They remained friends, and John bore no grudges, as is shown by the fact that she gave him her next book, *The Master of the House*.

Both John and Una remained on friendly terms with Harold Rubinstein, who was, unbeknown to them at the time, to play a most important part in Una's future life.

Insofar as John had thrown down the gauntlet to the Establishment, its retaliation and exaction of retribution were predictable. What was perhaps far less predictable was the support of ordinary people for both author and book. The case had caused 'widespread sympathy in all directions . . . miners and railwaymen were amongst her most ardent champions',[9] and public collections were made towards her legal costs. These she would not, of course, accept. For the second time in her life John found herself 'in urgent need of ready money'[10] and had to sell another house due to 'financial embarrassment'. This time it was 37 Holland Street which had to go, 'to meet the legal costs of the defence of *The Well of Loneliness.*'[11] The long lease, being valuable, was easily sold, and Una remembered afterwards that 'two applicants collided on the doorstep disputing as to which of them could claim priority.' Holland Street had been beseiged by reporters and photographers during the trials, but now returned to normality. The winning applicant was a Mr Laskey to whom number 37 was sold on November 13th, a day on which Una noted pointedly: 'we had tea with Jonathan who said nothing anent finances.' Six days later, on the 19th, things had to become financially explicit: 'we to Harold [Rubinstein] and Howard [of Cape] anent expenses of cases . . .'

They had spent four fairly happy years at Holland Street and Una regretted that 'it went just after John had fitted out a sunny little back room as a sitting room for me.'[12]

They went back to Kensington Palace Mansions as their London base. Just after the publication but before the trials of *The Well* John and Una had motored to Rye, on August 9th, at the invitation of Anne Elsner, an acquaintance, to spend a few days at her rented cottage. They both fell in love with Rye, which was to figure largely in their lives for the next ten years. On this first visit Una recorded: 'All very delightful, and we longed for a cottage there . . .' They continued to visit Rye, sometimes staying at The Mermaid, which was, at that time, like Hucksteps Row, owned by Mr James Macdonnell, a local solicitor and property speculator. They met him on September 22nd and 'decided to try to buy the Hucksteps.' On the 25th they went to see Mrs Mary Harvey at Hastings, the owner of the cottage then known as 'Journey's End' and let to Anne Elsner. This house was destined, though not for another five years, to become Una's 'beloved "Forecastle".'[13] They got it on latchkey loan for six months with 'an admirable servant', Mabel Bourne, and it became a much-frequented haven of rest during the trials later in the year. They took temporary possession on October 25th.

After the trials were over Una was left to comfort the battered warrior, who was, 'not unnaturally, exceedingly tired . . .' and 'in all her life . . . had never needed a rest so badly . . .' A holiday in France could profitably be combined with business as offers were being made for the translation rights of *The Well*, but John delayed going for several months. 'Well aware of the notoriety that attended her wherever she went . . .' (and Una also, in her capacity as consort) 'she had a consuming fear that if she left England someone would say that her courage had failed, that she had gone abroad to let things blow over.'[14] Six days after the failure of the appeal John, Una and Andrea drove down to the cottage to spend their first Christmas in Rye. The next day, December 21st, Audrey (now known, for some reason, as 'Robin') arrived; and on the 22nd, Patience Ross (also of the Heath Agency) and her friend 'Mornie'. 'Robin' left on the 24th but the other two stayed to make a Christmas houseparty of five.

On the 30th they all returned to London, and there John and Una stayed, and showed themselves in public at first nights, restaurants and functions, to dispel any possible accusation of loss of moral courage. A considerable number of letters were received, mostly from well-wishers, and John later told Ethel Mannin that 'the most cruel and abusive letter she had was from a Jesuit priest, as was also the most beautiful and understanding letter.'[15] The latter may well have been from their friend Father Thurston.

John was also asked to lecture on the theme of *The Well* by 'various societies' and did so. 'Micki' (Naomi) Jacob, who was to become a close friend, and to remain one of Una's after John's death, recalls attending one of these lectures. She had written to John after reading the book but they had never met until, staying in Southend, she saw a poster in the hotel advertising the lecture. She recalled:

I saw Lady Troubridge passing through the hall and, introducing myself, asked if it would be possible to get seats. She told me that she believed that the hall was completely sold out, but she would do her best, and leave tickets, if two were procurable, at the desk. She was successful and we went to the lecture . . . I don't remember that John was a particularly good speaker. She had a clear, pleasing voice, she did not fumble for words, but she seemed to me to lack fire, and . . . to try to 'get a quart into a

> pint pot' . . . to attempt to cover more ground, to give more facts, quote more authorities than the subject . . . would carry.[16]

A not dissimilar criticism to Sir Oliver Lodge's ten years earlier. Una's version, however, is a little different: 'The press to see John all morning . . . Robin came . . . we dined and went to meeting where John spoke on Sexual Inversion most eloquently and with immense success . . .' (Diary January 25th, 1929.)

Strangely perhaps, there is no record in Una's diary of what people closer to them thought of either the book or the trials: her own mother Minna, her sister Viola, Marie Visetti, or Andrea (now eighteen) . . . presumably they were either fully supportive or kept their views to themselves.

If they gained new friends through the book they also lost old ones. One of these was Toupie Lowther ('Brother'), their old friend from Chip Chase days, and for the oddest of reasons. They 'heard that she had resented the book as challenging her claim to be the only invert in existence,' Una recalled. The friendship had begun during the First World War, with Ladye as the common interest, apart from inversion. Una, at least, did not regret the passing of this friendship, as she makes clear from her description: 'A strange creature she was . . . essentially a crank. A compound of the very male and very feminine . . . Later still, when she was growing very old, I was told that she had moreover acquired the illusion that she had served as a model for Stephen Gordon!'[17]

Another mutual friend who came to dislike John was Romaine Brooks the painter, who, unbeknown to either of them, described *The Well* in a letter to Natalie Barney (her lover) as: '. . . a ridiculous book, trite, superficial, as was to be expected.' She described John as 'A digger up of worms with the pretention of a distinguished archaeologist'; and, like Toupie, was convinced that one of the characters was based on her, but was a poor likeness: 'She has watched me with the eye of a sparrow who sees no further than the window-pane. I find myself (?) chirping, pecking, hopping, just as she would herself.' With such 'friends' who needs enemies?

When they finally left England and arrived in Paris on February 5th, 1929, it was to find *The Well* and John's photograph displayed in every bookshop window, and everyone reading it. The trials had been well covered in the French press, and almost from their arrival, as Una said, 'there was no avoiding a continuous publicity'. However, it was a positive and therefore a gratifying publicity. Una describes how 'total strangers would come up to her in the street or in a restaurant and express their admiration of the book, their amazement and indignation at its persecution. She was lionised by English, French, and Americans alike . . .'[18] And Una, of course, was by her side to share in all this, as she had been in the English defeat. They saw a lot of John and Jeanne Holroyd-Reece in Paris; went to tea with Natalie, Colette and others of 'the girls'; to punch parties with 'the Duchess' (Clermont Tonnerre); met Louis Bromfield and Ezra Pound . . . John signed copies of *The Well* in bookshops, was interviewed by the press, including two reporters from the *New York Herald Tribune* . . . altogether hardly restful.

Uppermost in Una's mind was her knowledge of John's cumulative exhaustion, and the need 'to find some really quiet refuge' where she could recover her strength and relax from all the tensions. In addition Paris was bitterly cold with the Seine frozen over. While her mind was working on this, Una gave John two rather special presents at this time: sapphire and diamond cuff-links bought from the proceeds of the royalty account from her translations, which had just been paid; and the tiny Brabanconne bitch quickly christened Tulip, which Una later said was 'the dog she loved best of all'.

Colette told them about St Tropez where she had just bought a house and was 'wildly enthusiastic about the beauties of the Côte des Maures . . . its bathing amenities and . . . unsophistication'.[19] This planted the idea in Una's mind of a possible place of recuperation as John was becoming ill in Paris and 'far past any enthusiasm'. She decided that they should go there, and 'dragged' John with her to Thomas Cook to make the necessary arrangements. Her decisiveness and talent for organizing came into play, as it so often did at such moments. They were told that trains ended at St Raphael, beyond which they would have to go by road. Nothing deterred, even after John 'made a minor scene of desperation' in Cook's office, saying that Una was 'cruel' or 'crazy' to 'think of dragging her, tired to death as she was, to the ends of the earth and . . . landing her somewhere in the unknown . . .' Una was 'unconvinced and . . . clung to [her] plan'. She quickly developed this plan which involved going by road in the car they were already hiring; and by 'some juggling of mileage and charges' was able 'to dish it up as a positive economy', as an additional incentive. 'I have always been rather an adept at this type of arithmetic,' she explains blandly in her *Life* – no doubt due to necessity in the past, when the Taylor family income was such that economy was essential. John acquiesced, as she so often did when Una was adamant. 'John was always indulgent to me,' Una explains; adding, 'John was moreover full of the idea [which was surely true?] that I had suffered strain and stress as her lieutenant in the battle and that I also badly needed a holiday.'

This did, Una said later, turn out to be '. . . a holiday that we never forgot; not only because it was entirely delightful and because we needed it as perhaps never before, but because . . . it led to the writing of *The Master of the House*.' She describes the journey delightfully (and with typical vagueness regarding dates):

On a beautiful April morning – or was it May – we set out together in the car for St. Tropez, with Pierre the chauffeur driving, and our English maid beside him and John and I in the back of the car with Tulip . . . and plenty of impedimenta, for the leisurely and lovely journey to the south, punctuated by the best meals that can be eaten in France. Saulieu, Macon, Arles, Avignon, Aix-en-Provence. We stopped for the night as we felt inclined . . . and as the weather grew warmer we expanded, our tired nerves relaxed and we were very happy.

The date they left Paris was actually May 17th, and they arrived at St Tropez on the 22nd.

Such 'vicissitudes' as there were, were taken lightly due to their 'beatific frame of mind'. One of these concerns the maid (Barber) and is told by Una with succinct humour:

Despite grave warnings the English maid allowed herself to be 'treated' when we reached the wine country. I think it was at Macon that, when the time came to move on, she tottered into our room with a scarlet face and became strangely hilarious . . . over her own failure to stuff a left foot tree into one of John's right shoes . . . she was duly admonished and we resumed our journey. (I am, however, bound to admit that there came a time later on when her potations became habitual and she had to be shipped back to England.)

To Una, 'whose only previous experience of the south of France had been that disastrous visit to Monte Carlo (in September 1926), every mile was a joy and a revelation'. She records some of these: meeting for the first time the 'heavenly smell' of the *maquis*; the cherry market at Châteauneuf-du-Pape, where 'the minimum sale was ten kilos' but nothing daunted they 'had them poured into the bottom of the car and ate them steadily all the way to Avignon, throwing stones and stalks into the road . . . we sat with our feet submerged in cherries . . .'; Arles, which they 'simply adored', and where they 'drank much iced beer in a loggia at the Jules Cesar and walked the colourful streets until late at night'; but

the best of all that wonderful journey, in which every joy was doubled by being shared . . . was waking at the Napoleon at St. Raphael with the southern sky as blue as a sapphire, the warm air pouring in at the wide-open windows together with the multiple sounds of a harbour . . . And on going to the window the blue Mediterranean and the ships and boats of all shapes and sizes with their brilliant hulls and red or tawny sails . . . To see it all for the first time is truly an unforgettable experience.

Finding the English hotel recommended by Colette, Seaward Lodge, to be unsatisfactory, they went on to the Golf Hotel at Beauvallon, where they 'settled in beautiful rooms, with balconies overlooking the private bathing beach', and stayed there for 'several happy months'. They toured Provence, 'visited and explored all the little ports along the coast'; sunbathed and swam 'for increasingly long periods' in the which 'excess', Una tells us, 'John was the principal sinner'. John had certainly changed since 1919, when she had said of herself, 'I . . . cannot swim a stroke . . . I dislike bathing quite as cordially as it dislikes me.'[20] But it was Una herself who 'bathed in a state of nature at Les Salins' with several of their female friends, 'lay in the shallow pools among the hot seaweed and ate lobsters afterwards at the admirable restaurant . . . on the beach.' John presumably did not like to be seen naked except by her lover, or doctors when necessary. Nevertheless, she grew, Una said, 'brown as a berry and her hair got bleached and her eyes were clear and very blue and her teeth very white in her tanned face . . . All the lines of strain and anxiety seemed to disappear and her smile grew rakish and carefree again and I think I never knew her to be so well.' Una herself, always slim, 'had grown positively stout: I turned the scales at nearly eight stone, and was mahogany coloured all over . . .' On July 22nd Una noted, 'John and I bathed by moonlight . . .'

They returned to Paris on August 4th, then went from there to Bagnoles six days later on the 10th, where it was, Una recorded when they got there, 'hot as hell's kitchen'. They stayed at Bagnoles, which they always loved, until September 12th; and Una remarked thankfully, 'Not a soul here we know, very restful.' When they returned to Paris on the 12th they were briefly visited by 'Robin'; then Andrea, whom they had not seen since January, arrived to spend a week with them on October 1st. They showed her all round Paris, then she left in order to go up to Oxford on October 12th, having won a scholarship.

They relaxed and enjoyed this 'holiday of holidays', during which the battles over *The Well* must have begun to recede from the forefront of their minds. They were assured that it would survive, not just because banning a book is one of the best ways of ensuring its popularity, but because of its success in France and America, and proposed translation into many languages. Una herself was involved in the French translation. John was later to reclaim the English rights in 1938, but it was not republished in England until 1949, six years after her death.

Another major reason for the relative eclipse of *The Well* in their lives was the inception and gestation of a new book. To all authors the most important book is the one they are working on:

and no extant spiritual child can claim as much of its progenitor's attention as the child of the moment. Una recounts how,

> at the final stage of our enchanted pilgrimage . . . there occurred an incident which made me wonder whether . . . in my stubborn determination to come to St. Tropez, I had been influenced by forces of which I was unconscious. Many months before . . . John had said to me that she was haunted by the desire to write a book about . . . the son of a carpenter, who, as he grew up in the carpenter's shop, would have memories and impulses that he did not understand, that linked him with the Carpenter's Son of Nazareth. But she added that she was unable to begin the book as she could not visualise its geographical setting . . . as our car made its way through Frejus she suddenly grasped my arm and called to Pierre to stop. What had caught her eye was a low stone archway, and under the archway, half in and half out of it, a carpenter's bench and a carpenter at work. 'Look,' she said, 'there's my carpenter's shop. That's where Christophe Benedit was born . . .'

On October 14th, back in Paris, Una wrote: 'at 10.30 p.m. John began *The Carpenter's Son* and we talked till 3.'

This holiday then served not only its ostensible purpose, but also enabled John to collect copy for her next book, which, Una tells us, 'she herself, and I also, always considered her best book: *The Master of the House*' (as *The Carpenter's Son* became). It was a book which, like *The Unlit Lamp*, *Adam's Breed*, *The Well of Loneliness* and *The Sixth Beatitude*, Una herself named.

# 12

# *In Sickness and in Health (1930–33)*

On November 1st Una and John arrived back in London after nearly ten months' absence, and settled themselves into the Great Central Hotel in Marylebone Road. They had stayed there before, always preferring venues tried and tested by past experience. Old friends welcomed them as though they had never been away, and they were soon busy socializing, shopping, and house-hunting in earnest. One of their friends at this time and later was (Sir) John Gielgud, who remembers:

> I used sometimes to meet Una and John at the Ivy Restaurant . . . and they came together to drinks at my flat . . . John was usually in her black hat and black and white pinstripe coat and skirt with a black stock over a white shirt . . . Una with her monocle and leopardskin coat, both eye-catching personalities. Afterwards I met them again at Smallhythe at one of the annual commemoration performances on the anniversary of Ellen Terry's death in July.

They were to meet him at cocktails and parties during the early 1930s, and Una was to meet him again in Florence after John's death. He was one of the performers (the others were Sarah

Bernhardt, Nijinksy, and later Rossi-Lemeni) whose stage-presence Una most admired, and she was very pleased to number him amongst her friends.

The London house-hunting having proved rather unrewarding, they went down to Rye on November 29th to look for houses there, and booked into the Mermaid Hotel where they were to spend several months. They took a bedroom, number 3, over Dr Syn's room, and an adjoining sitting-room, number 12, in which John worked during the day.

Mrs Fisher, the housekeeper, was the only person who went into their rooms. She remembered that they had the fire lit at four, so that the room was warm to dress for dinner: 'They always dressed for dinner . . . quite stunning Radclyffe Hall was when she was dressed – frilly shirt, man's suit . . . always very smartly dressed. Lady Troubridge, she wore evening dresses . . .'

They had breakfast in bed, but other meals in the dining-room, always at their own table. Of Radclyffe Hall Mrs Fisher said: 'Proper mannish, she was . . . but you respected her.' She was 'kind', despite the exclamation, 'Oh, you fool!' so often said in her 'very deep voice', and of Una: 'I didn't like her, she was rather "superior". The waiter felt the same. She only spoke when she had to.'

This curious impression was partially confirmed by Mrs Gwen Bligh (née Macdonnell) who worked in the hotel at the time, then in her teens: 'Radclyffe Hall was like a husband, always asking for things for Lady Troubridge: "Lady Troubridge must have more fires," and so on.' She also preferred John to Una: 'She was very nice, although she was always calling me "You fool!" as though that was my name! Lady Troubridge was very much the Lady and was finicky . . .'

Asked if the staff or other residents had any knowledge of the real nature of their relationship, Mrs Fisher replied: 'You heard the occasional "dear" or "darling" but thought nothing of it. You were too busy to worry about it. In them days we had to work! When you work in a hotel you see all, hear all, and say nowt! Guests in the hotel were like guests in your own home – you didn't enquire into things.' The waiter enlightened her eventually, and she was shocked: 'I couldn't take it in.'

*The Well . . . and After (1926–34)*

Mrs Bligh remembers that in late 1929, lots of young women were clamouring to get into the Mermaid to see Radclyffe Hall, and that some would come in shouting, 'Where is she? I must see her,' and try to get up the stairs. She formed the impression that 'Radclyffe Hall was "not allowed" by Lady Troubridge to give autographs', and that 'Lady Troubridge kept people away', being both protective of her, and 'very domineering in a subtle way'. She offered it as her 'personal opinion' that 'Lady Troubridge was the boss', although Radclyffe Hall 'took the lead'. This is an interesting if not entirely accurate insight. The curious fact, in retrospect, is that despite the publicity about the trials of *The Well*, and John's personal appearance, many people at the time were oblivious of the nature of their relationship. 'Inversion' was not just unmentionable, but unrecognizable. However, Mrs Viola Bailey, a teenager in Rye at the time, knew 'a certain lady' who had obtained a copy of *The Well* from America, and lent it out at a penny a time!

The day after John and Una arrived in Rye they viewed 'The Black Boy', an ancient house in the High Street, which had originally been part of the nearby monastery; cottages in the Hucksteps, and furnished houses in Watchbell Street. 'The Black Boy', so named because of its association with Charles II ('Black Charles'), who reputedly stayed there, appealed to Una partly because of this association. As a left-over from her hero-worship days, she felt a 'posthumous friendship'[1] with him, a sympathy and affinity. As a house it was tall, dark and narrow, and in need of some renovation. On December 23rd and 24th, she and John went over it again, measuring, and inspecting the drains; and on the 28th Una recorded: 'John bought "The Black Boy" for me.'

It was the first house that John bought in Una's name, so that she was the legal owner, and only her name appeared on the title deeds. It was a very generous gesture on John's part, and one of the best 'presents' Una was ever to receive. (See plate no. 21.)

Andrea had been home from her first term at Oxford to spend Christmas with them, and visited them again in mid-January, but their relationship with her was becoming strained, and trouble was brewing. Her natural spirits, and new freedom as an undergraduate, made her increasingly restive about strictures; and she

196

was later to spend her vacations flat-sharing in London, where she could live her life as she wished. On January 24th, after Andrea's departure, they took possession of 'The Black Boy'; and the following day obtained the keys and met Breeds the builders there, as arranged. Macdonnell, known as 'Mac', and Freddie Fisher, the husband of the housekeeper of the Mermaid, also worked for them, tearing out old fireplaces, and putting in the oak beams so loved by Una and John, to give it a 'period' flavour. In the course of this work, which was to take eight months, a priest's hole was discovered, a fresco, a Henry VIII gold coin, a buckled shoe in the chimney-breast, and other minor items of interest.

John's work was well under way with *The Carpenter's Son*, and while she wrote, Una went each day to direct and often partake in the work being done at 'The Black Boy'. Her own work, translating, was in temporary abeyance whilst this new, practical project absorbed her attention. The previous year she had shown an unprecedented degree of personal ambition, and desire of acknowledgment in her own right, as her letters to Audrey Heath revealed clearly: 'Now, anent *my* affairs: . . . I've got Howard [of Cape] keen and *Mrs.* Howard crazy over "Chéri" so do let's strike hard . . . I've told them . . . that others are beginning to think of Colette so I think Howard wants to jump in! Of course I'm very keen to bring it off . . .' and also to Patience Ross, of the Heath Agency: 'Yes. *I want my name on everything now* so as to get known in case the Colette translations materialise. Tommy Smith is using it on *La Femme Qui Commanda* and is now advertising the fact that I also did the *Eunuch* and *Elegant Infidelities* – he is putting me as "Una Lady Troubridge" . . . though I'd rather be just "Una Troubridge" . . . the "Una" must be in because otherwise there will be confusion with my foul sister-in-law!'[2]

Never one to mince words where her personal likes and dislikes were concerned, she had no desire to be confused with Lady Laura Troubridge, the author of a book on etiquette and the pious *Memories and Reflections* of the Troubridge family. Una was also keen to make some money, having only Troubridge's pension which was her own, and a predilection for buying John expensive presents.

Realizing that renovations at 'The Black Boy' were going to be prolonged, they arranged to take a furnished house, 8 Watchbell Street, for three months, and moved out of the Mermaid on March 7th. Their social instincts could not long be suppressed by work, and they soon met E.F. ('Dodo') Benson, author of the *Mapp and Lucia* books, who lived at Lamb House, Henry James's old residence. They also met the artist Paul Nash and his family, inviting them to dinner. Later, 'Sybil Thorndike and her children came,'[3] and 'Axel Munthe came to tea and stayed til 7.'[4] As usual, they made friends with the local priest, Father Bonaventure of the Franciscan church of St Anthony of Padua. He dined with them, and was also invited to their parties. They had become disillusioned with the Church's attitudes by their experience with the leading priest of the English-speaking Catholic Church in Paris, Monsignor Jackman, of whom Una had written to Audrey Heath: 'I sometimes feel as if everything were conspiring to hurt us . . . from the church . . . I do not think that he [i.e. Jackman] would ever be willingly uncharitable – but he is of course one under authority, and I begin to doubt whether authority has any place where the invert may lay his head . . .'[5]

Perhaps, as a consequence, they did not discuss the problems of inversion with Father Bonaventure; and it is significant that they always went, not to St Anthony's, but to Hastings, for Confession. Their ultimate longing for 'some sort of marriage for the invert', has never gained a sympathetic hearing from the Church.

Audrey visited, and Una read her the first four chapters of the new novel, which she liked. Two days later they went to London to see Dr Dowling, a skin specialist, as John had severe pains in the palms of her hands. Una noted: 'He gave X-rays and irritated John's hands and she had a very painful evening.'

The 'sharp stabbing pain' soon gave way to 'an angry looking red stain . . . in the centre of both palms.'[6] What had happened was that John, working intensely for long hours (e.g. 'John worked from 2pm to 2am') on a book that, Una said, 'was written as an amends for that insult to her Lord and to her faith' which *The Well* had caused, had inadvertently and hysterically over-identified with Christophe Benedit, the Christ-figure in the book. John was writing it with 'conscious solemnity of purpose', and 'her life while at work upon it was deliberately austere,' Una stated.[7]

This 'austerity' did not extend to social occasions, as on April 13th, 'We gave our first Rye dinner party at the Mermaid.' They hired a private room, and invited between seven and ten carefully selected guests. Mrs Timmy Pitcher, born in 1896, first met Una and John when they were all living in Watchbell Street. She and her husband Bill were artists, and very poor, 'and painting like mad to keep going!' Timmy did a woodcut for a bookplate for John as a commission, and as fellow-artists they became friendly. Timmy remembers that she and Bill were invited to one of these private dinners at the Mermaid, on June 14th, 1930. Present were Father Bonaventure, 'Mac', Sheila Kaye Smith, one of John's publishers, and the Pitchers themselves. John was resplendent in a ruffled shirt, satin breeches, silk stockings and buckled shoes. Her 'mannish manners' and 'pose of male chauvinism' especially struck Timmy. Una wore an evening gown, and said in conversation that she thought *Adam's Breed* was John's best book; and Timmy's husband Bill, who hadn't read it, agreed readily! It was an enjoyable occasion, with much good-humoured banter. 'They were so rare in those days . . .' Timmy said; and their style was impressive.

Whilst 'The Black Boy' was in preparation, Timmy was shown over it by John and Una, and afterwards, when they had moved in, remembers being invited to tea. She arrived on time, but Una was still out shopping, so there was just John at home. Shortly afterwards Una burst in full of apologies, with a large paper bag behind her back, saying: 'I'm afraid I've been most dreadfully naughty – I've bought a hat!' John exclaimed, 'Oh, not *another* hat!' Then, relenting, commanded, 'Well, put it on then!' Timmy was amused by this scene but thought that Una perhaps 'overdid the "little woman" act'.

They began to have sittings again with Mrs Leonard, who was at that time living at Tankerton, outside Canterbury. They hired an Austin from the Central Garage in Rye, and Mr Donald Hughes acted as their chauffeur, and drove them there and back once a fortnight. They sat in the back divided from the chauffeur by a glass partition. Mr Hughes remembers that on one occasion when driving them to Tankerton in a snowstorm, Radclyffe Hall wound down the partition and asked him why he was not wearing gloves.

He replied that he did not have any, and Radclyffe Hall spoke to Lady Troubridge in French, not realizing that he understood, to say that they should buy him some in Canterbury. The sequel was unfortunate in that the sun came out and he never got his gloves, but it does show a charitable interest on their part. On the way home from one of these visits to Tankerton, they called in to see Timmy Pitcher, who had by then moved to her present address, Ship Cottage, Playden. Timmy was boiling up a sheep's head for the dogs, and there was therefore a most appalling smell all over the house. It was early afternoon, and John and Una called unexpectedly. Una, noticing the smell, said, 'Oh dear, I do hope we haven't interrupted your lunch, Timmy.' Timmy was so embarrassed, she remembers, that she didn't know what to say!

At Watchbell Street Una secured the services of Mabel Bourne, who had been 'lent' to them before with the Hucksteps cottage. She was to become their longest-serving domestic, being with them for a total of seven years, in both Rye and London. She got on well with them, but said that they couldn't keep maids for long, especially London ones who answered back! 'Everything had to be just so – they were very particular,' she said; and of the maids, 'No sooner I'd showed 'em what they had to do, than they cleared off – !' One was sacked, she remembers, for leaving a dustpan and brush on the stairs, and answering back when told in no uncertain terms to move it! Mabel never lived in, and started as a 'maid of all work', cleaning, cooking, washing and pressing their clothes, and generally 'looking after them'. There was also a ladies' maid, and Mrs Hobbs, a char who did 'extra cleaning'. They were especially fond of baked potatoes and chicken, Mabel remembers, and there was 'always plenty of butter to use, and the fish was always done in wine.'

'I used to like doing for them . . .' she said, as they were good employers, and always giving her things: the remains of joints ('they never ate the same thing two days running') occasional theatre tickets, and Una gave her dresses. John, always 'very smart', wore trilby hats; and Mabel proudly showed me a photograph of her father in a large black trilby which had been Radclyffe Hall's! Asked about her working day, she answered that she arrived at 9 a.m. and prepared breakfast; washed up; cleaned the house; got lunch, washed up, and went at 2 p.m. She returned at 4 p.m. to get tea, then dinner at 7 p.m. leaving at about 10 p.m.

John gave the orders and, as Una preferred, did the hiring and firing; and this gave Mabel the impression that Una 'had to do what Radclyffe Hall told her to do . . . sometimes she was scared of her . . .'

The picture is of a fairly stable but not a rigid domestic routine, with John and Una as basically benign, kindly employers; but John's temper was inclined to flare up when she was crossed. When John and Una had 'tiffs' and used to throw scones at each other, the maids were afraid to go and retrieve the tea tray!

Una wrote enthusiastically to Jacqueline from Watchbell Street, whilst they were still preparing 'The Black Boy': 'We found a secret room, a priest's hole and about a dozen Jacobean shoes and clay pipes among other relics . . . Of course Rye is par excellence the home of history, you can't dig in a garden without finding old coins and other trophies, and it is the place in all England where you can get away from this hideous age of progress – that is why we have come to it!'

They began the move into 'The Black Boy' on August 14th, but it was not until the 28th that Una recorded: 'John and I slept our first night at "The Black Boy" – in my room.' As was their usual custom with new residences of whatever description, the Church was in evidence with incense and holy water: '17 Sept. Fr. Bonaventure came and blessed "The Black Boy".' Mabel Bourne remembers the procession round the house, led by the priest, followed by John and Una, herself, and two giggling maids.

They were on particularly good terms with Bonaventure at the time, as John had presented the church with a very large, handsome rood cross in red and gold on which hung a clothed Christ. It hung, and still does, from the sanctuary beams. Beneath it, engraved on a brass plate in the floor, are the words: 'Of your charity pray for the soul of Mabel Veronica Batten/In memory of whom this rood was given. 1930.'

201

On October 7th John paid off the church's remaining debt (from its building in 1928), and on the 12th Father Bonaventure gave them and Ladye a special Mass of Thanksgiving. Relations with this priest were to remain amicable until his general competence was called into question two years later, followed by his removal.

Once settled into 'The Black Boy' friends and neighbours were often invited to it, and most expressed their admiration, to Una's gratification. She was especially pleased when 'Noël [Coward] and Lord Amherst turned up for tea – howls of laughter. Noël *adored* "The Black Boy".'[8] Their other visitors included Lady Gregory, Lady Maud Warrender ('Maudie' in the diary), 'Dodo' Benson, 'the Small Fry' (a family so nick-named from their surname), and the 'three boys' (all girls!) from Smallhythe: Edy Craig (Ellen Terry's daughter), 'Christopher' St John, and Clare ('Tony') Atwood; 'the famous trio' (as Sir John Gielgud called them) who founded the Barn Performances at Smallhythe in Ellen Terry's memory.

In October Una again turned her attention to Colette, and organized a theatre version of her translation of *Chéri* as a private performance, inviting the press and theatrical people who might be interested in staging it commercially. On the 24th and 25th dress rehearsals were held, John outfitting the cast and Una superintending the rehearsal. On the 26th, the day of the performance, Una was approached by four interested managers, but noted cautiously: 'not to my mind a warm reception . . .' Two days later her worst fears about its reception were confirmed: 'Press for "Chéri" unspeakable – not one decent critique except *Daily Herald* –' and as a consequence the four managers 'faded out'.

It was a bitter disappointment to all Una's high hopes, and was to be the first and last such venture in which she was involved. It may even have deterred her (temporarily) from further translations, as she declined a request from Gollancz in the middle of the following year.

The year 1931 began with John working very hard, often thirteen or fourteen hours a day, on *The Carpenter's Son*, by then renamed *The Master of the House*. Una, ever-vigilant, worried about her:

'John worked after tea til 2.30 a.m. I to bed at 11.30 but staid awake til she came up as I am worried when she works so late. At 12.30 I got up and went down to find as I suspected – fire out – bitter cold, and she had made no effort to light the electric stove.'⁹ Una was often lonely or at a loose end: 'I up at 8.30 and down to breakfast alone . . . I sat in library – read – played gramophone and bizzed . . .'¹⁰ 'Bizzed', meaning 'kept busy', is a word she always used to describe essentially futile activity – often a desperate keeping busy for the sake of it. They often slept apart or had meals alone, and it was with increasing frequency that, 'John worked late'. Una took refuge in socializing and shopping: new hats always made her feel better, and she must have had a considerable collection, as they were often multiple purchases.

When John was not working during the evening they would sit in front of their log or peat fire while Una read to John: her own work, other novels, or biographies such as *The Ladies of Llangollen*. Una also occasionally read aloud her diary to John, since it was not hers alone but a record of their lives together. One aspect of their lives together at this time is certainly open to interpretation: it appears that John kept celibate during the writing of *The Master*, either to concentrate all her energies upon it, or for reasons of ascetic principle due to its religious subject. This implies that, in true Roman Catholic fashion, she did in her deepest mind associate sexuality with impurity; and it is doubtful whether or not she considered Una in the matter, as the following reveals: Mrs Edith Lawrence-Jones, landlady of the George Hotel in Rye at the time, told her niece Marya Burrell much later about one of her maids, Bessy, who went to work for Lady Troubridge at 'The Black Boy'. Shortly afterwards Bessy told her: 'It was very difficult last night – Lady Troubridge was lying outside Radclyffe Hall's door saying, "John darling, let me in!"' It seems unlikely that the maid, who was obviously perturbed by this incident, could have made it up; and assuming that she did not, it shows a very unhappy Una, and a very hard John not so much nobly self-denying as ignobly denying Una.

As a departure from their usual habit of buying or selling houses for their own occupation, John and Una bought the 'Santa Maria' in

West Street, Rye, as an investment, and spent time and money converting it before letting it furnished on a fixed tenancy at £70 a year. The process of buying and converting houses was almost endemic to their way of life, although they were happily settled in 'The Black Boy' themselves and had no intention of moving. John was a diligent landlord and they got on amicably with their tenants, who often invited them to tea. Eventually the house was sold through a London estate agent.

By the middle of the year Una was having gynaecological problems and consulting a Mr Raby, 'who said it was [a] pinched nerve but could not examine me because of period.' Ten days later she recorded, 'John kept me in bed all day as I was so stiff inside . . .' then it seemed to clear up, but all was far from well. Una, accustomed to pain and discomfort in that part of her anatomy, could hardly have thought to what serious consequences it was to lead within a year.

Shortly after Una's 'indisposition' had temporarily abated, John announced that she was within five chapters of the end of *The Master*, a book destined to be as long as *The Well*. Una was busy doing its preface on Provençal language, and also trying to keep abreast of John's letters. She wrote to their old friend John Holroyd-Reece, answering a letter about contracts for further Paris editions of *The Well*: 'John has asked me to reply to your two letters as she is still hard at work and not dealing with any correspondence herself. Also, as she has just had to change her secretary . . . I am kept very busy trying to supplement la nouvelle . . .'

Two months later, on November 25th, Una recorded with relief: 'John finished "The Master of the House" at 3 o'clock in the morning.' By the end of November it was in Audrey Heath's hands, and a month later they were busy correcting proofs.

Una had seen very little of Andrea that year, as when not at Oxford she was living at an address in West Kensington. She was now twenty-one, and her own mistress and very conscious of the fact. She paid a rare visit to 'The Black Boy' on December 11th, and whatever she revealed about her private life shocked them both, and emphasized the increasing generation and empathy gaps. Una's diary entry is strangely formal and uninformative: 'received Andrea at 11.30 in the library. She went at 3.30 leaving us appalled . . .' She was out of favour and spent Christmas elsewhere. The 'Cub' had become a lioness.

Both Una and John had frequent colds, influenza and other ailments, and took to their beds for days on end, with a succession of doctors and usually a nurse in attendance. Such indulgence was expensive, and a prerogative of the rich. They tended to confine each other to bed and send for the experts at the first signs of impending indisposition; and cosseted each other with a rare devotion. Una would sit by John's bed reading to her for hours; John would sometimes write in Una's sick-room, and always bought her flowers, fruit and other little delicacies. Una both enjoyed and came to expect this attention, although there were times when she realized that she was burdensome: 'John kept me in bed . . . and I quite submissive as I feel like hell! – We sent for Dr. Hartley in early afternoon who prescribed seven tiresome remedies which my poor John worked till past 11 o'clock to apply' (January 7th, 1932), and the next day: 'John still applying remedies and I still abed; this is becoming silly!' (January 8th, 1932.)

Una spent most of January in bed, but the focus of attention changed sharply in February: on the 10th Una's own French translation of *The Well* was published by Gallimard. Cape published *The Master of the House* on the 29th, and there was also a special limited edition with photographs taken by society photographer Howard Coster (see plates nos 18 and 20), for which there were 7,000 subscribers. On the 28th the book had leading reviews in the *Observer* and the *Sunday Times* (despite the recent death of their friend Leonard Rees). The reviews in many of the national and provincial papers were, Una declared, 'magnificent', meaning approving; but *The Times Literary Supplement* 'went for' both the book and John. What really incensed Una, and John, was 'a vicious review in *The Times* containing two deliberate misstatements anent the Palestine campaign' which John had carefully researched. They went first to Cape then to Harold Rubinstein to draft a denial; and the following day: 'Harold rang up to say *The Times* will put in John's corrections of the mis-statements made by the reviewer in yesterday's issue.'[11]

Twelve days later this minor storm was forgotten as John was guest of honour at a Foyles Literary Luncheon where, Una recorded, 'she spoke most admirably' to nearly 700 people, including many of their friends, then after lunch, 'signed books for nearly an hour'.

Within a month another minor catastrophe threatened: Cape's American subsidiary Cape-Ballou was again 'going bankrupt', thus threatening John's American rights. Una recorded: 'we spending the evening making plans for saving *The Master* in America and for going to London tomorrow to see Cape who has bolted home.'[12] When they saw him Cape 'admitted Cape-Ballou goes into liquidation, either equitable or bankruptcy, next Tuesday –' so they cabled to Audrey Heath full authority to transfer to another publisher, and later that day, 'Cape came and signed a release.' Una went with Audrey to Cape's offices to see about advertising, 'while John waited in a taxi' outside. Una was a diplomatic negotiator on John's behalf when necessary. This business seemed to take its toll, and six days later Una noted, 'My beloved tired and anxious'.

They had been contemplating going again to Bagnoles to take the waters, but decided instead to go to Bath ten days later. They set off in the car with the chauffeur, Bertha the maid, and three dogs, to arrive after a nine-hour drive 'to find awful, stuffy room at Grand Hotel'. Una went out and reserved a room at the Empire Hotel for the following day, and they moved. As soon as they were settled in the new hotel they called in a Dr Baker to attend them both, and began their 'cure' at the baths. One day whilst they were there: 'John and I spent entire morning writing letters and sending photographs and autographs to her public.'

This was an aspect of her life as a writer that John took very seriously, and even on holiday it could not be ignored. The 'public' took it seriously too, and wrote her thousands of letters (an estimated 10,000 after *The Well*); some even sent more tangible evidences of their appreciation: 'Ten dozen carnations came from her Prague fan.'[13]

Una was at this time aged forty-five, and although not yet menopausal, began to suffer from one of its possible symptoms, menorrhagia (excessive menstrual bleeding). Whilst at Bath she was twice confined to bed with this complaint within seventeen days, then consulted a Dr Conran at Brighton who prescribed iron tablets for the resulting anaemia. When this happened again for the third time, after only a two-week interval, he decided that she ought to see a gynaecologist. Accordingly Dr Seymour examined her and diagnosed fibroids (as Ladye had predicted many years before), recommending an immediate hysterectomy. Una took a second opinion from another gynaecologist, Dr Hedley, through Sachs, and he upheld Dr Seymour's conclusions. It was arranged that Hedley would operate at the Welbeck Clinic on Tuesday July 5th, five days later. They made their plans accordingly, and Una rang up Audrey, asking her to be with John during the operation. She also saw her mother and went to Confession at Brompton Oratory.

On the 4th John took Una to the nursing home; they saw each other briefly at 8 a.m. the next morning, Una went to theatre at 9 a.m. and John stayed there the rest of the day so that Una saw her when she woke up later. The following day the diary entry is brief, and strange: 'John with me all day – a good day, too good.'

On the second and third post-operative days, the 7th and 8th of July, there was some complication, possibly a haemorrhage: 'John with me all day and all night. I was very ill. Sir Thomas Horder called in. Hedley came four times and Sachs several times.'

After these two days the real danger was past although it was to be another eighteen days before she was allowed to get up for even half an hour; and twenty-two days before she was allowed out: 'John . . . took me a drive in a Daimler on Hampstead Heath for an hour . . .' Una recorded on July 27th.

John lodged near by at the Welbeck Palace Hotel, visiting Una early in the morning and usually staying with her most of the day. Una was 'petted and cared for and made much of' by John, who frequently bought her 'bedjackets and fruit', 'peaches', 'Carnations pale and dark red, and lemon yellow', and once 'a wonderful "Victorian Posy" of many coloured flowers in a silver basket'. Many other people, friends and relatives, wrote, visited or sent flowers. In the back of her diary Una kept a list headed, 'Sent Flowers during my illness' followed by names with numbers beside them, for example: '3 Andrea. 3 Mother. 1 Sheila (2 dead sweet peas and a withered rose),' and at the end of the list, underlined,

*'John so many times that I could not possibly count.'* It is curious, and perhaps calculating, that Una judged people's regard for her by the number of their gifts; unless this list was to confirm what she already knew – that John's gifts and regard outshone everyone else's.

Comparing this to childhood illness, Una wrote, 'loving and thoughtful care provides flowers and fruit and books to help pass the time; skilled attendance is forthcoming as a matter of course and any necessary change or journey that may be suggested can be contemplated without financial panic,' yet she regretted that: 'I share with unerring intuition the miserable fear and anxiety I am causing someone who loves me . . .' so that despite being 'lapped in love and luxury . . . all serious illness is completely spoilt for me now, there is no fun left in it.'[14]

'Fun' or not, Una does seem to have enjoyed John's undivided attention ('the warm, happy consciousness of being absolutely essential to the one being on earth who is all in all') and she was in no great hurry to recover and return to normality. On August 2nd she finally left the nursing home, and John took her in the Daimler to Brighton, with Nanny Richardson in attendance. When they got to the hotel they put Una to bed for tea, and Nurse Dawn arrived to take over; and a Dr Cummings called by arrangement to take her blood pressure, temperature and pulse, all of which were normal. Four days later Una recorded: 'Afternoon she [John] took me in Bathchair to Black Rock and back for tea. – Nurse Dawn left in evening and we are at last alone together. Deo Gratis.'

John persisted in pushing Una about in the bathchair, despite a heatwave with temperatures in the high 80s and low 90s Fahrenheit. At last, on the 23rd, 'John went to return my bathchair,' and on the 24th, 'We got home to glorious Rye and our own "Black Boy" for tea and found flowers from . . . Smallhythe and roses from Dodo [Benson]. We were so *so* happy to be home . . .' Una visited friends locally and pottered gently, and they motored to Smallhythe and Winchelsea. Within a week of being home again, Una was in bed with shingles and an abcess, and in 'pretty severe pain'. When she was over this, she caught influenza; then started having headaches and resting a lot. This may perhaps subconsciously have been a way of re-focusing John's attention back to herself, as John was absorbed in revising and rewriting her short stories. She had also been asked if she 'would . . . go and do scenarios in Hollywood for 3 or 6 months', and they discussed it. As nothing came of it they presumably decided against it.

In early November Una went to Hedley for a post-operative check-up; and she recorded that he 'hurt me a lot'. For some reason, presumably infection, douches were begun and saline baths, of which she quickly grew tired; and on December 16th she went to him again for her 'final overhaul'. He 'cauterized again but thinks all is well and going on normally . . .' she recorded in her diary. This had been one of the most major and gratifying illnesses of her life, so predictably she had made rather a meal of it, and who can blame her? Her gynaecological history altogether had not been the most fortunate.

Attention turned from Una's health to Andrea, as it so often did at Christmas or New Year; on Christmas Day itself 'Andrea came for an hour.' She could have driven from London, but it is equally possible that she had only come from Camber Sands where, it has been suggested, she was temporarily living in a caravan (probably not alone). Her behaviour the previous year had given rise to alarm and censure, but Una at least was more sympathetic towards her, recording on Boxing Day: 'Andrea lunched and tea'd and we talked over her problems poor child . . .'

She was at that time aged twenty-two, and had left Oxford that year, her future uncertain. In the January of the new year, 1933, Una and John saw a lot of Andrea in London, usually together but occasionally Una alone. Their fondness extended to buying her a fur coat at Harrods. Whilst in London they looked for a flat as a London base for periodic visits from Rye, and John made an offer for the lease of 17 Talbot House, a fifth-floor flat in St Martin's Lane. The offer was accepted and they went to Harold Rubinstein to act on their behalf, then on January 17th went happily home to Rye in the Daimler. Even whilst they had been in London (just over a fortnight) Una had been unwell and confined to bed for several days. John, as usual, 'went and got me peaches, scent and spray, and peppermint creams –'

*The Well . . . and After (1926–34)*

On their return to Rye the situation was temporarily reversed: 'John abed with 'flu and I nursing her all day, intensive, with a view to scotching the germ,' (January 24th.)

'John still abed being nursed – I kept going until I had secured promise of a nurse tomorrow, then collapsed into bed with temperature of 101 at 7 in the evening . . .' (January 25th), until predictably: 'John and I abed with 'flu – nurse Chapman came at noon . . .' (January 26th.) For the next ten days they lay, 'side by side in the big bed', John recovering first, and Una nursing, in addition to influenza, styes and boils, the classic symptoms of a 'run down' state. Whether these frequent illnesses were the result of particularly sensitive constitutions, too hectic a way of life, or poor nutrition (i.e. over-rich foods) is impossible to ascertain; but certainly in Una's case they were becoming almost habitual. Late hours and stresses and strains did not help, and their tendency to do everything in extremes: total overwork or complete inertia.

As a distraction from their own problems there were always periodic bouts of Marie Visetti's: 'John and I awoke to a letter saying Mrs. Visetti had fallen off a chair with a wardrobe on top of her and broken 3 ribs and wants at least 100 pounds! We have wired to get name and address of Dr. in charge as the letter tells nothing and is more or less illiterate –'

Though a quasi-humorous instance, this was typical of her tactics to extort money and draw attention to herself, a tendency which increased after Visetti's death. Despite the mutual absence of affection John worried about her mother and felt duty-bound to help her; and Una resented both her manipulativeness and her effect on John's peace of mind.

John had become quite a celebrity and was often asked to speak to university societies as well as at literary luncheons and dinners. In late February she and Una went to Oxford, staying at a 'very comfortable, hideous hotel' (the Randolph), so that she could speak to the English Club on the following day. Una recorded: 'Dinner was at 7 and after she spoke to over 500 in Taylorian Hall. Then they had a reception to meet her at The Randolph.'

Two days later, back in London, John 'was sick and terribly tired,' so Una called in a Dr Curtis who, 'said she must have 3

210

months rest for complete nervous exhaustion.' As on previous occasions such advice was completely ignored, and the following day John, with Una at her side, went to lecture at University College, Gower Street, giving a paper of just under an hour, followed by tea and socializing.

Their pace of life went on the same as ever: Andrea had joined a repertory theatre company, and they went to her rehearsals and first night at Wimbledon; to parties where they met John Gielgud and other friends; to matinées; to the obligatory seven churches on Maunday Thursday, and to Highgate with flowers for Ladye's tomb. They were essentially creatures of habit, still frequenting many of the same haunts and restaurants (such as the Eiffel Tower and the Ivy) as they had during and just after the First World War.

Restless as ever and tiring of the quiet country life in Rye, they tried to let 'The Black Boy' furnished; and whilst their London flat, 17 Talbot House, was being renovated by builders, they took a furnished flat downstairs, number 8, on a temporary basis: 'John and I and Mabel [Bourne], Charlotte and Gabrielle [birds] to London to furnished flat 2 p.m. . . . .' Una recorded on March 25th. On May 18th they completed the final move into number 17. Not having managed to let 'The Black Boy' they commuted frequently between London and Rye, meeting many of the same friends in both places: the Smallhythe crew, Edy, Chris and 'Tony', and Lady Maud Warrender. They also saw much of Andrea, Minna, and Audrey Heath; went to late-night parties; and still visited Mrs Leonard at Tankerton every fortnight. On July 15th, 'we both lunched with John Gielgud,' Una recorded; and ten days later Madame Nijinksy, on a visit to London, dined with them. She stayed for four hours and was 'very interesting'. Una no doubt learned, if she did not know already, of Nijinsky's sad history[15] since she sculpted him as 'The Faun' in 1913.

In the middle of the year Una received the illustrated version of her translation *The Grand Eunuch*, and began translating *The Child of Consolation*. John was busy finishing the short stories which were published the following year under the title of the first one, *Miss Ogilvy Finds Herself*. In late August the publisher's copies arrived for checking; but as Cape tried to bargain for it,

John instructed Audrey to offer it elsewhere, and eventually, Gollancz having refused it, it was placed with Heinemann.

While all this was going on Andrea was courting 'Toby' (Theodore Egerton Nicholson) Warren, son of Lord and Lady Warren. He was said by one of Andrea's nephews[16] to be 'intellectual' and to look 'like a Greek god', but made his living as a caterer. On June 29th and again on July 6th, 'Andrea brought Toby Warren to tea.' How they all got on is not known, but on September 2nd something certainly went wrong: 'Lady Warren and Toby lunched – a most uneasy and disconcerting seance –' Una's use of the word 'seance' is curious here, as presumably it was a meeting for matrimonial rather than spiritualistic purposes; and whatever was 'disconcerting' is not revealed. It left bad feelings, as on October 3rd, 'Andrea lunched and left very insolent,' and on the 21st, 'from Andrea came another insolent letter.'

Several weeks later, on November 7th 'Andrea sent *me* an invitation from Tom [Troubridge] to her wedding.' This was deliberately insulting as the invitation did not include John, and certainly shows ingratitude for all that John had done for Andrea, both *in loco parentis* and financially, since she was five years old. This implies perhaps that John was at the root of the 'disconcerting seance'; and it may well be that she had refused to foot the bill for the wedding. Una, sensitive to the implied insult, did not attend the wedding, as Andrea must have known that she would not. She merely noted in her diary on November 15th, 'Andrea's Wedding Day', beneath a mundane three-line entry of engagements. What she *felt* is not stated. Her step-son Tom, and his wife Lily Kleinwort, gave the wedding reception at 14 Egerton Gardens, after the marriage at St Mary's Catholic Church, Cadogan Street. Their son, the present Baronet Sir Peter Troubridge, remembers being a page boy, aged six; and still remembers his Aunt Andrea with affection.

In August 'The Black Boy' had been viewed by agents preparatory to selling, after only two years of occupation; and they had 'looked over the Hucksteps cottage' in which they had first stayed in Rye. In mid-November John made an offer for what was to become 'The Forecastle', two Elizabethan cottages knocked into one, on the edge of the cliff overlooking Romney Marsh and

212

commanding a distant view of the sea. On December 5th, Una recorded: 'We learned that Mrs. Harvey had accepted John's bid for "The Forecastle".' John's offer was £750, approximately twice the average house price at the time; and like 'The Black Boy', she gave it to Una, whose name appears solely on the Deed of Conveyance from Mrs Harvey. They remained as busy as ever, leaving the move until the new year, John lecturing on 'The Historical and Period Novel' in November, and on 'Novel Writing' in December. As well as going sometimes 'to John Gielgud for cocktails at 6', they invited another actor, John Wyse, and his friend Gordon Stannus, to cocktails with them; then in turn went 'to cocktail party at John Wyse's', then invited them to their own large party on December 6th.

Gordon Stannus modestly remembers that 'Radclyffe Hall struck me as handsome with dignity and a certain charm, and rather "tailor made" in her appearance, rather "mannish" for those days. I was very shy at meeting such a famous and grand person!'

John Wyse, who respected them both, had more to say about Una:

It is my opinion that the depths of her character were never properly recognised by many, if any, of their coterie. Johnny's personality was so astonishingly vivid and I think it says a lot for Una that she held her own so well through all their long years together, knowing too jolly well that she just must stand up for herself in that adoring world of Johnny's hungry admirers. And hungry they were most of them – just for a crumb, which is all, I am sure, that any of them ever got.

Ironically perhaps, and contrary to this impression, it was not to be any 'hungry admirer' who would be a threat to Una, but a complete outsider of the sort who wins the Derby against all predictions.

On November 30th Una and John organized a party of their own, their guests including Pamela Frankau, Ronald Armstrong, Wallace Wood and Princess Troubetskey. On December 6th they had another party with nineteen guests; and again on the 13th, with a huge list of guests. Christmas was as usual a quiet affair: they went in the morning to give 'sweets and sixpences to the Hucksteps children' for the third year running, then met 'Mac' for sherry at the Mermaid, and lunched there with two friends, dining later with 'Dodo' Benson.

The year ended with Jack Raymond of British and Dominion Films asking John to meet a scenario writer in London, and she and Una duly went on December 29th, but it appears that, as on previous occasions when such offers were made, nothing came of it. On New Year's Eve Una noted that they 'corrected page proofs' but made no reference to seeing in the new year as they always had before. It was almost as though this was an unconscious omen of the year to come: a year which was to be cataclasmic, and to bring Una the greatest unhappiness she was ever to know.

# 13

# *So Vast a Need (1934)*

There is a drawing by Van Dyke, dated 1634, of the south-east prospect of Rye, showing the Ypres Tower and an untidy huddle of houses on the cliff, subsequently known as The Hucksteps or Hucksteps Row. Three hundred years later, in 1934, when Una and John moved there, it was a clutter of about a dozen slum cottages very close together; lived in by 'fisherfolk', two families to a cottage, with shared outside toilets and no gardens. They were let furnished at between 2s. 6d. and 3s. 6d. a week, being owned by James Macdonnell ('Mac') whom John called 'the happy-go-lucky landlord'.[1] It was to be portrayed by John as Crofts Lane in her last published novel, *The Sixth Beatitude*, in 1936. It was an unlikely place for them to make their home but 'The Forecastle', despite its surroundings, was a large and picturesque period cottage standing detached in its own modest garden; and it was the cottage in which they had first stayed in 1928, and had always wanted to buy. The deposit was paid by John on December 27th, 1933, and the final Deed of Transfer signed by Mrs Harvey, the vendor, and Una, on February 2nd, 1934.

Una records that they were, 'told . . . the local name for the Hucksteps is Jolly Sailor Lane . . .' after the one-time pub of that name, but it was also known colloquially as 'Fishgut Alley'. It

215

boasted twenty-nine children, wild urchins of whom Dr Alec Vidler, as a boy, was in trepidation as he passed its entrance on his way home to 'The Friars of the Sack', the oldest house in Rye, in Church Square.

As soon as it was finally theirs, Una and John set about the 'exhausting and entrancing orgy' of doing it up, much as they had 'The Black Boy'. It was to become what Una called 'our beloved Forecastle', and they wanted to make it beautiful. Macdonnell acted on John's instructions and had the work carried out for her, supplying as usual old and new beams from his woodstore in the Strand, Rye. Mrs Gwen Bligh remembers John saying to her father, 'Mac, I must have more oak,' and that he often said afterwards, 'Any more oak in that house and it'll go down the cliff!' They restored its Tudor character inside and out, and when they had finished, 'everyone who saw it exclaimed with delight and admiration,' Una said; but 'in the end we looked at one another and confessed to a curious misgiving' that it might have become 'something of a museum piece'.[2] They were restless perfectionists when it came to houses, and seemed never wholehearted or unqualified in their satisfaction with either their purchases or renovations. The repeated 'raptures of home-making' were perhaps a palliative against other problems in their relationship.

They moved into 'The Forecastle', which was to be their last and most permanent home in England, keeping the flat in St Martin's Lane as their London base. Mabel Bourne had become ill and left their service in December 1933, so they returned to Hucksteps Row without her. The moving and renovations had made inroads into John's writing time and she was keen to settle into 'The Forecastle' for the summer to resume her work; but Una, noticing that 'she was far from well', and that 'her old enemy the "hunting vein" was giving her trouble', tried to persuade and 'put great pressure on her' to 'postpone her return to work and . . . do a cure again at Bagnoles de l'Orne.'[3] Una was always to remember how 'earnestly' John opposed her, and how she 'overbore her protests' in her concern for John's health. Only afterwards did John tell Una that 'she had had an almost overwhelming instinct against leaving England on that occasion.' At the time she kept this feeling to herself, and gave in to Una as she had before about St Tropez. It says much for the strength of Una's personality that she could manoeuvre John round to her point of view. It may be that John, knowing her adversary, realized that resistance was useless; for Una, once decided, especially with John's welfare in mind, was like a dog with a bone, worrying at it until she achieved her end. Una was well-practised in the subtle art of persuasion. Having won the day she made, as usual, all arrangements for their journey. She was playing into the hands of fate without knowing it.

They left England on a hot June day and after a good crossing went to Paris, meeting as usual the old familiar friends: Natalie and Romaine, Colette, the Countess de Clermont Tonnerre, as they had for the past twelve years. Despite a heat-wave with temperatures of 93.2°F they had a hectic but enjoyable forty-eight hours, and then went on by train to Bagnoles little knowing what lay ahead. Something rich or sour that Una had eaten in Paris had upset her stomach, and she felt unwell on the journey. The heat-wave, interspersed with violent thunderstorms, continued, and when they arrived in the 200-room hotel, occupied by only twenty people due to the weather, Una felt worse and went to bed with 'a violent attack of enteritis', and summoned the doctor. It was ironical, Una's concern for John's health having brought them to Bagnoles, that she should become ill on their arrival; and even more ironical that Una herself, from entirely altruistic motives, was directly responsible for what happened next. John was nursing Una, who was 'soon too weak to stir from my bed'. This defeating the object of their visit by preventing John herself from either resting or taking the waters, Una rang through to the American Hospital in Paris to ask them to send her a nurse to relieve John. 'This they did and on the following day Evguenia Souline arrived . . .'[4]

The die was cast. She was to prove a catalyst in both their lives. A thirty-year-old, unmarried White Russian, the daughter of a Cossack general, a refugee and officially stateless, she had the slanting eyes and facial features of the Mongolian races, and her temperament was fiery, erratic and passionate. However, even

217

Una had to concede that 'she was a devoted and admirable nurse', who soon made her comfortable. She spoke in broken English, wore glasses, and was far from beautiful; but as Una said, 'the utterly unexpected does happen.'[5]

One has to reconstruct what did actually happen from the limited evidence available. Una, not surprisingly, is silent on many points, but the first mention of Souline is in Una's 'Daybook of Rye and Bagnoles', dated Thursday July 5th, 1934: 'we now have a nurse from the American Hospital in Paris . . . a treasure and charming . . .'

She made a favourable first impression, and three days later Una wrote: 'My nurse a strange woman . . . More efficient than either of us would have believed possible and . . . quite unmistakably of our own class, but while she is obviously friendly she has sudden inhibitions and reserves which baffle one; John and I think that she saw much horror in Russia during the revolution until she left in 1922 . . .'

In the intervals between Souline's attendance on Una, and in the evenings when Una had been settled down for the night, John and Souline spent time together, in walks, or in Souline's room, Una blissfully ignorant of John's growing interest in her nurse. They had elicited her biography, and as Una recovered Souline dined with them and they walked together after dinner. On July 10th the three of them 'lay gasping like fish on the terrace seeking the cooler spots and walked at tea time into Bagnoles, dripping as we went . . .' and later that evening, 'We decided to keep nurse a few days longer, as she reassures us with her experience.'

But this could not last for long as with her hotel board she came to 175 francs a day, and had stayed nearly a fortnight. Besides, Una was all but recovered, and as she recorded on Friday July 13th: 'I am really on my feet again so that I think nurse goes tomorrow . . .' Evguenia Souline left by the evening train on July 14th. Those were the external events, but during her stay the world turned upside down for all of them. It is not certain exactly when John told Una of her infatuation with Souline, but it may well have been the very evening she left, as Una recorded enigmatically on July 14th, 'We talked very late in evening,' or certainly shortly afterwards.

The primary source material of the 'internal' events consists of John's letters to Souline, written in retrospect. They were disparate beings with little in common to converse about, but John's reactions were immediate and extreme: 'I fell madly in love . . .' she confessed in a letter later.[6] Whether she actually 'made a pass' at Souline is not certain, but she made the nature of her interest perfectly clear. Souline seems to have been somewhat taken aback, and although she did not give 'Come hither' signals, she did not give 'Go away' ones either. Perhaps an undecided reaction is the most tantalizing of all – it certainly had that effect on John. The part of her that 'feels young, absurdly so for its age, and . . . demands the pleasures of youth', asserted itself with renewed vigour, 'reckless of consequences, greedy of happiness . . .'[7] 'Her hot youth'[8] rose up again to confront her in middle age; and she was so carried away by the force of her feelings that she was initially almost oblivious of disloyalty to Una. Souline quickly became 'an obsession', and John convinced that they had been 'foreordained to meet'.[9] She told Souline later that when she met her, 'I was empty, finished . . .'[10] and that, 'this thing has just swept me clean off my feet – it has made me come alive again.'[11]

It is necessary to step aside momentarily from the narrative of events to consider how and why this situation arose, and what were its predetermining factors. Looking first at John's nature, it is clear that she had a low threshold of sexual boredom, and found fidelity difficult, being naturally, like her father, a 'squire of dames'. But at the same time one has to balance against this the fact that Una had held her undivided erotic attention for eighteen years, for as John told Souline, during that time 'my union has been faithful'.[12] It is possible that this 'repression' of John's nature had created 'so vast a need', that it only took a spark to ignite her desire, and that once ignited it erupted like a non-quiescent volcano; and that, had it not been Souline, sooner or later it would have been someone else. It has to be asked how far Una herself was culpable for this state of affairs, since 'so vast a need' in John must have been cumulative. 'She has given me all of her interest and indeed of her life ever since we made common cause . . .' John told Souline, and this had certainly been true;

but she also told her: 'I am not and have not been in years the least in love with Una . . .'[13]

This may have been simply because erotic disinterest and boredom is a real danger in all long-term relationships; but it could also have been that Una, who had so carefully made herself indispensable, John's companion of the revels and the doldrums, had become too much the capable, organizing 'wife' and forgotten that John needed a lover too. Certainly she had never been too keen on the closeness of the shared bed, preferring 'comfortable repose' alone to sleeping 'with one's head "pillowed upon another's breast" or with someone else's head riding upon one's bosom.'[14]

Una's 'endless neurotic symptoms'[15] and frequent ill health must have been a strong contributory factor towards John's 'vast' need, and must have occasioned much 'forced abstinence'.[16] She also recognized 'the undeniable fact that anyone who is constantly being ill must inevitably end by becoming a bore',[17] but ironically did not seem subjectively to realize it. It is also a fact that some women seem to suffer a loss of libido following hysterectomy, although there is no evidence that this happened in Una's case, or that she ever lost erotic interest in John. In fact diary entries late in 1933 suggest that, despite John's subsequent claim of no longer being 'in love' with Una, they were still sometimes lovers: 'John turned in with me in the big bed . . .' (August 12th, 1933.) 'John and I breakfasted in my room where we had shared the big bed –' (October 14th, 1933.)

Novelty, inevitably, had long worn off, and had not been replaced, on John's side at least, by that mellow, deeper love which grows, rather than diminishes, with time. She had come to take Una, and her devotion and fidelity, for granted; to regard her as 'a comfortable habit'. The fire and urgency had gone, as had the stimulus of adversity. John had written, perhaps prophetically: 'to find oneself lonely with the creature one loves is to plumb the full depths of desolation,'[18] and also paradoxically of 'the infinite sadness of fulfilled desire . . .'

John was less able than Una to live with this 'infinite sadness', or to accept the changing seasons of love. For her it had to be spring and freshness for ever; urgency and longing; ardour and youthfulness. Souline was thirty, and 'untouched by human hand': virginal, and thus full of promise; Una was forty-seven, long known and familiar. John's palate was jaded, and needed a rejuvenating experience. Una had failed to see the signs, or perhaps John had disguised them out of kindness.

The marriage bed can be one of the loneliest places in the world when the real loving has stopped; and nothing so confining as a relationship in which part of a person's nature can no longer be fulfilled. Claustrophobia, restlessness and disinterest are bound to follow. In this connection, time had dealt unequally with them: Una's poor gynaecological and nervous history had taken its toll; whilst John, still lithe and handsome, was as highly-sexed as ever. Chronological and biological age are not the same thing. Una, though chronologically younger by seven years, was biologically older than John, who at fifty-four looked remarkably youthful with a clear, unlined face. Her pattern of ageing was gradual, and more like a man's; whereas for Una, the forties were proving a difficult time. This disparity had occurred with Ladye, where both the chronological and biological 'age-gap' was more pronounced, and John's 'fancy did stray . . . but it was a trivial, passing lapse, broke no bones and left no aftermath.'[19] Una herself had been initially such a 'fancy' or 'lapse' of John's; but *this* 'straying' with Souline was to be neither 'trivial' nor a 'passing lapse': it was to be serious, permanent, and to disrupt three lives. What was to be 'broken' was Una's heart; and yet, paradoxically, refined by that very pain, her love was to grow even deeper.

# IV

*Life Together:
the Last Years
(1934–43)*

# 14

# *This Agonized Bliss:*
# *the Bitter Cup*
# *(1934–5)*

Evguenia Souline returned to the American Hospital in Paris leaving emotional turmoil behind her. John was firmly 'in the grip of . . . the most relentless of all . . . human emotions',[1] and had already started writing the first of the 600 letters she was to pen to Souline over the next nine years, pouring out 'all the pent-up passion', and 'all the terrible, rending, destructive frustrations . . .'[2]

Una was stunned and desperately unhappy. The world seemed to have come suddenly to a nightmarish end. It was unimaginable that her John could be interested in another woman in this way, yet there it was: a cold, hard fact. She was deeply shocked. It had all happened so suddenly, so unexpectedly. She had held John for nearly nineteen years, and had come to expect her exclusive devotion and loyalty, even as she gave her own. She had trusted John with an absolute trust.

Referring to this period in the wake of her departure, John wrote to Souline some months later: 'At Bagnoles I knew I had found a woman who was going to move me very deeply, and after you left I nearly went mad, feeling so terribly uncertain of our future.'[3] This was as nothing compared to Una's uncertainty and fears for *her* future with John, and for the whole basis of their union.

They were shortly to follow Souline to Paris for a few days stop-over on their way to visit 'Micki' (Naomi) Jacob at Sirmione, and John determined to see Souline while they were there. Although Souline had signed some of her letters to John, 'Your obedient servant', this formality did not hide her interest, and she co-operated in the proposed meeting, even sending a welcoming note to the Pont-Royal Hotel to coincide with John's arrival. In reply John wrote on July 24th: 'Darling . . . Yes, I am here in Paris, and it seems so strange that only a few weeks ago I did not know that Paris meant you . . . it's red hell to be here and not to be able to see you until the day after tomorrow and then only for a few hours . . .'

John gave her instructions to take a taxi for which she would refund her afterwards; and they met for lunch, but Souline could not eat, presumably due to nerves. They went back to her sitting-room where John tried to engage her in passionate kisses, but Souline was frightened, and returning only innocent child-like kisses, declared, 'I don't know how to kiss any other way . . .' This riveted John. Here, for the first time, he encountered a woman who had never been initiated into the mysteries of sexual love; one who was still, in effect, a child at thirty. Things went no further, but John left determined to claim that virginity. Una marked this occasion by commenting laconically in her diary: 'July 26th. John gave my ex-nurse luncheon at Lapeyrouse . . .'

A few days later John and Una went to Sirmione, and stayed at the Albergo Catullo recommended by Micki Jacob, whose own villa was near by. Known to them only by correspondence since their meeting in 1929, Micki Jacob soon became a close personal friend. She shared with them not only inversion, but Roman Catholicism, a great love of animals (she kept eleven cats and various dogs), and writing. Her appearance was even more mannish than John's since she was darker, more heavily set, and wore full male suits and never skirts as John did. She had made her home at Sirmione since retiring from the stage, and Sir John Gielgud recalls that she was a 'rather endearing character of great kindness . . . and one of the few people who rescued Mrs Patrick Campbell in her last penurious days.'

She was later to work for ENSA during the war, where, Sir John remembers that 'A naughty legend of her, when working for the troops in Italy, had her opening her caravan door one morning with, "Sergeant, where is my shaving water?!"' Una wrote of Micki in her diary at Sirmione: 'I could not be in love with Mike in a hundred years if there were no one else in the world; but I do love her and admire her deeply and sincerely.'

John and Una had a beautiful room in the hotel, with two windows overlooking the lake. They 'came up every morning to my villa before luncheon,' Micki Jacob wrote later, where usually, 'John pounced on *The Times* and immersed herself in it,' while 'Una inspected the cats having their dinners. One day Una, always a keen amateur vet, successfully removed a painful tooth from one of them! 'We went for excursions,' and 'In the warm, quiet evenings after dinner we foregathered in the Piazza,' and 'there would be good talk, a great deal of laughter,' and 'once or twice John would declare that we must have a "beer party",' Micki wrote cheerfully.[4] On August 1st Una noted in her diary: 'nineteen years today since we met.' Outwardly, all seemed calm and normal, but inwardly it was very different. Some of that laughter must have been forced, or pure escapism, since John was 'half mad with longing and very near despair',[5] and Una, euphemistically, 'in the midst of distress and anxiety'.[6] John was working on a seventh novel, *Emblem Hurlstone*, but they spent much time with Micki or sitting in cafés, almost as though they could not bear to be alone too much. Consequently they spent many sleepless nights talking things out, and eventually both had to resort to 'Neurinase', a sleeping draught.

There was no doubt in Una's mind as to the degree of John's obsession with, and insistence on continuing to see, Souline. She began seriously to fear displacement, and knew that she had ceased to be the emotional centre of John's life. Her natural and 'inevitable jealousy'[7] was getting the better of her, and she flatly refused to let John see Souline in Paris on their return home from Sirmione. Shortly afterwards, feeling that perhaps she was being harsh, or asking too much, she conceded that they might write to each other.

John was distraught at this unexpected turn of events, and wrote to Souline in histrionic vein:

My beloved. I do not know how I have the strength to write what must be written . . . I cannot see you in Paris on my way back to England – I had been counting on this . . . it was something that Una said that made me dare to hope. And then in Paris she seemed so merciful . . . I thought Una would consent, for she knows how it is with me, with us . . . Then I found she means to keep us apart . . . I am almost too desolate, as it is, to go on living . . . I think that in parting with you I am finished . . .

In the same letter, dated July 31st, 1934, John described 'the hell that I went through last night and this morning' with Una. Although she conceded that Una had 'the right to do what she is doing', in keeping them apart, by virtue of her long-held position, she seemed totally oblivious to, and even callous about, Una's feelings in the situation. All she could see was the potential thwarting of her own 'extra-marital' desires: 'It has been very terrible,' John continued, 'she has reminded me of her operation, of every illness she has had through the years. She has told me that she is very ill now, that Sachs warned her to avoid all emotions, that if I do see you everything will happen between us, and that then she could never be happy again but would fret herself until she died.' John did not care to see how 'very terrible' this all was to Una, only its effects on herself.

Una was obviously searching desperately to find leverage to move John from her set course of action: '. . . she has reminded me over and over again until I have nearly gone mad, that I have always stood for fidelity in the case of inverted unions, that the eyes of the inverted all over the world are turned towards me . . .' John admitted that 'when she says this I can find no answer . . .' but although she could not justify herself, she would not give up Souline. Una, highly-strung and deeply distraught, had even 'suddenly hurled herself onto the floor and behaved as though she were going demented'; but John's explanation for this disturbed behaviour was not to see it as a response to her own, but that 'her operation has made her more excitable', and she added with characteristic 'male chauvinism': 'women are like this after this operation.'

228

Consciously or otherwise, Una was trying vainly to appeal to one of John's 'most deeply-rooted instincts: that of protection towards anything weak or helpless.'[8] However, John's protective instinct was working overtime in Souline's favour, since she had 'neither money nor country nor home'.[9] John would have given her all three if she could have done so, but contented herself with sending Souline £100, ostensibly for stamps, stationery and telegrams. Towards Una she felt 'a debt of honour . . . a terrible obligation', adding, 'it is less whether I can shirk my load than whether I can bear it.' This makes it sound as though Una had become a burden which duty forced John to carry; but it is not certain whether this was what she really felt, or if it was merely a plausible and placatory explanation for Souline.

'I am longing to get away from here,' John wrote to her when they had only been at Sirmione for a matter of days, but added that, 'for some reason Una wants to stay on . . .' The reason was clear enough: the longer they stayed at Sirmione the longer Una could keep John away from Souline.

Souline confessed to John in a letter dated August 5th that she 'loved her too much', and asked, 'When shall I see you?' but the following day wrote to say that she would *not* see her on her way back to England via Paris. This should have been just what Una wanted: a refusal by Souline to see John could settle the whole problem; but Una herself had relented and agreed that John *could* see Souline in Paris, on condition that she solemnly promised not to be unfaithful 'in the fullest sense of the word'. Una did not want to be thought 'devoid of all heart – a hard, cruel woman without compassion'; and once John had 'made her the promise that she seems to cling to above all else'[10] she relaxed her strictures to the point of offering to write to Souline to *ask* her to see John!

'Honestly, she *is* willing that I should see you as she wants to spare me unhappiness, and I have told her that I will honourably keep my promise,' John pleaded with Souline. She also spoke of 'the great denial duty and honour impose upon us', as if to reaffirm it; and emphasized that Una 'well knows that we could not help this thing and that she still has from me a real devotion.' John saw herself as the passive victim of an irresistible event: 'falling in love', exonerating herself from her actions by a plea of 'diminished responsibility'. She expected the same tolerant 'understanding' from Una that she had expected from Ladye in similar circumstances. Una was both generous and trusting, unable to believe that John would ever demean 'her high code of honour'.[11] In a typical 'wifely' protectiveness of that very honour, Una discreetly maintained in her *Life* of John many years later that 'She was incapable at all times of considering herself alone . . .' but this was blatantly untrue in the matter of Souline.

John's letters to Souline from Sirmione continued to be full of those 'things that all lovers, even those who are not free, have a right divine to say to each other . . .' Fortunately Una did not see the written results of John's 'divine right', as they would most certainly have upset her. Almost as a distraction, one suspects, as well as a genuine admiration for the man, Una urged John to seek a meeting with the well-known 'poet-patriot' Gabriele D'Annunzio, who lived at a 'palatial villa . . . a few miles from Sirmione.'[12] They were both keen literary and ideological supporters of his, and it seemed too good an opportunity to be missed. On the advice of Romaine Brooks, who had been his mistress many years before, Una sent a copy of *The Well* and a letter asking if they might call on him. The reply was almost immediate and in the affirmative, but for John only, presumably because she was the writer. John kept the appointment, stayed for some hours, and eventually arrived back at the hotel showered in gifts. Una was glad for her, but very disappointed at not meeting him herself. He was plagued by an 'incubus of hopeless melancholy and isolation',[13] and was virtually a recluse except for his current mistress, Louisa Baccarra, who kept them informed of his progress and eventual death. Despite several subsequent summonses and false alarms, they were never to meet him again.

Due largely to Una's influence, their visit to Sirmione lasted well into September. On September 19th, despite her promise to Una, John wrote to Souline of 'the longing to feel you in my arms, to feel your body against my body and your lips on my lips –' Hardly chaste thoughts, but in keeping with John's determination not to 'leave untasted,/One drop of sweetness life may hold for me.'[14]

The following day, September 20th, they finally left Sirmione, sleeping at Milan, and arriving in Paris early on the 22nd. On the 23rd John went out at 11.30 in the morning and, as Una noted later in her diary, 'came in just before midnight'. The next day John 'went out for afternoon and evening'. And so it continued for the duration of their stay in Paris: John spent a large part of each day with Souline, and broke her promise to Una. Recalling the events later, John wrote to Souline:

> . . . how virginal and innocent you were, how ignorant of physical passion – you the most passionate of all women . . . I was your first lover . . . Step by step – very gently I led you towards fulfilment . . . I found you a virgin and I made you a lover . . . I have made a new discovery through you – I find that to take an innocent woman is quite unlike anything else in life, is perhaps the most perfect experience in life . . . Your . . . innocence was a revelation to me – I had never met anything quite like it before.[15]

For John this set the seal on everything. Yet on October 2nd, while they were still in Paris, Una wrote: 'In spite of everything we are close, close: one spirit and one flesh, indissoluble and indivisible for ever. She said to me yesterday: "Remain with me for ever and ever throughout eternity. Amen!" She said: "*You* are permanent!"'

And so it was to prove.

Back in St Martin's Lane on October 4th John wrote to Souline of 'our love's completion', and reminded her that 'we have slept in each other's arms . . .' Round her neck she wore a little Russian cross given her by Souline, and placed her photograph on her desk. Already a visit to England was planned. She told Souline that she 'couldn't go on living without you'; and offered her 'my most faithful love of soul, mind, and body': very ironically in the circumstances.

'How often have you said: "I can't believe it – this love of ours seems to me like a dream,"' John reminded Souline in the same letter, adding: 'Dear fool who I love – it is not a dream but a strong and insistent reality.' To Una, despite John's assurances, it was more like a strong and insistent nightmare.

Una's love for John was exclusive and unconditional; and its physical expression was to her sacramental. This sacramental bond had now been fully violated by another woman. Thinking things through, she realized on October 8th that she was one 'who will never in a hundred years respond to or even see anyone but John . . .' How she behaved is clear from John's letters, but what she felt and thought is far less explicit, her diaries and Daybooks recording mainly events and other people's reactions, particularly John's and Souline's when they were all three together.

John had told Souline, 'perfect love . . . knows only that while it would give all things it would also gladly accept all things . . .'[16] 'Gladly' accept Una did not, yet, within a fortnight of the *fait accompli* she was actively helping Souline to obtain the necessary visa for her visit to England, and wrote to her on October 19th: 'Now about this question of your visa for England. John has told me you fear delay and difficulty and as I have some standing as the widow of an Admiral I have slipped in and taken a hand!' Una had been to the Passport Office to make inquiries, and gave Souline careful instructions, adding: '*I* have written guaranteeing your identity and that you come as a guest for a few weeks, are not destitute or likely to be so and will not seek employment here.'

Una had to keep the Under-Secretary of State at the Home Office informed of Souline's whereabouts whilst the visa application was pending, and it was uncertain whether she would be in Zurich or Paris. She was being employed at the time by a princess, but of which royal house is not clear, presumably through the American Hospital. On the 24th Una wrote to her again confirming that the Home Office had assured her that 'they . . . anticipated no difficulty and . . . would put the matter through as quickly as possible.' Despite Una's apparent matter-of-factness, there is something strangely, sadly paradoxical in all this. John also wrote to assure Souline that 'Una's name is even more valuable than mine in a case like this because of her title . . .'

She also added that 'you . . . must be naturalised French as I can't marry you and make you English!' By implication, if there *had* been a form of 'marriage' for inverts, John would certainly have 'divorced' Una in order to 'marry' Souline to give her British citizenship; and no doubt she would have expected Una to *understand* her motives.

The visit was scheduled for November, and as it drew nearer John wrote ecstatically to Souline: 'Darling, I am wild with excitement, aren't you?'

There was an oblivious, almost adolescent quality to John's exuberance, but Una was far from ecstatic. She had co-operated in the matter of Souline's visa, but even she refused to vacate 'The Forecastle', *her* house, to allow John and Souline to use it for their love-tryst. It says much for the depth of Una's feelings in the matter that she stood on her dignity and refused: it was probably the only thing she had ever refused John. Consequently John and Souline spent ten days together in the London flat in St Martin's Lane, leaving Una alone at 'The Forecastle'. Those ten days must have been among the bleakest and loneliest in her life; knowing that the person she loved was making love to someone else.

No sooner was the visit over than John was making arrangements to spend a fortnight in Paris with Souline in January 1935. On November 28th she wrote no less than three separate letters to Souline, in one of which she bewailed how 'crippled . . . we are by circumstances . . .' The visit had only inflamed John still further: 'I am mad with love for a Chink-Faced White Russian who lives in Paris . . .'[17] and her mind ran in a single track marked 'Souline'. Nothing could remain the same, even her work had to be incorporated in her: 'out of ourselves I will make a book,' she promised.

Souline said that she felt like 'a stray dog' in the situation; that she often missed John at night, and read and re-read her letters. John hastily reassured her that 'You've got me completely – body and mind and soul you've got me,'[18] and she always signed her letters 'Your John', to emphasize her possession by Souline. But Souline wanted undisputed possession and hated to be *à trois*: 'we will talk of "*we three*" as you call it –' John assured her, and tried to clarify the situation by explaining: 'I feel a deep gratitude to-wards her [Una], a deep respect and a very deep affection – also an enormously strong sense of duty . . .' whereas 'my love for you is more like "first love".'[19] Perhaps the contrast is even better

pointed by the ending of the letter: 'Darling and most Chink-
Faced little Tartar I must stop – I must dress and take poor Una to
the dentist . . .'

'Poor Una' was struggling with herself and often floundering
helplessly in these early days of the new situation, and there were
scenes between her and John. John was beyond all appeals or
deterrents: Una had played all her cards in that direction. On one
occasion: 'There was a scene which left me so shattered that I
couldn't attempt a letter to you,' John told Souline, but did at least
admit that 'I was very inconsiderate to Una – said something in the
end that I should never have said . . . It was largely my fault . . .'
In the same letter John added wistfully: 'I wish we could be
together at Christmas.'[20]

John and Una went to their pre-Christmas Confession on
December 15th, and it is tempting to wonder whether John
mentioned her 'infidelity' with Souline and hurting of Una. Their
Christmas that year was quiet: on December 24th they went 'to
Midnight Mass our 20th together and never one missed Thank
God.' Afterwards they went to a party then walked the streets of
Rye until 3 a.m. On Christmas morning they distributed sixpences and sweets to the children as usual, went for a walk, then
home to mid-day lunch. On New Year's Eve they went to friends
'for champagne and cake and to see the New Year in,' and Una
added hopefully, 'May it be happier than 1934.'

By the end of 1934 John was giving Souline £10 a month and
paying for the flat in Paris, and in addition she had made her
presents of money for a 'nest-egg'. It was obvious that Souline had
come to stay.

Not unnaturally, Una's view of Souline was bound to be biased.
Looking back in her *Life* of John eleven years later, she described
Souline as 'a creature of impulses and violent surface emotions
. . . as violent and uncontrolled as a savage . . . headstrong and
wild and inconsistent . . .' and strangely enough this was echoed
in one of John's own letters to Souline, where she described her as
'so terribly apt at wounding – so thoughtless, so much a creature of
moods, so terrifyingly a creature of impulse.'[21]

The similarity of these statements, given their writers' totally different viewpoints, argues for their veracity. Quite apart from Una's self-admitted jealousy, she regarded Souline as an unworthy love-object; and one of the things that most irked her was Souline's almost total disinterest in John's work, and her devastating effect on its continued production. Events were to prove her right for John produced only one novel during the last nine years of her life. After all, Una had devoted herself to what she believed to be John's 'genius' and now it seemed to her that it was being thrown away.

The new pattern had been set: the pattern of John's 'agonised bliss' (that contradiction in terms from one of her early poems), and of Una's bitter cup. The paradox was early evident in John's letters to Souline where she calls her, 'my most sweet load of grief and of inexpressible joy'; 'my sweet torment'; and 'my heart's joy and heart's ache . . .' She was never to be really sure of Souline, who over-drank vodka and led her own life in Paris, going to dances, theatres, the races, with other friends and possessive patrons of whom John was often jealous.

For Una, after living with Ladye's 'ghost' for so many years, came the awful reality of Souline: it was still 'our three selves' though the persons of the 'trinity' were different. She was to tread the penitential way, the north aisle of life; as she had usurped, so she was usurped in turn, suffering the humiliation of displacement by a younger woman. The bitter chalice from which Ladye drank had come to Una herself, and she must have seen with unerring clarity the irony of it all. Nemesis was satisfied.

It was the old story in unconventional guise: the erring 'husband', and the 'wife' and 'mistress' who resent each other's existence but are ironically united in the common love-object. In the role of 'mistress' herself Una had disregarded other people's feelings but suffered emotional insecurity; as the 'wife' she was to be 'so loyal and . . . so gallant'.[22]

John began 1935 by sending Souline 1,300 francs on New Year's day, presumably in anticipation of her two-week visit to Paris on the 15th; but also because she was as 'jealous as a schoolboy!' of the fact that a Mrs Baker had sent Souline 'a fat cheque'. In April another Paris visit was arranged: 'I am going to stay about two weeks in Paris,' John told Souline, 'not longer as I must get Una down South – this is absolutely my duty.'²³ Just before this they gave up the St Martin's Lane flat, and Una recorded in her *Life* of John how on the very morning they were moving out John 'through sheer cussedness . . . it seemed . . . elected to choose that morning for work,' and sitting at her desk, the last piece of furniture left in the flat, began writing the Rye novel, originally called *Hannah*, which Una later renamed *The Sixth Beatitude*. She wrote it in seven months, just over a quarter of her average novel-writing time, and it was heavily imbued with aspects of her relationship with Souline. Parts of it read remarkably like her love-letters to Souline: 'Body close against body, mouth against mouth; one desire, one breath, one body, one joy.'²⁴

May and June were spent at Beauvallon, with John trying desperately to persuade Souline to join them there, and Una presumably glad of Souline's reluctance. 'My moody and tiresome little Cossack child,' John wrote in exasperation, 'I know there are things in our situation that gall and wound – but think, darling think – we are better off than hundreds of lovers. If I were a man and married what then?'

How would the situation have been different, one wonders, since she regarded herself as morally if not legally 'married' to Una?

'I need the vitality and health that you give me,' John told Souline imploringly, 'and this was to be strangely prophetic, as she ailed as the relationship did and survived its eventual demise by only nine months.

'When we're too long apart I feel ill – ill with longing – ill with fretting about you,' she added.

Problems began between them as Souline was wilful and easily bored. During Souline's brief visits her behaviour was such that it left John so bemused that she turned to Una as a confidante and adviser. Una wrote on May 4th, 1935: '. . . she [John] said she was quite worn out by Souline's moodiness, obstinacy, and uncertainty of temper – that all day she had been impossible – . . . John kept on saying, "and yet I do think she cares for me . . . and I *am* kind . . ." I told her part of the trouble was that she was *too* kind and had spoilt the girl rotten so that she just indulged every mood at her expense . . .' After this common-sense analysis of the situation Una added hopefully: 'I am inclined to think that this is the first sign of the eventual rupture –' then observed: '. . . if John lived with her she would find her very tiresome to live with . . . she will suffer less if the girl proves thoroughly unstable and unsatisfactory . . .'

But it was not to be so black-and-white.

'I expect the affair will drag on for some time with halcyon periods of lessening length . . . and lengthening intervals of dissension when John says, as she said last night, that a mistress' place in a man's life is to be responsive and soothing and provide relaxation . . .' Una remarked in the same entry. This chauvinistic attitude revealed to the 'wife' about her rival contrasts markedly with the impassioned statements made to Souline herself in letters, and also with the placatory and often dismissive remarks made in those same letters about Una. John was uncomfortably poised between two rival camps, and not really true to either, trying diplomatically to disarm the criticism of each whilst protecting herself in the middle.

'Not for years has a woman made me feel as you do, and you mustn't play me up, beloved,' John wrote in May, then in June: '. . . we punish each other, we get angry and inconsiderate of each other. Then we come together again in the body and our union is closer and more violent than ever –'

This pattern was to continue. 'Almost from the first she and John were oil and water and their relationship, after a very brief spell of relative peacefulness, became chiefly an affair of storms and reconciliations,' Una observed accurately. She saw the effects it had on John but had to keep silent since to criticize Souline openly would be to court disaster. Despite her own feelings, she was far too sensible a woman to do that. John had to be allowed to go to hell her own way.

From Beauvallon they went to Sirmione for the second time, taking Souline with them. Micki Jacob had moved to Merano but Una had written to her asking her to join them there, saying: 'Can't you come too? Sirmione won't be Sirmione without you, Mike.' Una prevailed.

Micki Jacob recalled later: 'I joined them in Sirmione, back at

237

the Albergo Catullo. Somehow the thing wasn't a success, Una and John had a friend with them who apparently disliked all Jews – practising or otherwise.'

Souline made no effort to moderate her typically White Russian anti-Semitism, and an unpleasant scene occurred. Whatever Souline said John defended her, and was, Micki Jacob thought, 'unwarrantably pontifical', and 'Una – whose complete loyalty to her friend never faltered for an instant – naturally was in agreement with John' – whatever her private thoughts. Micki Jacob was 'simply furious at what I felt had been an insult . . . and . . . left in . . . a blaze of righteous anger.' Of Souline she wrote, perhaps hardly surprisingly, 'I disliked her with the utmost cordiality.' The friendship was not to be resumed until the beginning of the war, when Una wrote commiserating on the death of Micki's favourite dog.

Souline's moods and behaviour must often have been an embarrassment, as she did not observe the Western courtesies of civilized life.

After Sirmione they returned to Paris, where John wrote to Souline on August 12th: 'Later I will be with you. We will have a part of my birthday evening in each other's arms.'

In October Una and John went back to Rye where John finished *The Sixth Beatitude*, leaving Souline in Paris. Placating her as usual, John wrote on November 5th: 'May be later on Una will get more reasonable . . .' By implication, she thought Una *unreasonable*!

With a generosity which surprised even John, and certainly surprised Souline, Una decided to give the latter a diamond safety-pin for Christmas. John then wrote: 'Una is being extremely good – she speaks of you often and with real affection. She has got the diamond safety-pin out [i.e. from the bank] – the pin she is going to give you for Christmas.'[25]

John was determined to have Souline with them for Christmas, and Una co-operated, writing her a formal letter of invitation to enable her to get a visa for a month. Una's reactions are charted in John's letters: '. . . now Una does not seem to resent my talking of you . . .' but in the same letter: 'There is something I want to say about Una. I know that you feel that she has exaggerated reactions and that you dislike such reactions . . . try to remember that Una is not English but Irish . . . the Irish are the most emotional people God ever created . . .'[26]

What these 'exaggerated reactions' were is not stated but it seems extraordinary that neither John nor Souline see their own reactions as in any way 'exaggerated' whilst viewing Una's as almost pathological. John never suggests to Souline that *their* behaviour might be responsible.

Two days later John wrote: 'Poor Una, her nerves are very bad again at the moment – one never knows when a storm will blow up. One minute she's so good, so marvellous to me, and the next she's almost a devil.' John's terms of approval apply to a Una who accepts the situation; and her terms of disapproval to a Una who opposes it. Una's repression of some of her own reactions lead to '. . . a constant violent headache . . . which nothing seems to have any effect on', and the old hysterical tendency to convert anxieties into physical symptoms. John tells Souline without any apparent sense of irony that she is afraid that 'I sympathise too much very often . . .'

On December 19th Souline arrived in England for a month, and they all lived *à trois* at 'The Forecastle' for the first time. John and Una determined that Evguenia should enjoy her first Christmas at Rye, and as well as buying her expensive presents they also gave her a 'fun' stocking, eagerly collecting its items, which included pink sugar mice and smelling salts. Una wrote in her Daybook in December 1935: '. . . except that I deplore this affair with Evguenia as a blemish upon our complete mutual faith and as a thing that wrongs it and her integrity, there are times when I weakly feel that I have not the heart to grudge her the pleasure . . . that she gets out of it.'

The four-bedroomed cottage with thin plaster walls, wooden stairs and creaking landings, does not allow much real privacy, and sound travels very easily. Una, always a light sleeper, must have heard John negotiating the floor boards between her room, opposite Una's own, and Souline's: a sobering and melancholy experience.

Una tried to accept the new order of things and to *like* Souline, but this could not last and John was to remark to Souline two years later: 'If only there had been friendship between you and Una . . .'[27] John expected rather a lot of them both!

Harold Rubinstein said of Una that she was 'an exceptionally trusting and affectionate woman', and that 'the shock [i.e. of Souline] to her when the truth came out, was distressing.'[28] This was certainly an understatement: it was one of the most profoundly shattering experiences of her life.

# 15

# *Our Long Pilgrimage Together (1936–40)*

It may be pertinent to ask at this point why Una did not leave John. There is no evidence to suggest that she ever seriously thought of doing so; neither did she deliver any ultimatums of the usual sort. Indeed, apart from extracting the promise from John which the latter subsequently broke, and refusing to give them 'The Forecastle' for ten days, she did little to oppose John's will, and at times positively co-operated to aid the situation. The reasons are not far to seek. She was firmly ensconced as 'wife' with her rights and privileges, and was not going to step aside for a rival whom, in any case, she held in contempt. Secondly, she trusted in John's continued 'devotion' to her, despite Souline, for she knew that in John new desires did not cancel out old affections. Then there was the matter of loyalty, one of Una's sterling qualities. They had been a bonded pair for eighteen years, and even though no longer lovers still shared companionship and home, which Una would have been loath to lose. John could have made a settlement on her as she had on Dolly Clarke, and Una owned 'The Forecastle' so she would have had a home, but it was a home which only had meaning by being shared with John. John was her whole life. She would have said, as Stephen did to Mary in *The Well*, 'How could I leave you and go on living?'

She also thought, and certainly hoped, even by 1936, that John's relationship with Souline would not last. John's 'fancies' had been fleeting in the past, with the exception of Una herself, and she could see that Souline was unsuitable for John in so many ways. What she may not have fully appreciated was the fact that John had changed, had, in fact, 'ceased to take love lightly'.[1] Neither could she have known or understood the importance and binding power of Souline's initial virginity, for John.

Why, as at times she must have longed for her freedom, did John not leave Una for Souline? This is very much the same question as why do some people prefer to stay married and have an extra-marital affair than to divorce and re-marry? Firstly there was, as she stressed to Souline, her sense of 'duty' and responsibility towards Una because of their long years together. It also seems clear that she still wanted the advantages of Una's companionship and of their shared life and home together. In addition, she still had the legacy of guilt from her hardness towards Ladye and its consequences, and could not bear to cause another catastrophe of any sort. But far and above these reasons was the motive of preserving the *status quo*: not for the usual reasons, but for her 'fan-public', since after *The Well* she had become 'a kind of legend', a mouthpiece for inverts everywhere. Her own union therefore had to be seen to be faithful, or the 'cause' would suffer, and her integrity be called into question. She did not want to be seen to 'pension off' a faithful middle-aged spouse in order to live with a sexy, younger woman. That would have given ammunition to critics and opponents eager to prove all inverts 'moral lepers'. That this was in her mind is clear from an early letter to Souline: 'If my fan-public knew the condition to which I have been reduced by a Chink-faced Tartar what would they say?'

Her own words from *The Well* also came back to her, and she knew that she had to take the advice which Puddle gave to Stephen: 'for the sake of those others who share the same burden . . . show the world that people like you . . . can be quite as selfless and fine as the rest of mankind. Let your life go to prove this . . .' It is at best ironical, at worst hypocritical, that John took this line of reasoning; and it is certainly no compliment to Una that John stayed with her primarily for reasons of public relations rather than personal sentiment. Una was aware of this, and had used the power of this argument initially as a means to deter John from infidelity.

It was to remain an unhappy situation without solution, and no one was to be either contented or at peace for long. John could not leave Una and would not give up Souline. Souline resented Una and the fact that she could not usurp her any further; she was possessive and wanted John to herself. When she realized that this was impossible she made a life of her own in Paris among other emigrées and grew to resent John's interference in her affairs. Una, throughout what was left of their 'long pilgrimage together',[2] went on loving, serving and supporting John as before, and kept her very real griefs to herself.

'Evguenia remained with us wherever we went, either staying with us in hotels or occupying quarters of her own nearby. This was in accordance with my wishes . . .'[3] Una explained later, but this is rather misleading. Souline was with them less as the years went by; and 'compliance' would be more accurate here than 'wishes'.

After a spring in Grasse, chiefly for Evguenia's health, they all three spent the summer of 1936 at Trois Epis in Alsace, and during their absence an extraordinary occurrence took place. Lydia Allison, of the Boston Society for Psychic Research, visiting England, went to see Mrs Leonard at Tankerton on Sunday August 9th. Although she was a friend of John and Una she did not know any details about their private lives, but they had arranged for her to take a proxy sitting for them with 'Ladye'. The information which was received was not known to either the sitter or the medium, and was therefore quite remarkable for its accuracy.

'Ladye' says to Lydia Allison through Mrs Leonard: 'Tell Una I have been helping her, to cheer her, in my special way. I've helped them both. They know; and I have been helping our third one. They will know.' That is clearly a reference to Souline, whom she claimed to be trying to 'help': 'I have had to make an alteration in some of the arrangements because of the formalities I was trying to make for the girl . . .'

'Ladye' confides that 'I have had some strained and anxious times with them . . . So much trouble between them; no one knows. Lately, you see. But I'm trying to help things because they must see things through . . . I hope they may go on some time together. They will go on together.'

Lydia Allison's ignorance of the meaning of the information given is confirmed by her letter sent to Isabel Newton, the Secretary of the S.P.R. in London, accompanying the notes to the sitting: '. . . as you know, I am very fond of Una and John . . .' she wrote, and went on to express concern that they might be in some sort of trouble. As indeed they were. Presumably they received a transcript of this proxy sitting in Alsace. While they were there things between John and Souline became increasingly difficult, with John often beside herself with anger or jealousy. On the night of June 22nd, 1936, John arrived back late from Souline, looking pale and troubled, and quickly confessed to Una that she had been

> engaged in systematically breaking up in Evguenia's flat everything that she had ever given her – tearing up all photographs of herself, all her own books, all pictures and etchings, breaking the frames, destroying most particularly the bag of crocodile which was so ungraciously received at Christmas, she then systematically hunted the flat for any evidences of some other presence, demanded Evguenia's keys as an alternative to breaking open her . . . wood cabinet, and found . . . nothing at all except some letters in Russian which she could not read and eventually returned . . .

This kind of violence was uncharacteristic of John and its relation must have surprised Una, who commented in her Daybook: 'She appears to have wrecked the whole place with incredible strength and persistence . . . she is now ashamed and regretful . . . but I think she had had long and sore provocation. I myself have watched the girl baiting her for hours and days at a time.'

Five days later, Una noted: 'At 3 she went off to her Tartar Torturer, promising me she would leave at once if there were any signs of bullying and baiting and would not be drawn into dispute – but I have little hope she will be able to keep her word.'

Una's role seems strangely protective, almost maternal; and the portrait of John hardly fits that of the carefree philanderer going off to take her pleasure! On August 10th Una asks herself rhetorically: '. . . is she learning, in a series of bitter realisations what Evguenia is really like, and will she free herself in the end?'

They journeyed from Alsace to Merano in the Tyrol, arriving in November and staying for seven months. While they were there John showed signs of the eye affection which was to bedevil her last years and to cause Una concern. A spasm of the eyelid turned the lashes inwards against the eyeball, causing intense irritation and pain, and was eventually to require operative intervention. In April 1937 they spent a week in the Grand Hotel at Gardone waiting for a summons from D'Annunzio which never came. Una was particularly disappointed as she was eager to meet him, having missed him the first time. Before they left Merano John had an idea for a novel set there, about the life of a shoemaker, but she was destined never to complete it; and Una was to burn it after her death, in accordance with her expressed wishes.

In May they went from Merano to Florence, travelling in a fifteen-seat motor coach specially converted for the three of them and their luggage. The people of Merano who watched it thought their departure quite a sight! Una and John had decided to settle in Florence as they both loved it, and the climate was suitable for Souline who had to be careful with her lungs. Neither Una nor John had been to Florence for fifteen years, and it must have reminded Una, sadly, of happier times, especially their first visit together in 1921.

At first they stayed in hotels, the Albion, then the Gran Brettagna, where Una had another attack of enteritis. They were soon flat-hunting, intending to settle their winter quarters before returning to England for the summer. As usual they were fastidious in their requirements. John, Una recalled, 'developed a craving' for a flat opposite their hotel, in the Borgo San Jacopo, but as its rooms were 'small and dark' Una 'managed to head her off', having ideas of her own: she had 'more than a fancy for another apartment that . . . boasted three rooms on the Ponte Vecchio'[4] but these were also very small, as well as damp.

Eventually they found a suitable flat for themselves at 18 Lung 'Arno Acciaiuoli, next to Berchielli's Hotel. It was on the second floor, and John's study and Una's sitting-room 'opened on to one of the loveliest views in the world', of the Arno with the Ponte Vecchio in the distance. They engaged an elderly but superb cook and Maria Prosperi as general maid. Maria called them 'Donna Una and the Signorina', and was to prove very capable and loyal. A flat was also found for Souline near by, 'a flat with which she was highly delighted'.[5] Having settled matters satisfactorily they all journeyed to Paris, where John reluctantly left Souline on July 15th. Souline made it quite clear that she had had far too much *à trois* at Merano for her liking; and so, no doubt, had Una. Souline was glad to be left in Paris to live her own life, and Una must have been very pleased at the prospect of having John to herself at 'The Forecastle' for the summer; but the very next day, July 16th, John was writing to Souline: '. . . this cottage is full of reminders . . . of those early days of our loving . . . Separation for me is just another word for hell . . . I think of what might have been but what is not.'

Referring regretfully to the end of 'the period of our life lived closely together' at Merano, John reminds Souline that this was 'the period you hated and longed to be released from, yes, and begged to be released from many, many times, often telling me to go back to England.'

This was a proof, if John needed it, that the *à trois* solution was no solution at all; and she conceded that, 'never again will we live three together, this I have promised so do not fear it.' '. . . you were deeply in love . . . three years ago . . .' John reminded Souline wistfully, adding that many 'things bitter and sweet' had happened since then.

The question of Souline's visa was uppermost again, this time the Italian visa for the winter in Florence; '. . . until you . . . get it I shall have no peace,' John told her anxiously. She also gave vent to her suspicion that to Souline their 'temporary partings are . . . a relief.' The reason was clearly Una: '. . . there are circumstances in my life that outweigh everything else with you, that over-shadow everything else.'

Souline was very jealous of Una: '. . . you want me all to yourself, don't you darling?' John knew the answer perfectly well and reassured her that 'you get much more than half, and in many, many ways . . .' These 'ways' included love, time and attention.

'I am trying to be reasonable, but finding it hard . . .' John confessed. Her interpretation of the word here is curious; above all, she was being *un*reasonable, especially in expecting Una and Souline to be amicably disposed towards each other.

At Rye everything went on ostensibly the same. They visited Edy Craig at Smallhythe, and Andrea paid them a rare visit. They had seen little of her since her marriage, but the insult of the wedding invitation had been patched up. Una was pleased to see her and gave her a little clock case, and they were both sympathetic to the fact that she was out of work and down at heel. Toby Warren was not proving a good breadwinner and acting was a precarious profession. In addition she had an infant son, Nicholas Vincenzo Troubridge Warren. She noticed a picture of Souline and commented that she had an amazing Tartar face, but was not, of course, told about the circumstances.

They were quite well-known in Rye, despite their absences. Old friends welcomed them back, and new people were interested in them. For some they were colourful figures a little larger than life. Mrs Wethey, who met them casually, thought them 'charming', but 'a bit odd'. What seemed to her particularly 'odd' was their habit, when out walking or shopping in Rye, of shouting to each other across the road, which was 'not quite done!' Another memory is provided by Mrs James, of 'The Jolly Sailor', Hucksteps Row, who met John and Una in London in the mid-1930s. She knew the Webbs and the Shaws, and was invited to a literary party, by her friend Katie Gardner. The party was somewhere near the Law Courts, and the Webbs were there, but the people she most remembered were John and Una.

I can remember to this day exactly what they were wearing . . . Radclyffe Hall wore a beautifully cut man's dinner jacket and skirt, a stiff shirt and bow tie . . . all in black, and wearing a monocle. Lady Troubridge wore the most glorious dress, and looked like a bride. It was an evening dress in cream coloured soft satin. She wore only pearls: earrings and two or three strings of pearls round her neck . . . she looked beautiful, almost over-dressed. Everybody's eyes were riveted on her. They cut a tremendous dash as a pair. I was introduced to them, and told Radclyffe Hall how much I admired her writing. She was very gracious and charming. I never forgot her, and read all her books . . .

She felt that they rather 'gave audiences', but were much sought after.

The dichotomy between the public and private life was marked. Writing to Souline that summer, John said: 'I think very often of our future, but know that for the moment we must just mark time. I am convinced that we shall find a solution.'[6] She was less 'convinced' herself than trying to convince and pacify Souline. Her dependence on the relationship with Souline was total, and her great fear was that Souline would tire of the situation and leave her. 'I think that had we really parted . . . I should not be alive now,' John told her melodramatically in the same letter.

In August John slipped in the garden of 'The Forecastle' and hurt her ankle, and what was initially mis-diagnosed by a local doctor as a sprain was later found to be a triple fracture. Una took her to London where an X-ray confirmed the real diagnosis, and the ankle had to be broken and reset. They were at the London Clinic for some weeks, and John's foot was in plaster and she on crutches for an abnormally long time. Una noticed that John seemed to have no reserves of strength and that her recuperative powers were far less than expected, but saw no reason for or sinister significance in this. As always, Una coped and organized their arrangements. John was anxious that her injury should not delay their projected return to Florence in October as in that event Souline would have to winter in Paris. Una arranged for relays of carrying chairs *en route* and for nurses to accompany them, and they returned to Paris in October. They were delayed there a week when it was discovered that one of John's Achilles tendons had shrunk, and a very painful intensive course of physiotherapy was undertaken at the American Hospital.

They collected Souline and all three returned to Florence in November to settle in for the winter. As soon as they arrived in Florence Una sent for their doctor to take John's health in hand,

and various tonics and treatments were undertaken, but it was not until the following summer that John was fully recovered. John and Una had a ready-made circle of Italian friends, largely through Una's connection with the Tealdis and the Massolas, and through them with the Corsini, Imperiali, Piccone and Capponi families. They had a good social life and John was happy to enjoy the advantages which Una's connections brought as well as the other advantages of having Souline at hand. Una was thankful that she and John still shared a home and spent much time together: they liked walking and exploring, which Souline did not, and still went out socially as a couple to visit people like the Berensons, and Isabel Graham-Smith at Fiesole. They also visited Sienna and Viareggio alone. But there were problems too, arising from their changed domestic situation. On January 13th, 1938, Una wrote:

Today John has gone off with a suitcase to stay two nights with her . . . It feels very odd and strange that she should be staying away from me with Evguenia and all over Florence friends know it – but as it happens it is much easier here than it would be elsewhere, as they do not know the revolution it constitutes from our inseparable years – and I am quite successfully convincing when I say how glad I am she should be able to get a change of scene and variety with someone experienced like Evguenia! More lies . . . more subterfuge . . . life seems these days to be made up of them, and I a lover of truth compelled to be a master dissembler. Yet how could I say when the matter is discussed, 'I loathe her going; it is unprecedented in all our years of union, I am hurt and miserable and in any case Evguenia is selfish and unreliable and I neither like nor trust her'?

The infatuation had not fizzled out as she had hoped it would, but was in its fourth year: 'There are miserable hours when I feel that the long mutual trust and confidence between John and I has degenerated, in spite of all our affection . . .' The situation also necessitated a degree of hypocrisy on Una's part: 'I . . . cannot like Evguenia or respect her . . . but I must tacitly – and sometimes even actively, pretend I do or life with her always a third in everything would be impossible . . . I must conceal my views.'

They remained at Lung 'Arno Acciaiuoli until July 1938, when they discovered that the heat, noise and smells made it untenable. Una, as usual, determined to find somewhere else before they left Florence for the summer, and eventually succeeded, after much footsore searching, in finding a large, luxurious second-floor apartment in a 'beautiful trecento palace'.[7] It had communicating bedrooms, and a vast study in which was a curious little annexe or 'cell' in which John was to write. They were to move into 8 via de Bardi in the autumn.

Souline had taken herself back to Paris by June, as she always hated 'being chock-a-block with Una'.[8] So intolerable did Souline find the situation (having far less patience, tolerance or selflessness than Una) that she threatened to leave John because of it. John replied hastily and desperately: 'No, no, Una does not hate you. But can we never get away from Una and think of ourselves? . . . I know it would be happier for you if my circumstances were different – if I were free . . . but am I to be sacrificed to my circumstances?'

She tried to reason with her: 'Had I been a man I should have married Una . . . the result would have been that I could not have divorced a faithful Una even had I wished to . . . she is a Catholic and would not divorce Troubridge . . .' then to coerce: '. . . all you need do, just be on terms with Una. She matters so little to you really . . . you give her undue importance . . .' then to caution: 'Are we really to part? Think long and think wisely . . . Four years – it's a big thing to smash . . .' and finally to plead: 'I am nearly broken and you alone can mend me. If you leave me I break completely . . . I am a violent and passionate woman . . . Don't drive me to my death . . .'

Of Una she said blithely: 'If you leave me because of Una you can't love me . . . Because of Una, incredible! She has never harmed you seriously, she was terribly jealous and hurt just at first but not now . . . never mind Una, only love matters . . '

It is clear that the only thing which mattered in John's life was not losing Souline. She would use any ploy or pressure to keep her, including the financial: '. . . my allowance has made you free –

given you your freedom on conditions that are merciful . . . I could have said: "No me, no money," but I do not and did not want to buy you . . ."[9] Nevertheless, John was not above reducing the allowance when displeased, and of using the promise of an eventual inheritance of English money to draw Souline to England.

In July, as usual, John and Una went to Rye for the summer, and as usual there were problems about Souline's visas, this time the renewal of her English one as John was trying to woo her to Rye. John instructed her, as before, to use Una's name because '. . . her name as Troubridge's widow and her father's daughter carries a certain weight in Government circles,' and blatantly appealed to Souline's prejudice by explaining that delay was due to a Foreign Office 'distracted' by 'Jews! Jews! Jews! Millions of them trying to push their way into England, and dozens and dozens managing to slip in without papers or passports via Ireland, or by arriving at small villages on our coast in fishing boats . . .'[10] John explained, in addition, that 'I am always telling the authorities . . . that you have been adopted to all intents and purposes and I therefore want you in my own country.'

Souline was less than willing to commit herself to a visit to Rye and the old à trois situation all over again, and must have delayed, to Una's delight, since John was still writing to Souline on September 13th: 'So far no news from Whitehall about the English side of your life . . .' Una, always glad to have John to herself, must have regretted the end of the English summer, and the end of Rye each year and the return to Florence in the autumn, much as she loved Florence. Both Paris and Florence now meant Souline. John's despairs and distractions when things were going wrong between her and Souline were difficult to live with, and Una knew all the signs, reading the state of play from John's moods. Una was disappointed that in three years John had started several books but finished none, and her work habits had become increasingly erratic. Either she did not work at all, or she drove herself in manic fashion, working all night until six or eight in the morning. Her chronic lack of sleep may well have contributed to the weakness in her health, about which Una continued to worry as of old, but she was fighting an increasingly losing battle.

In November they were all three back in Florence, and Una wrote on the 12th: 'John and Evguenia went out to dinner and I had mine in bed where I read and fell asleep very tired before nine. At ten came John, or even earlier, and I awoke – She sat down on my bed and took me in her arms and kissed and kissed my eyelids – my forehead, my lips, my hair – and said nothing. What is in her mind and what is going to come out of this visit . . . of Evguenia's?'

It is not surprising that Una was confused, for John was too. Three days later Una observed in a tone indignant on John's behalf:

> She is being quite outrageously treated. Evguenia has come here – resumed relations with her and then announced that they are to end. A) She is 'off sex' altogether. B) She will marry and settle down if opportunity should occur. C) She is more normal than John thought . . . She will have John's 'friendship' i.e. money and help while refusing not only to be her lover, but even to remain in the same town and give any companionship . . .

On a more personal note Una bewailed on November 27th: 'The bitter thing is that all this *should* be so happy – our lovely flat, nice acquaintances eager to make much of us, admiring John and liking us both.'

Some of their closer friends did know the whole truth, and sympathized with Una. Jeanne Holroyd-Reece said it was like some 'dreadful game that may go on forever . . .' Souline went back to Paris leaving John and Una alone in Florence at the end of November, but by the middle of December the question of Christmas arose: 'I know beforehand if Evguenia comes and does not change her mind, what will happen,' Una declared. 'She will come here for a spree – very likely see comparatively little of John – hurt her at every turn – keep her at arm's length and go away leaving her more unhappy than ever. Meanwhile she is all agog for the coming visit and everything that did not seem worthwhile when we were alone is no trouble at all now that Evguenia will share it!' If there is a hint of irony here it is understandable. On December 22nd there was yet

> Another Evguenia fuss. A letter from her this morning dated 20th says she is 'flying out now' to get her ticket and send a wire – today, two days later, no wire – ergo, as *of course* she would never have failed to send it' something terrible has happened to her and John is crazy with anxiety, a long telegram is prepared, and I suggest telephoning – we wait half an hour and Evguenia's landlady says Mlle. Souline is perfectly well, is out, and leaving Paris on Friday – at luncheon we receive the telegram despatched at noon *today*! Is it wonderful that I feel I could strangle her? And after all as Don Rinaldo said to me two days ago in the confessional, 'no one can be asked to *like* anyone to order – Our Lord does not ask or expect that.'

Just as well, perhaps; but this entry does show their three behaviours rather well: Evguenia thoughtless, slapdash, inconsiderate of John's feelings; John highly-strung and extremist in her emotions about Souline, unable to be calm, rational, or to see the woman as she really is; Una full of practical commonsense, knowing the others' reactions so well, naturally angry at Souline's behaviour and its effects on John.

In January 1939 John and Una went to Viareggio to stay, and John wrote to Souline holding out financial bait: 'You have had War Loan . . . bought for you . . . and ample provision after my death . . .'[11]

On February 9th John mentioned that she had been 'discussing with Una what was likely to happen if war broke out,' and that she was worried about Souline's French money, and glad that she had the English 'nest-egg'. She emphasized that 'Una never presumes to question me about it', and that her financial provisions for Souline were entirely private between them. Souline was obviously touchy about this, and John anxious to pacify her since, as she said, 'you so frequently get angry these days.' The phrase 'never presumes' is revealing of the nature of John's and Una's relationship at this point.

John expressed bitterness that Souline preferred to remain in

Paris, and that her taking a flat in Florence had therefore 'failed so miserably in its object'. John thought it her 'duty' to stop Souline's allowance if she persisted in remaining in Paris, then relented, changed her tone, and remarked, 'I would *like* you to be out of Paris during March . . . but you will decide this for yourself . . . my wishes will not weigh with you I fear . . .' in the end she pleaded, '. . . you promised to come at Easter . . .'

John was also concerned about Souline's national status in the event of war, and advised her to 'think many times before you decide to refuse to take out your English Nansen . . . it will soon be now or never for England.' She was careful to emphasize that England was 'the country that is your soul [*sic*] hope financially.' She was disappointed at Souline's long reluctance to seek British naturalization, or ever really to like England.

On February 10th John and Una left Viareggio and returned to Florence, where Souline eventually joined them on April 3rd. Her visits were now only occasional, as she wanted more and more to live her own life, to John's dismay and Una's joy.

In May John's health was again in question and Una took her to Professor Lapiccirelli who examined her chest and lungs. A radiological report by Dr Enrico Cumbo showed evidence of more than one episode of tuberculosis which had left considerable scarring and calcification of the lungs; and also that the heart was enlarged, presumably in order to compensate for the reduced lung efficiency. This meant that lung function was reduced and very restricting in terms of energetic activity, which perhaps accounted for John's general weakness at this time.

As usual, Una sought a second opinion, and on Lapiccirelli's recommendation they went to Rome to consult Professor Frugone. The findings were confirmed and northern winters definitely vetoed for the future. This twenty-four-hour visit was to Una 'one of the good memories' of these years; not only were the specialists 'kind and efficient' but they also 'treated John as the great artist that they knew her to be', which delighted Una whose faith in John's abilities never wavered despite the latterly unproductive years. In addition, they enjoyed Rome together, going to Mass in the crypt of St Peter's, breakfasting in the sunshine at a pavement café near by, then wandering in Rome, and dining at the famous Alfredo's where John's picture was on the wall with other celebrities who had dined there. It seemed almost like old times.

Souline was becoming less and less of a threat to Una, due to her increasingly long absences; and although John was often not easy to live with, Una had stood her ground and retained her position. John's affections might be elsewhere, but John herself was with Una, who now had more of her company than had Souline. Souline had found Una a force to reckon with, and had failed finally to draw John away from her. Realizing that Una's claims were stronger than her own, that precedent and 'duty' would ultimately outweigh the fluctuations of passion, she had retreated into a life of her own, fighting fiercely for her independence from John's strictures, whilst retaining what advantages she could. John wanted desperately to believe the best of Souline, but it became more and more difficult to maintain the fiction. A rare surviving letter from Souline, dated June 7th, 1939, shows to what a state the relationship had come: although headed 'Darling Johnnie' it is a catalogue of complaints, and shows more coldness than real feeling. 'My plans are unchanged, as I told you . . . I shall come to England for a month . . . if you prefer to take it as a drama, then do it . . . I am not going to repeat again what I have already said about it . . .' she insisted categorically.

The dispute was partly about her going out of Paris into the country for weekends with a person called Lisa: 'I am only going there for week-ends . . . You make everything so unpleasant that I begin to wonder why on earth have I written to you about it . . . it is too innocent a fact in itself and you take it as a tragedy,' she complained, adding: '. . . as I am getting older there is nothing else for me to do but have something of my own.'

About the old question, she prevaricates: '. . . in connection with my taking English Nansen I have not decided yet any-thing . . .'

In conclusion she states: 'I've written to you solely because you've asked me to . . .' and admonishes John: 'Let live, and you shall be happier yourself.' John seems to have clung on more tenaciously as she sensed Souline slipping away from her. Bitter-ness and recriminations had become more frequent between them;

and John may have realized that she had loved Souline unwisely and Una latterly not well enough.

That year, in the preparations for their summer trip to England there were 'conflicting elements of precaution and bravado'.[12] Rumours of war vied with the hope that such a thing was impossible. They had bought in fuel for the following winter but at the same time Una gave 'a dozen or so very special treasures' to Maria, the maid, with instructions to take them in a taxi to Baroness Massola if 'the worst' came about after all. John's doctors advised a summer in the Italian mountains instead of England, but she ignored their advice. They intended to spend only eight weeks in Rye, having reluctantly decided to sell 'The Forecastle' and to live permanently in Italy.

'We left Maria and Teresa and our home in July 1939 and that was the last time John was ever to see them,' Una wrote six years later. They collected Souline in Paris, saw the usual friends, put Fido, their large white poodle, in charge of the head keeper in the Bois de Boulogne, and crossed the Channel, unknowingly for the last time together. They arrived at 'The Forecastle' on August 4th, and were to be uncomfortably *à trois* there, despite Una's and Souline's dislike, and John's previous assurances to the contrary. Una had 'misgivings' about John remaining in England even if war did break out, feeling strongly that her primary duty was not patriotism but to preserve her own health in a suitable climate. John's own misgivings concerned not herself but Souline, and she sent for 'Mac', who was a solicitor, to help sort out Souline's papers and position. Mrs Bligh remembers that her father was hastily summoned by John to deal with an emergency concerning a third person, a foreigner, but at the time did not know the details.

The three of them heard the outbreak of war announced by Chamberlain on the wireless as they 'sat in the little "Forecastle" parlour'. The rumours had been correct, the unimaginable had happened for the second time in their lives. They were trapped in England by events: their only hope was to try to return to Italy, which would surely remain neutral? In any case, neither John nor Souline should winter in a northern climate.

They put 'The Forecastle' on the market and it was sold for

£1,650 in late November, the final deed of conveyance from Una to Lionel Browning being signed on January 4th, 1940. It had more than doubled its value since 1934, when they had bought it for £750. Whilst investigating the possibility of returning to Italy they decided to winter in the west country, going at first to the Cottage Hotel at Lynton, where Una and John had had so many happy holidays since the middle of the previous war. It was anathema to Souline from the beginning: she felt bored and trapped, and was 'fretting for Paris'. There was little to do except read, ride or walk, and John was 'fully launched upon a new book'.[13] In addition, Souline was incensed by the fact that because of her 'stateless alien' status she had to register her address with the local police station wherever she went. John and Una, her official sponsors, were responsible for her, and also had to know of her whereabouts. She resented this, and took herself off to the Hotel Osborne in Queen Street, Exeter, where John and Una shortly followed her.

Soon after their arrival, John contracted 'severe influenza . . . the first of a long succession of disasters,' Una noted later with hindsight. Predictably it soon attacked John's already weak chest; and ironically, as they had gone there for the warmer climate, it was one of the worst winters ever known in the west country. The pipes were frozen solid in the hotel, and electricity was rationed. Una felt the stirrings of 'all those latent fears of losing what I loved', and remembered 'all John's long-past predictions (and Ladye's also) that she would die before me . . .'

Una persuaded John to allow her to make inquiries about returning to Italy; and when John was apparently recovering, they made a series of trips to London, staying at the Rembrandt Hotel in South Kensington, to try to 'co-ordinate our permits and visas with those that were being granted to Evguenia Souline'.[14] She was the real problem. The result of all their endeavours came in March, when they were told that as they had then been in England for over six months they could no longer be regarded as 'domiciled abroad', or given financial facilities in Italy. Una records that John 'heaved a sigh of relief' at this outcome, happy to stay in England for the duration of the war. They returned to Exeter but unable to find a suitable abode went back to Lynton, leaving Souline in

Exeter as she would not consent to return with them. Despite this, she wrote complaining of the insecurity of her position, and John replied: 'Darling, of course I am all you have got, and surely I have taken good care of you? These are very grim days, I must admit, and I do understand that at moments you feel the lack of intimate friends but I am here and we will of course see each other . . .'[15] but they were to see each other less and less.

On their return to Lynton, John and Una went first to the Imperial Hotel, finding the Cottage Hotel 'much changed' in a short time. For the first time in many years Una's heart began 'misbehaving'; hills and stairs were forbidden, with riding the recommended exercise. John was solicitous, and after hiring ponies for them both, bought 'Star' for Una and 'Tommy' for herself. They rode on the moors much as they had done in their early holidays together, and it must have seemed strangely sad to Una to do so again in such totally changed circumstances. The six years since 1934 had changed everything except the quality of Una's love; she had mellowed, learned to suffer in silence, to smile and carry on, and to co-operate with the 'enemy' just as much as was necessary to maintain her own position.

Rumours of possible enemy invasion in mid-1940 led John to persuade Souline to take a room in Lynton to be near them as her guarantors. Looking for a room for her led John and Una to discover 'The Wayside', a cottage near the Poor Clare Convent and Church, belonging to Jack and Marjorie Hancock. They took it for themselves in June, and Souline found another address locally. They were to become the only 'permanent lodgers' of the Hancocks, with whom they got on well; and they took at first all the bedrooms and the bathroom on the first floor, and the sitting-room, then later the dining-room as well. John, Una, a grey parrot and three dogs moved in, and how the Hancocks themselves managed to live there as well is a mystery. It was an amicable arrangement, and John and Una were to lodge there for three years, until 1942. Souline stayed in Lynton as short a time as possible.

Their faithful servants in Florence, Teresa the cook and Maria the maid, when told that John and Una could not return to Italy, 'both offered to apply for daily work and to remain and guard our home without wages . . .'[16] Una recalled. Other expatriate friends of theirs did manage to pass the war peacefully: Natalie and Romaine were left unmolested by Mussolini's government in their villa, Sant Agnese, in via San Leonardo, possibly because they had been friends of D'Annunzio; and the Berensons lived in their villa, I Tatti, on the outskirts of Florence. Similarly Gertrude Stein and Alice B. Toklas lived undisturbed at Culoz on the Rhone. No doubt had John and Una been in Florence as they had at first wished, they would have been accorded the same treatment, being also distinguished foreigners and known admirers of D'Annunzio. But that was not to be their fate, they were to face the last crisis of their 'long pilgrimage together' in their own country.

# 16

# *Much, Much Stronger than Mere Death (1941–3)*

Despite wartime privations, inclement weather, doubtful health, and frequent worries as to Souline's whereabouts, John and Una made the best of life at Lynton. They had their dogs, their horses and riding, their books, the haven of 'The Wayside', and a few friends. Above all, from Una's point of view, they had each other's constant companionship, and in a place which they both loved, and which Souline hated, her dislike keeping her away.

John 'toiled on doggedly'[1] with her book, needing both a focus for her mind and a distraction from the problems with Souline. Her eye troubles were increasing, and Una removed some of the offending eyelashes each day in an attempt to ease the discomfort; then later offered to take John's dictation in order to spare her eyes. To Una's surprise John accepted gratefully and they achieved an 'eminently workable combination'; and Una knew 'the joy of being brought closer to her than ever before in the creative work that was an essential part of her being.'[2]

During the summer the pain and discomfort of John's eyes became acute, and Una took her to Bath where they consulted an eye surgeon by the name of Tizzard. He seemed confident that he could cure the trouble not by medical but by surgical means, and warned that unless this step was taken ulceration and consequent blindness would occur. He was keen to do both eyes together but John insisted that they should be done one at a time, so that one eye could always be in use. The arrangements were made, and Una booked them in to the Francis Hotel in Bath, from which John was to go to Church Street Nursing Home for the operation, then return to the hotel a few days later when the stitches were removed.

John wrote to Souline from Bath the day before the operation: '. . . Una is half-dead with worry and making endless difficult arrangements for this operation tomorrow. So better stay where you are and I will send for you if absolutely necessary . . .'[3]

The first operation to the left eye was carried out by Tizzard on August 26th, under local anaesthetic. Una wrote to Souline on August 27th:

> Dear Evguenia,
>     Just a line to tell you that the first operation was done this morning and that Mr. Tizzard is satisfied . . . both he and the doctor said she was an admirable patient and so brave. She had some pain for a few hours afterwards, rather severe . . . but the actual operation she says she only felt a little just at the end . . . She sends her love to you. Yours in haste, Una.

This was the first of seventy-one letters written by Una to Souline on John's behalf between August 27th, 1941 and April 6th, 1942. They are largely detailed medical bulletins, or instructions about the content of Souline's own letters, or intended visits. When John was able she would often add a note of her own on to the end of Una's letter. As well as writing on John's behalf, Una had to read Souline's letters aloud to her when she was either forbidden to use her eyes, or too weak to read. She therefore knew what was in Souline's letters, and also how much they meant to and affected John. Una's letters were usually written daily or every two or three days, and stopped when John was able to resume writing herself. Writing these letters must have been extremely difficult for Una in the circumstances, and that she did so shows the degree of her selfless devotion to John.

On August 28th Una wrote: 'John must not use her sight at all at

261

present, as the uncovered eye is inclined to water in sympathy and they want complete rest, so I am writing to tell you that both your letters came this morning and that she loved getting them . . . The oculist did the first dressing last evening and it was all right . . .'

Two days later she wrote to tell Souline that although 'The oculist is . . . well satisfied . . . the stitches will not be out in 5 days, probably 8 . . . as there was a lot of haemorrhage and therefore more swelling of the eyelid than usual . . .'

On the 31st Una reported: 'At present, owing . . . to her bleeding so much there is a blood clot . . . and great suffusion to be dispersed. He has started hot fomentations and drops . . . Tizzard says openly to her we must take no chances. She . . . must not be made to laugh, and nothing to touch her emotions in any way as tears are above all injurious . . . so . . . I read bits from papers and unemotional fiction . . .'

This was a hint to Souline not to write either emotional or worrying letters to John. This setback in post-operative progress was the first of 'the disasters that befell us in Bath . . .'[4] Una wrote. Fomentations were of no avail, so on September 2nd a light anaesthetic was given and a small incision made to drain the clot. Una reported to Souline afterwards: 'Needless to say John is being quite marvellously good and plucky about it . . . Dr. Aldred Brown told Kathy (Lady) Dorchester that she was the bravest woman he had ever known!' One can detect a note of 'wifely' pride creeping in here: Una was impressed by John's courage and patience, and pleased to be able to boast of it to Souline. 'They are keeping her absolutely quiet – seeing nobody and in a chair for only 1½ hours daily . . .' she added, in case her own enthusiasm should prompt Souline to make a visit. She enjoyed being at hand herself and having bona fide reasons for keeping Souline at bay.

On September 5th Una wrote: 'John has asked me to send this line . . . to say the stitches are now out . . . and her eyelid which I was allowed to look at before it was bandaged definitely . . . much better . . . The stitches were deeply buried and it was a very unpleasant affair, but she sat like a rock . . . There were nine stitches. Una.'

262

When able, John wrote herself or dictated a letter to Una. On September 10th Una took John from the nursing home back to the Francis Hotel, where it was intended she should stay for a fortnight before the operation on the second eye, the first one remaining bandaged for a week. John was forbidden to wear glasses or use the good eye more than absolutely essential. After telling Souline the medical news on September 11th, Una added: 'She goes out a bit now in the streets with the nurse and myself either side . . . Our room is small but rather attractive and very airy . . .'

On September 18th the bandages were at last removed and the other eye was operated on twelve days later, on September 30th. Two hours afterwards there was another haemorrhage and Tizzard returned and applied a painfully tight tourniquet so that John had 'a most tormented night'. After the stitches were removed, John was back in the hotel on October 6th. '. . . thankful to be out of the nursing home of which she was heartily sick – she has had so much of it, so much more than was expected . . .' Una informed Souline, adding: 'Dr. Brown is going to try to get her strength up as she has gone very thin under the strain . . .'

John was also very weak and tired, and Una monitored her convalescence carefully to avoid over-taxing her. There were car drives, and visits to the Roman Baths and to Downside Abbey, before the return to Lynton. After October 19th John was able to resume letter-writing herself, although her eyes were still uncomfortable and sore. On November 7th she wrote to Souline curtly and critically: '. . . regarding any future plans you may have in mind I shall be willing to discuss these with you when I am feeling better. I must say that your new friends and political views are both highly objectionable to me, also I wonder whether you have fully realised the extreme heartlessness of taking advantage of my operation . . .' As a reprisal, John cut her allowance by £5. This letter was indicative of the strained nature of the relationship, and reads more like that from a parent to an errant child than between lovers.

John and Una, dissatisfied with the results of Tizzard's operations, decided to seek more expert help in London, and went in mid-December to stay at the Rembrandt Hotel prior to consulting Sir Harold Gillies, an eminent specialist. Souline had gone to live

*Life Together: the Last Years ( 1934–43 )*

in Oxford by this time, but John wrote trying unsuccessfully to arrange to meet her at the Rembrandt.

Gillies, when they saw him, was horrified at what had already been done by Tizzard, which had apparently exacerbated rather than alleviated the original trouble. He offered, though reluctantly as he was devoting himself to work with the war wounded, to operate to correct matters, but this was destined never to be, as John became ill a few days later. It was an icy winter and what began as influenza quickly developed into bronchitis, as before; then on January 11th, 1942 pleurisy set in, to be followed by double pneumonia.

Una wrote to Souline on January 12th postponing her proposed visit to John, and saying that they had two excellent nurses for night and day, but that if John was not soon recovered she would call in Lord Dawson, the King's physician. No one was too good or too expensive for her John. When she had summoned him she wrote: 'All this is exactly what Lapiccirelli feared might happen in the English climate, and Lord Dawson says the lungs are badly damaged . . .'

Una exercised that part of the 'wifely' instinct which is almost maternal when the beloved is ill: she protected John from stress, discomfort, intrusion, called in the highest medical experts with equanimity, cooked for John herself on a spirit stove, and helped with the nursing. 'For 17 weeks I fought for her life, with her own gallant assistance as soon as she was conscious enough to give it,'[5] she wrote later. She also wrote frequent bulletins to Souline, as before, but sparing her none of the details: '. . . she is very weak and exhausted and in much pain and suffering so terribly from retching and nausea caused by the sulphonimide . . . Lord Dawson . . . said that she had been terribly run down and weak before the infection began and that the operations on her eyes had pulled her down and diminished her resistance . . .' 'This morning she is beginning to expectorate and the coughing is very painful. A sputum test is being made . . .'[6]

On January 15th Una wrote: 'As well as congestion of lungs and pleurisy there is acute influenzal poisoning which causes much pain in head, ears, and limbs . . . also when she coughs a tendency to vomit.' As a nurse Souline would have perhaps appreciated the

264

unsavoury details; but neither nurses nor doctors saw the true significance of such details: 'her face is dreadfully wasted and drawn . . . she feels worse and suffers more than she did earlier . . .'

Una managed, with the rationing, to get a milk order for John by getting a doctor to certify that she was 'seriously ill with congestion of the lungs and pleurisy'. She then made John milk puddings on the spirit stove in their bedroom. Lord Dawson ordered John to eat sweet apples but as there were none obtainable in London Una wrote to ask friends in the country to send what they could spare. Mrs Hancock and Lady Dorchester obliged.

Una took Souline to task when necessary for John's sake:

I have wired you this afternoon asking you please not to fail to write to John, if only a line, every day and to post early. No letter arrived yesterday . . . She looks for letters – wonders if anything is wrong if they do not come, and she is so very very *weak* . . . that the smallest anxiety or disappointment might sabotage her recovery . . . I also asked you to send one or two affectionate telegrams as I can read them to her in some interval when she is in less pain and give her pleasure.

Una pocketed her pride, resentment, jealousy, and all her natural antipathy, in her overriding anxiety and concern for John's health and well-being. This co-operation with, and coercion of Souline, to this one end, shows the depth of Una's love and contrasts with Souline's.

John's own concern was still for Souline, and Una must have been pleased to have to tell her: 'She [John] whispered to me again today that *on no account are you to come up*, especially as the hotel is full of influenza.'[7]

Una gave Souline regular reports of John's pulse, temperature and respiration, Lord Dawson's pronouncements, and new developments. It would be many weeks before John could be moved, and her convalescence would be long, they were told. When well enough, she was to be taken back to Lynton, on Lord Dawson's orders. An air of benign conspiracy sometimes crept in: 'She *does not know* she has had pneumonia and is not to know at present.

265

Una.'[8] She was happy to be in control of the situation, and declared with an almost maternal possessiveness, 'I am taking no risks with her extreme weakness . . .' and, 'She slept badly last night and so I am trying to keep her very quiet today . . .' Then, 'How we are all working and watching night and day to avoid any relapse.'

Una was also acting on John's authority at the bank during her illness, and had to sign cheques for her and pay bills. This also included Souline's finances: 'Will you let me know . . . the amount she sends you for a month's heating, so that I may add it to your allowance cheque at the end of the month, please?' Una asked matter-of-factly on January 25th. She was detached and business-like, never in any of these letters revealing her own feelings. She behaved with admirable dignity. She safeguarded John by amending Souline's letters when she read them aloud to her, and told Souline: 'I read your letter to her omitting the sentence about your trachea feeling better owing to change of weather. I also omitted . . . such sentences as that you "had had a slight cold", that the English "houses are like ice". All these . . . would upset her terribly and she would be worrying and fretting . . .' To make her point clear, she emphasized that 'It is absolutely essential to her recovery . . . that she should have peace of mind so I wired you today not to put in anything that may alarm or worry her – at present I read her the letters, but anyday she felt stronger she might ask to *see* them and then I could not prevent her being upset . . . write her only the most cheerful unworrying letters you can think of . . .'[9] It is clear that Souline was thinking of herself, and Una of John.

John's extreme weakness remained to worry Una, who tried her best to obtain such foods as eggs to build up her strength. She was unable to wash or feed herself, and was only lifted into an armchair for half an hour a day; and was dosed with pain-killers, expectorants, purgatives and sleeping draughts. After a long description of John's bowel troubles, Una launched into a diatribe on doctors to Souline in early February: '. . . these English doctors, except Dawson, are very helpless. I cannot have discomfort and pain and lack of rest holding back her recovery, so Dawson comes tonight . . .'

In a very full letter summing up the present and the probable future, Una told Souline:

> The truth is that she has been *terribly* ill and very nearly went out of this world . . . It will be many weeks . . . before I can get her home, and even then it will mean a dreary time for her staying indoors at the slightest sign of bad weather, and unable to work or to read much because the eye . . . is still wrong and must eventually be operated again . . . When she gets home everything possible will have to be done to ensure such comfort and palliatives as can be contrived – and above all to shelter her from the smallest anxiety or distress . . . I think it right to tell you what Lord Dawson and the other doctors say, as you must want to know the exact position now and in future . . .[10]

The situation was abundantly clear, and to Souline it must have sounded extremely boring and prohibitive; but she visited them for the day in mid-February, and for three days in mid-March when John booked a room in their hotel for her. Just before this Gillies and Williamson Noble checked John's eyes and told Una that there was a distinct possibility that the condition was inoperable. Una however kept this to herself, to spare John. It was not until the end of March that John was allowed up, first to have lunch downstairs, then a few days later to go out for a few minutes.

On March 28th she was well enough to write to Souline herself, and of a proposed meeting on April 8th, said: 'Ask your friends to join us at tea at 4 o'clock.' These were the friends of whom she had already made it clear that she strongly disapproved. Una's last letter to Souline is dated April 6th, 1942. At first it explains that John's exhaustion has necessitated a heart stimulant, and that she may not be fit to travel as anticipated. Then she says:

> After her very grave illness of nearly four months . . . I think it only right to repeat what I have already told you: that Lord Dawson warned me that . . . her convalescence could only be a very lengthy one. He is sending her to Lynton to recuperate . . . and if, in such circumstances you decide to go away

without keeping her informed of your address (and this at a time when air-raids are frequent) and if the strain breaks her down and she dies it will be your doing and on your conscience all your life. Una V. Troubridge.

It was a fitting, seemingly final, letter and the nearest Una ever came to expressing her true feelings; she had kept them in check for so long, feigning friendship for this woman who had taken John's interest away from her, who had thrived on John's support and given so little in return, and whose behaviour now seemed to threaten John's very life.

John wrote to Souline herself two days later threatening to cut her allowance from £250 to £100 a year if she persisted in her wish to live in another country; and five days later wrote a very sharp letter setting out the conditions on which the allowance would be continued.

Micki Jacob, meeting them at this time, thought John looked much thinner and had a strangely frail look. Una put this down to the fact that John had 'managed to crawl back to life' having nearly left it; and 'drove her back triumphantly to Lynton'. Although John was weak and emaciated the summer lay ahead, and they had both 'acquired a measure of confidence that we had met and overcome the worst that could befall us . . .'[11]

Sadly, this was not to be the case.

On their return Una was 'to exercise increasing care and vigilance', and 'Marjorie [Hancock] was to prepare good and nourishing food.' John on her part 'was to display courage and patience in a life that seemed chiefly made up of restrictions: she was not to work . . . she was not to smoke, she was not to leave the house in rainy or windy weather . . .'

John took up knitting as she could do this automatically without looking down, and Una would read to her the favourite books which they had read and re-read over the years: Alison Uttley, Margaret Irwin, Daphne du Maurier. In addition they took up their riding again, which John found less effort than walking; and Una was to remember John's last ride, on October 28th, 'only five months before she was smitten down and the mysterious cause of her illness revealed', and how much, weak as she was, she enjoyed it.

On November 9th John invited Souline to join them at Lynton for Christmas, adding rather pathetically, 'I don't think I take up very much of your time these days.' In the event the visit was called off by Souline, who had taken a secret government job, presumably in order to leave the country as she wished. She wrote coldly to 'Dear John' on December 15th, in an envelope marked by the censors 'Italian Section'. John replied on the 17th: 'I feel as though a thick dark curtain had dropped between us – so strange after all these years.' The end was sadly formal: 'God bless you and your new work and keep you safe. I send you a heartful of sincere good wishes for your success in what you have undertaken . . .'

John's last known letter to Souline was written on December 26th: 'The Christmas Dinner prepared in the wild hope that you would share it, we are having in an hour's time, and our very nice little new priest is coming to help eat it . . . God bless you and keep you safe. I miss you even after all these years. Your John. P.S. Enclosed is a bit of the white heather you gave me.'

This was the end. The lovers had finally parted.

At the end of March 1943 John was suddenly taken ill. Local doctors mistakenly diagnosed a severe chill, and for the first ten days Una devotedly nursed John herself, before seeking nursing assistance. She obtained a nurse from London, Nurse Baldwin, whom they both vaguely remembered from the London Clinic. John was to nickname her 'Little B.' in the months that followed. After three weeks with no improvement, Una made 'a lightning resolve to get John to London',[12] and made the long journey by ambulance with Nurse Baldwin's help. On arrival the problem was finding 'any hospital or nursing home that would not separate us'. Una was determined not to give John totally over to other people, and John herself agreed with her. After many unsuccessful phone calls and near despair, Dr Armando Child came to the rescue. He told Una to take John to the Ritz, and after asking many questions as to John's symptoms and condition, said that he would try to find both a surgeon and accommodation for the two of them. He was as

269

good as his word, and that same day he and Cecil Joll, a senior surgeon at the Cancer Hospital, examined John thoroughly – and told her the truth. John was not surprised, and had already said to Una, 'You know, don't you, that this is probably cancer? And if it is, that it's God's will and that it must not only be accepted but welcomed?' John was more able to welcome it than Una, who recalled: 'Dr. Child . . . examined her and told me at once that a colostomy was inevitable and to my horrified protest he replied, "It's her *only chance* . . ."'

It was decided to operate the following day. Una slept beside her that night, and next morning got Father Geddes from Farm Street to anoint her. John herself asked to see Micki Jacob and Una phoned her and she came:

> Una met me, and in the sitting-room of their suite told me what the trouble was. She was very brave, though I remember that her face was like chalk . . . John was in bed, immaculate as always, her hair shining and sleek, her pyjamas the last word in silk elegance . . . She looked tired, thinner, and fine-drawn, but she smiled, held out her hand and said, very cheerfully, 'This is a nice kind of ending, isn't it Mike?' . . . Just before I left she again gave me her hand, and said, 'Good-bye, Mike. If things – well, if they don't go quite as Una hopes they may, take care of her Mike, won't you?' . . . That was the last time I saw John.[13]

They went from the Ritz to Lady Carnarvon's Nursing Home in Hadley Wood, which must have reminded them of Chip Chase twenty-three years earlier. The same day Joll operated, performing colostomy and laparotomy at 9 p.m., but it was a palliative measure only. An abdominal tumour was removed, but John's condition had gone too far and was basically inoperable. For Una this realization opened up a 'bottomless pit of horror and despair.' Immediately after the operation John was given morphia, but in Una's absence it failed to take effect: 'before long I was told that she kept asking for me and would not rest unless I came to her. I think she would have slipped away that night if I had not sat beside her and held her hand till morning; every time she opened her eyes she . . . knew that I was there and drifted back to sleep. In the morning they told me that she would live.'[14]

But no one knew for how long, and Una tried desperately not to see the grim truth that the sand in the hourglass was rapidly running out.

They moved from the Carnarvon Home to one in Primrose Hill, but finding it gloomy soon went to the London Clinic to a suite of adjoining rooms divided only by sliding doors. John had 'another . . . terrible dilating operation later.' Una helped with the nursing and usually slept on the chair at John's bedside, although a divan was provided for her next door. Nurse Baldwin remained with them. On Sunday afternoons Micki Jacob used to go to the Clinic and Una would meet her downstairs to give her a progress report on John. During the six and a half months of life that remained to John, Una was with her night and day. It was what Una later called their 'Garden of Gethsemene', in which 'a strange and fulfilling happiness' blossomed for them. They were fully reconciled, talked, and became closer than they had been for many years. On June 21st, Una wrote: 'Today she said suddenly to me: "I want you, *you*, *you*; I want only you in all the world . . ."' and so often she has said, "You may flatter yourself, Lady Troubridge, I'm not sticking this for Evguenia, of whom I'm intensely fond, but who is on the very outskirts of my existence . . . It's only for your sake I'm sticking it, entirely for your sake . . ."'

And with even more conviction on September 1st: 'never in all our 28 years together has she given me such perfect assurance that of everyone on this earth I only am necessary to her. I alone have her entire love and devotion.' Una said afterwards: 'This strange joy and peace that had come to us in pain and sorrow was so precious that we could not bear to lose a moment of it.' They shared the new, deeper intimacy of imminent death.

Dr Armando Child told Una several merciful lies, notably that John might hang on for a long time, and that when the end finally came it would be painless. For a time, the extremity of her 'grief and fear' for John allowed her to believe these things. John's cheerfulness and sense of humour did not desert her, and nurses and doctors were equally amazed by her. Una recounts that Dr

Child asked her one day, 'Isn't she afraid? Surely she must be afraid
. . . everyone is with cancer . . .' Una's answer was unhesitating:
no, she had never shown any signs of fear, day or night, to Una's
knowledge. If John was ever afraid, she hid her fear from Una. The
courage of her death matched that of her life.

'It was not within the power of her love to spare me her
suffering, but at least she could spare me the knowledge of her
fears,' Una acknowledged later. Her own 'special anguish' at the
time was her powerlessness to alleviate John's sufferings. John's
faith was as impressive as her stoicism. She believed unequivocally
in a loving and merciful God, and was not afraid to meet Him
when the time came. Her Catholicism had been of the constant,
deep-growing type and it gave strength and solace in these last
grim months.

'She had no fear of death and no desire to live . . .' Una
realized. John had lost Souline, her creative powers had waned,
and she had nothing left to live for. She did not want to die in
hospital, and asked Una to move her from the London Clinic into
some accommodation of their own. Una accordingly found a
furnished flat, 502 Hood House, Dolphin Square, and moved John
there with Pippin the canary and Fido the poodle. 'Little B.' went
with them, and her sister who was also a nurse. Una wrote
poignantly in her Daybook from 'Beside my John's bed' in

> The flat to which I brought her by ambulance on August 3,
> 1943, expecting her to recover. I was so happy at securing the
> flat, which seemed ideal for illness and convalescence; I visual-
> ised her being wheeled about the garden before the warm
> weather went away . . . It is *September 29th* and she is dying. My
> John is dying. She is going where I shall not see her or touch her
> hand or hear her beloved voice again until God allows me to
> join her. The Doctor says she may go any day, or more likely
> any night, and my whole soul shrinks from what must
> come . . .

She shrank equally from the prospect of John's lingering 'for weeks
or months' in 'utter wretchedness'. She was being given pain-
killers freely but they were unable to alleviate 'incessant, devastat-

ing nausea, vomiting and retching'. John was patient under appalling suffering, courteous to her nurses, and solicitous of Una's tiredness, and 'several times she has cried at the thought of my loneliness when she is gone.' Una, as she sat by John's bed day after day, also thought of 'the future and its terrors . . . with ghastly clairvoyance of what the days and hours and minutes are going to be like without her constant and familiar sharing of them.' The Daybook served a therapeutic purpose: 'the waves of fear and anguish wash over me and I must write to keep my misery at bay.' But even in the midst of all this there was for Una, 'one consolation that will abide . . . and that is the certainty of the perfect union and love and understanding that is between us, that has swept away for ever any possible differences or disagreements, that has left us seeing each other in perfect love, face to face.'

Shortly before John's death she and Una discussed the possibility of post-mortem communication via a medium. John asked Una if she would attempt it, and Una answered that she would not as she disliked the processes associated with it, and hoped that her faith would be sufficient to sustain her in her loss. John answered that if the positions were reversed she would not seek to communicate either but rely upon the Communion of the Saints. After all their previous psychic experience they had both come to a final position of scepticism on the matter, preferring after all traditional Catholic consolation. Perhaps John was wandering in her mind when, 'as she lay in bed a few days before she died she said to me [Una] quietly: "Rufus [her long-dead Collie] is standing beside me with his head on my arm."'[15]

Sometimes when John was asleep, Una sat for a short time in the adjoining room with Andrea or Viola, who came daily to see her to ask after John. They meant well and tried to cheer her:

They are very kind, but what have I in common with them? They try to turn my eyes to a personal future. Viola tells me I shall live a long time . . . that I have Andrea and her child to live for. Why should I live for them? They have no need of me and are just externals to whom I feel a cool friendly affection. Andrea tells me it is a good thing that this bereavement is happening while I am still young enough to reconstruct my life

273

. . . none of them has ever begun to learn what love means; they do not conceive of it. Of a love that may begin in youth and health and physical . . . attraction, but that takes gradually unto itself roots deep in the soul until it becomes an integral and essential part of being . . . Until one's whole heart yearns and aches with pitiful adoration for the beloved body that is ageing, worn, battered, mutilated and humiliated . . . until the most menial of services become as the service of the altar of one's love . . .

Una could only watch and wait; pray, and write. She had 'kept most amazingly well' during John's six months of illness, having had little air or exercise, and barely a night's unbroken sleep. She transcended her own physical limitations in order to serve John's need, but hoped that the cumulative effects of those months would, after John's death, quickly bring her own 'release'.

Seven days before her death John made her last Will, revoking all previous ones. She had promised Souline 'ample provision after my death', and had probably divided her estate equally between Souline and Una in the previous, 1939 Will. Now that was all changed. Instead she appointed Una her sole Executrix, and in a Will of twelve lines only stated: 'I Devise and Bequeath to her all my property and estate both real and personal absolutely trusting her to make such provision for our friend Eugenie Souline as in her absolute discretion she may consider right knowing my wishes for the welfare of the said Eugenie Souline.' The signature was surprisingly firm, despite her weakness, and Dr Child and a nurse witnessed it.

Una knew its contents and John's wishes, and wrote: 'Evguenia, as I long hoped would be the case, is now for her merely a responsibility which she will not abrogate, the object of a mild benevolent and tolerant affection . . . I shall of course, and how gladly, do just exactly in every respect as John has instructed me.' A little later she added: 'Sometimes I wonder what will be Evguenia's future. John wants her taken care of and her earnings supplemented . . . but does not want her so provided for that she is idle, as this in the past only led her to degenerate into discontent, ill-temper and misery . . .'

274

John fluctuated between being almost her normal self – calm, collected, rational and relatively comfortable; and being racked with pain, then delirious with heroin. Una fluctuated between being unable to let John go, and praying for her release from 'a prolonged agony'. She had much time to think: 'The more I reflect the more I am inclined to believe that this cruel parasitic disease has had a hold on her for years . . .' she wrote, being unable to remember when John had last felt really well. John began to sleep more and more as the days passed, and relatively peacefully as she grew weaker in early October.

John died, clasping Una's hand, at 8.07 p.m. on October 7th, 1943, from carcinoma of the sigmoid colon. She left an estate of £118,015. 19s. After her death Una found that John had left her a letter. As this has never been found among Una's surviving papers it is impossible to know what it contained, but Una told her readers later that it ended with the words: 'and believe in my love, which is much, much stronger than mere death.'

# V

# 'Widowhood' (1943–63)

# 17

# *Utter Bereavement: Early Years (1943–53)*

Death is always a shock to the survivors however much it is expected and prepared for, and although John's was a merciful release from a life of increasing suffering, Una's sense of loss and desolation was immense. They had sat together in the shadow of impending death for months, and had found a new intimacy and peace; but Una had kept a tight rein on her feelings of grief, and her fears, in order not to upset John. She had tried to keep calm, even cheerful; and the cumulative strain of those final months left her both exhausted and numbed. Their 'long pilgrimage together' was over and she had to face the prospect of life alone. She had grown accustomed to a kind of loneliness during the last nine years, to the fact that John's passions lay elsewhere; but even this 'moral death' of their union had not been so complete, so final, as the physical death of one of its partners.

The news of John's death was not released immediately, but Micki Jacob arrived on October 8th, the day she was going overseas, anxious to see Una before she left. She wrote later:

Una . . . was calm, steadfast, and able to tell me all she could about John. I asked if I could see her, Una met my eyes very steadily, and said, 'No, Mike.' I suppose I was overwrought, and

> I admit that I behaved very badly. I said that she had no right
> to prevent my seeing John. She answered very quietly, and
> with a grave dignity which I can appreciate now – even if
> then I was blind to it, 'I have every right. Now, Mike, please
> go.'[1]

This is the only picture of Una recorded so near John's death and it
is a revealing one. She is collected, firm, and in full possession of
herself. Her refusal to allow Micki Jacob to view John's body may
have been because she wished her to remember how John had
been in life, but is more likely to have been her natural desire for
privacy, and her strong sense of having 'every right' to be alone
with her dead without the prying eyes of even the closest friends.
She was not only John's chief mourner but in a sense her 'widow'.
She forgave Micki Jacob and they were to remain friends.

Four days after John's death, on Monday October 11th, 1943, a
brief obituary notice appeared in the *Daily Telegraph and Morning
Post*, listing her publications but offering no commentary; but a
much longer, evaluative obituary was offered by *The Times* on the
same date. Her work, it stated, 'had real merit and originality', and
after a full *curriculum vitae* of her achievements, concluded that:
'Radclyffe Hall had abundant sympathy and pity, and views on her
controversial book [*The Well*] should not be allowed to rob her of
credit for her sterling literary qualities, her well-controlled
emotional pitch, her admirable prose style.'[2]

Other tributes were to follow; and in addition Una found herself
'besieged by the press', who wanted to know what John had been
writing at the time of her death, and whether it would be
published. John had, in fact, asked Una to destroy the book about
the shoemaker of Merano, which was only half-finished, and Una
had promised to do so. Not being her usual discreet self she
unwisely told the press the truth, and this unfortunately led to 'a
spate of press comment' and 'some tedious letters'[3] of protest from
the public. Burning the book regardless, Una argued that she 'had
no alternative to that of honourably carrying out her wishes', but
also stated later that 'the true reason' for its destruction was that
John had 'almost unconsciously allowed . . . her personal suffering and natural resentment' pertaining to someone who 'during

the closing years of her life' had 'very deeply hurt' her, to enter into the book. There is no doubt whatever that this person was Souline. Una recorded that John had said to her, when asking her to destroy it: 'It isn't forgiveness if one leaves a record that might be recognised and give pain . . .'[4]

Writing a week after John's death Una recalled it: 'At one moment it was my beloved . . . wasted, drawn, lividly pale and at times distorted – the next, a stranger lay there on the bed. Very handsome, very peaceful, very calm, but with scarcely a traceable resemblance to my John.' So strong was this sense of strangeness that when she had been laid out Una and the nurse 'stood looking down at her and I said: "Poor boy; he must have suffered a lot before he died . . ." It seemed a young airman or soldier who perhaps had died of wounds after much suffering . . . Not a trace of femininity; no one in their senses could have suspected that anything but a young man had died.'

After embalming and a Requiem Mass in Westminster Cathedral, Una had John interred at Highgate in the mausoleum where Ladye had lain since 1916. Even in death John had to be 'shared' with someone else. Una must have felt as John joined Ladye again, for the last time, excluded, condemned to life; and it emphasized that, at the end of everything, Una was one of a number of women who had been loved by John in the course of her life; whereas John was the only woman, and perhaps the only person apart from her father, whom Una ever really loved. Una's distinction in John's life was due to the duration and closeness of their relationship; she was the only woman to hold John's exclusive attentions for eighteen years, or to live with her for twenty-eight years. Even though John at times did not appreciate it, Una was also the only one to give her a wholehearted and indestructible love. On John's coffin plate, as if to emphasize this, Una had engraved: 'And if God choose I shall but love thee better after death.'

When she thought over 'those recent years which were leading me step by step to bereavement',[5] she felt bitterness at the various medical mismanagements which had both increased John's sufferings and delayed the correct diagnosis. Una also asked herself the inevitable question: 'For how long must I expect to have to survive her?' The very phrasing shows her reluctance; for although she believed in their ultimate reunion in the hereafter, she was anxious that it should not be too long delayed. Although for religious reasons she would never for a moment have considered suicide, she was equally determined not to strive to stay alive; and in war-time London fully expected not to do so. 'Why do any one of the thousand actions or think any one of the million thoughts that go to make a day, if she is not there as a companion, a mate, a raison d'être for everything?' Una also asked herself, and answered: 'Only because the very pain is – must be – God's will, can it be faced up to and endured.'

Una could not bear to remain in the Dolphin Square flat for long after John's death, and took a flat in a Tudor house in Lincoln's Inn, feeling 'more lonely than I had ever thought it possible to be'.[6] She made a vow to herself never deliberately to seek safety, and went about her daily life as usual, never once going into an air-raid shelter. On October 29th Una went to Harold Rubinstein's office and signed a new Will, anxious to take proper care of John's estate, particularly her copyrights. She appointed John Holroyd-Reece literary executor because of his 'flawless trustworthiness' and sympathy towards John and herself in the past. Afterwards she wrote, 'I can now die with a quiet mind . . .' On October 31st, a little over three weeks after John's death, Una wrote the first of many thousands of 'Letters to John': an extraordinary one-way correspondence written almost daily for nearly twenty years. This first letter began: 'My beloved; today is October 31st, vigil of All Saints day and a Sunday, and I awoke as usual, very early, to a world that for evermore lacks your dear physical presence . . .'

On November 19th probate was granted to Una, and this brought problems with it. Firstly, there was John's request to Una regarding Souline. Una wrote:

As to Evguenia, I have done my best in every way, and can only believe that John must approve. Within a few days of John's death she came to 'ask my advice': in other words to demand my (financial) sanction to her . . . taking a flat immediately, on that day, on a minimum of six months agreement, in London, with the winter ahead and the possibility that the Foreign Office might offer her a job in the country (in which event, she said, she would turn down the job!) I protested that she should not . . . sign any lease until she knew the situation and nature of her future employment . . . Result: violent fury on her part; she had expected I should be against her and much more better left unrecorded . . . She . . . is quite ungovernable and I cannot think it right that this should be allowed to start . . . a series of distressing and purposeless scenes in which I can only arouse a fury of resentment if I try to do as John wished in her regard . . . Already, before John's body was buried, this resentment burst forth in undisguised rage and vituperation . . .

As a consequence she accepted Holroyd-Reece's offer to be her deputy and spokesman in all financial and business transactions with Evguenia, but this arrangement, like his literary executorship, was not to last, and Una wrote of Souline: 'I am afraid that any subsequent amiability or appearance of friendliness can only be suspect as the outcome . . . of her learning definitely from John Reece that her advantage lies with keeping on good terms with me, since her allowance is and will always be, at my discretion.' This marked a new departure in the old problematic relationship: between a firm but forbearing Una carrying out John's real wishes, and an unreservedly mercenary Evguenia, appealing to John's imagined wishes.

The second problem was Marie Visetti, who was then living in the Viennese Hotel in Hove. As she had grown older she had become more difficult, demanding and self-pitying. John had made her an annual allowance but otherwise had little contact with her in later years. In a catalogue of complaints written to her cousin Jane Caruth in July 1943, Marie Visetti had grumbled: 'I am literally here alone, no friends – I do not even know where Marguerite is . . . Naturally if you don't care, this is all right . . . I am debarred any, in fact every pleasure . . .' Six days after John's death she wrote again enclosing a cutting from the *Telegraph*: 'You will see by the enclosed that Marguerite is dead . . . I am worried about what she has done – this was her last chance to give me back what she was using that belonged to me . . . £2,000 . . . that I had

283

given up to secure her inheritance . . . but she *never did* . . . She allows me £200 a year . . . I will . . . be a beggar – you can imagine the anxiety I am suffering . . . it has made me . . . ill.' This letter, so self-centred, mercenary, and utterly lacking in any grief for the death of a daughter, is typical of the woman; yet, almost to justify herself, as much as to attack Una, she complained that: 'the Troubridge woman . . . had never even let me know she was ill – but how she dared to show me such disregard – I cannot think . . .' It is not difficult to see why.

Determined to look after her own interests and claim what she could, she went to see her bank manager and asked him to look into it. On November 10th she wrote again to Jane Caruth: '. . . the answer came this morning . . . Troubridge is the Sole Executrix and my name is not in the Will – what will become of me I cannot think . . .' By February of 1944, through her solicitors, Una had agreed to continue Marie Visetti's allowance, in return for her assistance with material relating to the early years of John's life for a projected biography, and a guarantee that she would never herself write or assist in the writing of anything detrimental to John. This was not at all unreasonable in the circumstances, but Marie Visetti was never satisfied, and told Jane Caruth: '. . . of course this harsh treatment my daughter has seen fit to make me suffer, has had a very detrimental effect on my health . . . the least she could have done was to leave me a decent income in her Will . . .'[7]

John and Jeanne Holroyd-Reece asked Una to live with them as a member of their household, and she considered doing so. After making her Will at the end of 1943, leaving him her diaries and appointing him her literary executor, it soon transpired that his only interest was to gain control of her money, and after an explosive argument with him she revoked her Will and asked Harold Rubinstein to try to find a trustworthy replacement to be her literary executor. It was John's literary property that she was determined to protect by placing it in safe hands. Early in 1944, with Wills and death still on her mind, Una sent Harold Rubinstein, her solicitor, a letter containing burial instructions, beginning:

Dear Harold,
   As you will in the event of my death be called upon to dispose of my body, should there remain (which in these days is definitely doubtful) any body to dispose of, I am writing you my wishes in the matter which I beg you to carry out as far as may be possible . . .

There followed details of the clothes and jewellery in which she wished to be buried after being embalmed, then:

On the Coffin Plate I want the following inscription:
   Una Vincenzo Troubridge,
   The Friend of Radclyffe Hall:
   Arrive at last the blessed goal,
   When He that died in Holy Land
   Would reach us out the shining hand,
   And take us as a single soul.

After this she specified:

I want to be buried in the Catacomb Chamber at Highgate Cemetery that already holds John's body; if necessary another shelf must be put in for the purpose, and I want the following inscription placed upon the front of the entrance on the side opposite to that which records John's burial:
   Una Vincenzo Troubridge,
   the friend of
   Radclyffe Hall,
   with whom she shared a home for nearly
   twenty-nine years. She survived her (years,
   months inserted here) and died
   (Date inserted here)
            . . . . . . . .

Referring to this letter in 'Letters to John' Una remarked: 'I think that will do very well, stating for the world the length and fidelity of our devotion . . . I feel I must leave an unequivocal record of our life and love, just as The Ladies [i.e. of Llangollen] did, to cheer and encourage those who come after us . . .'
   Ironically, in the event, this envelope addressed to Harold

'*Widowhood*' (1943–63)

Rubinstein and marked 'To be opened immediately after my death and prior to my burial', was only found after her death and burial in Rome.

Una, writing her 'Letters to John', described her days, her thoughts, her longings. They often open 'My darling', or 'My beloved', and end 'Goodnight my heart's love. Your Una,' or 'Another day nearer our meeting, my very dear.' Her sense of John's continued proximity was often very strong, as on November 3rd, 1943: 'My sweet. Here we are, alone together in the flat and I can talk to you in peace. Indeed I very often do talk out loud to you and there being . . . no one to hear me but you, what matter!'

During packing and unpacking she threw out many old papers, including her correspondence with Troubridge during their years of separation, and tried to put her house in order. She told John: 'I am well, and quite hungry, and I do sleep sometimes, but I am *broken*, as maimed as if I were helplessly crippled, without you, and there it is . . .'

She spent Boxing Day that year with Andrea and her grandson Nicholas, whom she described as a 'hooligan and most unattractive child'. His manners offended her old-world sense of what was correct: 'He does not say how do you do, or thank you for presents. He interrupts everything and everyone all the time, walks round the room during the meal . . . an altogether odious brat . . .' She was in no danger of suddenly developing into a doting grandmother in her bereavement.

On December 31st, 1943 she wrote poignantly to John: '. . . but oh, if I could take your dear familiar hand in mine and your head on my shoulder and feel your hair under my lips . . . dear human eyes and hands and lips . . .' There would be no more New Years for them to see in together.

Early in 1944 Una's initial busyness after John's death, which had been something of a therapeutic distraction, eased off, and she began to experience 'a persistent "spiritual dryness" that admits of no consolation . . . that gives me no blessed hours of spiritual consolation,' and she told John, 'I just plod through my prayers and masses . . . I feel no nearness to Our Lady; no consciousness of you being near me. It is all just sheer dull desolation . . . with recurrent waves of unendurable misery. I do *not* ask for death. I told Our Lord I wouldn't; that I would face twenty years of life if you might have a peaceful release . . .'

This was to be strangely prophetic, as she was to survive John by ten days short of twenty years.

Two vignettes of Una at this time survive from friends who knew her moderately well, although both men confessed to preferring 'Johnny'. The first is from John Wyse, their old actor friend: 'The last time I saw Una was about a year after Johnny's death. She came to tea and I was struck by the extraordinary sadness about her. She had always seemed to me so . . . superficial, albeit entertaining and highly intelligent. But here was a quite different person.'

The second is from Felix Hope-Nicholson, Jacqueline Hope's son, who met her through his mother: 'After John died Una used to often arrive at More House after breakfast and stay for lunch, tea and dinner – talking about herself and her grief. She adored Johnny and was grief-stricken after her death. My family were good to her . . .'

Una felt the need both to talk about and grieve for John in the company of sympathetic people who had known her, unable to bear the burden of her loss entirely alone. There had been many letters of condolence, but the war had scattered people and few good friends were at hand. There were many places and things to bring back memories: 'At Harrods in the late spring of that year [i.e. 1944] I was making my way to the nearest exit, having failed to obtain any one of the items on my household shopping list. . .'[8] she wrote, when she noticed oysters for sale at the then expensive price of 18s. a dozen. A flood of memories returned to her, particularly of going to Cheeseman's cramped little oyster shop in Brighton with John in the 1920s. . . Harrods had been so much a part of their lives that it must often have brought back many memories.

During that summer, at 8 o'clock one Sunday morning, Una had one of her many near-misses when a V1 flying bomb fell in Chancery Lane under the windows of her flat. A glass partition

wall was smashed and a 'jagged spearhead of plate glass some
fifteen inches in length' cut into her pillow, which she had left
only minutes before to make a cup of tea. 'An amiable member of
the ARP, who had promptly invaded the house, showed it to me
with a grim smile, remarking: "Might of cut yer 'ead orf!"'[9] Una
recorded much later. Almost against her will she was to survive.
On September 1st, 1944 Una wrote to John:

> as usual awoke to my loneliness and dreary thoughts at 6.30 . . .
> The early mornings are just damnable with their daily task of
> facing up to emptiness . . . But I would not have it otherwise. I
> would no more wish to be 'healed' of my love and sorrow and
> longing than St. Francis wished to be 'healed' of his Stigmata
> . . . for what is my sorrow but the stigmata of a great love whose
> pain is as much a privilege as its joys? . . . I would not become a
> lesser thing taking ignoble relief in forgetfulness . . .

On September 7th she remarked upon 'This strange feeling of
belonging to nobody . . .' In this same year, 1944, Harold
Rubinstein introduced her to Horatio Lovat Dickson, a publisher
who worked for Macmillan's, as a possible replacement literary
executor for Holroyd-Reece. They met for lunch. His description
of Una's appearance at this time is interesting: '. . . a thin slip of
an elderly woman with short-cut grey hair, wearing flat-heeled
shoes . . . she habitually wore a beret[10] . . . and underneath this
unbecoming pancake of a hat her small face peered out full of
determination.'[11] Her eyes were a 'faded blue', but her voice struck
him as unexpectedly rich, warm and vibrant. He perhaps did not
know that it had been well-trained. It was to be a significant
meeting. Una liked him and was prepared to trust him with John's
works and to leave him their copyrights, so that on her own death
he would inherit a valuable literary property, on condition that he
never allowed any bowdlerized or cheaply sensational edition of
John's works to appear, or anything which would be detrimental to
her as a writer. Una was relieved to have solved finally one of the
problems that had been uppermost in her mind since John's death.
After this meeting they corresponded, and Una told John in
October: 'Rache [Horatio's nickname] writes that I seemed too full

of vitality and "joie de vivre" . . . Poor lad; does he think real, abiding sorrow goes around in restaurants displaying itself with a pale, brave smile? And all the time my only thought was to weigh him up as to his value and capacities as the servant of your work . . .'

Late in 1944 Una gave up the Lincoln's Inn flat and went to stay temporarily with one of their old invert friends, Ethel. This caused her some anxiety, as she explained to John:

> I am just a little troubled, darling, lest anyone spiteful may say that in staying here with Ethel I have taken on a love affair . . . I don't *really* think they can . . . She is 60 and I am nearly 58; . . . I am elderly, gaunt, with neither make up nor lipstick, neat but now *very* plain with . . . a lined, drawn face, my hair unbecomingly short, always a collar and tie that never really became me and if I am not bare-headed, your beret in which Viola, Minna, Andrea and Nanny Peeke have all protested that I look like hell!

This is an interesting self-portrait, not unlike Lovat Dickson's, but showing an unusual degree of humorous detachment, and revealing that she had taken to wearing John's clothes. She also wore much of John's jewellery, especially the chain bracelet which Ladye had given to John and which John had worn until she died.

Early in 1945 Una moved to a small flat in Chelsea Cloisters, perhaps partly to facilitate her increasingly frequent visits to More House. There were a number of paying guests living at More House at the time, and one of these, Martin Bretherton, remembers: 'Una used to come to lunch every Sunday at Tite Street. I was very fond of Una.'

Another memory of this time is given by Mrs Marie-Jacqueline Lancaster (née Hope-Nicholson), Felix's sister and Jacqueline's daughter:

> I got to know her during the last war and in the late 1940's . . . when I became very fond of her. I met Johnny Radclyffe Hall only once that I remember, between 1940–42, when I was staying at my mother's home in Tite Street. I was about 18 and

they came to tea and I was fascinated but a bit nervous of meeting them. Una was charming and put everyone at ease . . . After Johnny died . . . Una would often spend Sunday afternoons with my mother. She adored children, especially my two daughters, and would knit them little socks of a special white silky thread. It seemed so out of character but she was very quick and efficient at it. She always looked smart and impeccable, getting her slightly severe blouses with high tied ends round the neck from that special shop in Knightsbridge . . . opposite the new Berkeley Hotel. I believe she has been rather under-rated in the existing biographies of her circle . . . all the 'stuffy' Troubridges were very anti-Una of course . . .

Una quickly discovered that, having sorted out all the concerns that immediately followed John's death, there was a void to fill: '. . . life is so *dull* without her,' Una wrote, 'I . . . lost my occupation as well as my infinitely beloved companion . . .'[12] In order to fill in 'those hours of leisure that are now only too often mine', she took up again her old habit of avid letter-writing: to close relations, and friends such as Edy Craig, Micki Jacob, Marjorie Hancock at Lynton, Romaine Brooks, Mother Mary Clare, Abbess of the Poor Clare Convent at Lynton, Lovat Dickson, Harold Rubinstein, and also Natalie Barney, with whom she was to keep up a correspondence which covered a period of forty years. With the help of photographs and information about John's childhood supplied by a belligerent Marie Visetti, Una set about writing a biography of John, in the form of a long letter 'to those who will read it'. She seems to have written it very hurriedly between February 19th and March 18th, 1945, fearing that if she did not commit what she knew to paper it would die with her. Despite her avowed intention in the Foreword to 'tell the truth, the whole truth, and nothing but the truth', the book *is* both 'expurgated' and 'idealised', and in a court of law some of her statements and omissions would amount to perjury! She should perhaps have said instead, as her grandfather Sir Henry Taylor did in his *Autobiography*: '. . . it has been no part of my design to speak the whole truth.' Una's *Life and Death of Radclyffe Hall* cannot be taken as either strictly accurate or objective: it is a public relations exercise on John's behalf, and often distorts, minimizes, or omits things in order to show John in the best possible light. This is hardly surprising in the circumstances: what 'wife' could write of her 'husband' without being frequently partisan and subjective? Una was particularly reticent about their private life, using euphemisms such as 'made common cause' (for living together) and 'our conviviality' (reason for sharing a bedroom). Never once does she use the word 'love' of their relationship, but 'companionship', 'friendship', or occasionally 'our union'. It meanders confusingly, showing little concern for accurate dating, but in fairness some licence must be granted in a 'letter'. What is never in any doubt is Una's partisan attitude to her subject, which any discerning reader will find hard to take.

Una herself never thought that she had written a perfect book, although it must have had therapeutic value at the time. She hoped that one day John's life would be professionally written by someone else, and accordingly refrained from publishing. There was also an even more pertinent reason for withholding the book: certain people, then still alive, notably Jane Caruth, Marie Visetti and Souline, were spoken of in terms that could be construed as libellous. Una had no wish to spend John's money defending lawsuits or paying compensation to such people. As John went into eclipse as a writer and most of her books went out of print, no one came forward to write about her until after Una's death.

Although Una had lost 'the be-all and end-all' of her life, and to some extent her purpose in living, life had to go on and it was not in Una's nature to give up when things became difficult. She decided to make the best of it and to keep busy. Relations with Andrea had been renewed in John's lifetime, and Una saw much of her in London during and after the war, and said in 1944 that Andrea had 'grown into an admirable, unselfish, generous woman'. In 1945 Andrea was a Talks Producer with the BBC. Mrs Joyce Mumford, who worked at the time as Relief Secretary in the Duty Room at Broadcasting House, remembers Andrea: 'Occasionally we both worked late . . . and stayed in the overnight accommodation at Egerton House, next to Broadcasting House, when she had the bunk above mine. I remember her as short, dark, plumpish, with a pleasant manner . . .'

She had mellowed, and like Una had a great affection for Jacqueline Hope and her daughter Marie-Jacqueline Lancaster, who remembers: 'She was charming and after she was grown-up grew to be very fond of Una . . .' They sometimes met at Tite Street, or entertained each other at their respective homes, and Una was not surprised to discover that Andrea was divorcing Toby Warren.

Una's 'widowhood' has surprising parallels with Alice B. Toklas's. Gertrude Stein died in 1946 after living with Alice B. Toklas for forty years. Alice and Una had taken similar supporting roles in relation to female 'husbands' who were writers, both of whom had coincidentally died of cancer of the bowel, leaving their 'widows' a protracted widowhood: twenty years in Una's case, and twenty-one in Alice's. Una and Alice suffered the same kind of loneliness: 'Nothing at all is the same . . .' Alice said, and Una would have agreed. Both of them still needed to feel needed, and were to encourage other, younger artists; writers in Alice's case, such as Otto Friedrich, and one particular singer in Una's case. Both Una and Alice appeared to have taken auxiliary roles during the beloved's lifetime, but showed their strength and independence, which had always been there, afterwards. Alice was very concerned about the republication of Gertrude's books and the preservation of her memory and literary reputation, just as Una was about John's. Alice hated living on without Gertrude, as Una did without John. One major difference was that Alice was ultimately buried beside Gertrude, whereas Una remains in Rome and John at Highgate. A second difference was that Alice *was* approached by biographers wanting to write a life of Gertrude, but she was suspicious of them and unco-operative! How co-operative Una would have been to a potential biographer of John remains uncertain, but at least theoretically she was hoping for just such an approach as Alice received.

On August 12th, 1945, John's birthday, Una wrote, 'The six hundred and fifty sixth of these letters that no one on earth will ever read . . .' but explained her motives for writing them: '. . . they have helped me to keep sane in my loneliness and have pitifully provided some poor outlet for the endless exchange of thoughts and ideas that were an essential part of our lives for so many years.'

On November 19th, after dining with Andrea, Una wrote to John: 'Going on for midnight and I am sleepy although I slept for an hour this afternoon. Result perhaps of Andrea's really sumptuous meal of which I will tell you tomorrow my dearest dear. Goodnight and be near me, please . . .'

In the spring of 1946 Una left London on an extended visit to Edward Marcus Worsley (younger brother of the Baronet Sir William) and his wife Joyce at their home, Cawton Hall, Hovingham, Yorkshire. She was trying to decide her future, and had time to spare. Writing to Jacqueline Hope on May 16th, she explained:

I have practically decided against returning to Italy and I want to discuss with my lawyers and shipping agents whether it is possible, by our furnishing the necessary legal documents, for them to claim John's property and mine on my behalf in Florence without my going there and ship it to England. The more I reflect upon the idea of going to Italy the more I funk it. Not only does it demand an energy and enterprise that are not now in me and never will be again: to 'break in' a new life in an entirely altered foreign country, take a flat or house, manage servants etc . . . would all seem quite motiveless without John: a travesty of our life together, a kind of trying for happiness that is fatal, and the thought of walking alone the familiar streets . . . and sitting alone in the familiar cafés is more than I can endure . . .

There is a certain heartfelt poignancy about this letter, revealed not just in what she says but in its very syntax: an artless flowing-on so untypical of Una. She had known Jacqueline since before her marriage to Troubridge, and hid nothing from her.

In July she gave the 'Relic of the True Cross' given her by the Smallhythe trio some years earlier, and subsequently authenticated by the Church, to Father Marcus at nearby Ampleforth, 'in memory of John'. She wrote to Jacqueline on July 24th describing how 'at 5 pm it was publicly venerated by Monks and 100 little boys of 7–12 years old – a *lovely* ceremony and I felt John so near that I was almost happy! . . .'

She intended to stay at Cawton Hall until October, then to have a few days in London on her way to Lynton. One reason for her extended stay was confided to Jacqueline five days later, on the 29th: '*Between ourselves*, the Home Secretary . . . is expected to come on an inspection of the local Civil Defence school of which my host is a senior officer and *if* he comes it may just conceivably be possible for me to speak to him personally anent the republication of 'The Well', so I shall hang on for some time anyway, in the hope . . .' When the visit took place she handed Home Secretary Chuter Ede a copy of *The Well* with a note. Later he wrote explaining that he had 'no authority to determine' a book's obscenity or otherwise, as this devolved upon the courts; but that any publisher reprinting *The Well* would 'do so at the risk of proceedings'. Nevertheless, she was to see the book republished three years later without any official opposition. Times had changed.

On January 30th, 1947, after Una had returned to Lynton, her mother Minna died at the age of eighty-six, at the Mount Carmel Nursing Home in Chalfont St Peter. Her Will, like Ladye's, was idiosyncratic: she asked to be cremated and that her funeral be 'as inexpensive as possible', and directed that 'no one should wear mourning for me'. Personal and household items were to be divided equally between Una and Viola, but her plate and her shop she left to her grandson Oliver Woods. J. L. Garvin, Viola's husband, was also to die that year.

On December 27th, 1947 Una's letter to John concluded: 'Goodnight my very dear; I am in bed and it is just past midnight, so another day is over. Four more days and it will be 1948 – a million years since 1943 when you were here – but suffering, my beloved, and now you suffer no more . . .'

Una visited friends in London and elsewhere, and wrote many letters, but was essentially restless and unsettled, as she exclaimed to John: 'Oh, this eternal restlessness, my dearest, that makes me neither want to go out nor stay at home, neither read nor write, play nor work, see people nor remain alone . . .' Lynton was as full of memories as Florence would be, perhaps more so due to their nearness in time. John's last days there would always haunt her, yet she was loath to uproot totally from places she knew. At times they were almost comforting.

On October 4th, 1948, Andrea, at thirty-seven, married Brigadier Douglas John Tulloch Turnbull, aged forty-six, in Kensington Registry Office. The witnesses were her cousins Oliver Woods and St Vincent Troubridge, and Una did not attend. This marriage was to be happier than her first one. 'Bull' Turnbull was at the time Military Attaché to the Emperor of Abyssinia, who became very fond of Andrea, bestowing gifts on her: so much so that their 'great friendship' embarrassed the Foreign Office, who removed 'Bull' and sent him to Ethiopia for two years. Later that same year, on November 28th, to Una's great delight, a selection of John's poems in English and Italian was published in Milan.

At last, early in 1949, nearly six years after John's death, Una found the 'energy and enterprise' to return to Florence. She was sixty-two and had been away from Italy for almost ten years, but what she had written about her Italian friends in 1945 was still true: 'I still feel that wherever they may be will be the nearest thing to home that I can expect to find on this earth.'[13]

That same year her old friend Natalie Barney, then over seventy, returned to her house in Rue Jacob, after almost as great an absence as Una's from Florence, and re-opened her salon on Friday afternoons to a new generation of notabilities, including Truman Capote, and some of the old survivors such as Alice B. Toklas. Natalie was to outlive everybody and eventually die at the age of ninety-five in 1972. Romaine lived in Nice, visiting Paris and Natalie every spring, then going on to summer in Fiesole, where she must often have seen Una.

There were many friends, both English and Italian, to welcome Una back to Florence. 'They are all out to be cordial and welcoming and I am warmly grateful,' she wrote to John. She had her furniture removed from storage and found a small flat at the Palazzo Guicciardini, 15 Via Guicciardini, owned by Paolo and

Augusta Guicciardini. Though impoverished enough to have to
rent out their house in apartments, they still had a fine galleried
library and many treasures, which Una admired when asked to tea
with them. There was much to do sorting things out and putting
them to rights, but she felt that she had come home. Florence was
the place, of all others, that she had always loved. She soon settled
herself into a routine of life with a resident maid, Prinetta, who
also did the cooking. She got up early every day and went fasting to
Mass, eating only two small meals a day. She walked more than in
the past, slept only five or six hours a night, drank very little, but
started to put on weight and had to have her clothes altered. She
rarely refused invitations, and in her turn took friends out to
supper, particularly Nino and Sandra Tealdi. When at home she
lived quietly, writing letters, reading, and listening to the radio,
especially opera. 'God knows I am grateful to the radio; I who used
to wonder why people listened to it,' she told John. She put up her
pictures: the Buchel portrait of John, pictures of Ladye and 'il
Commandante' (D'Annunzio), old masters she had collected; and
her many books, and wrote in her daily letter to John: 'at last I
have all your things round me . . .' and: 'So we are in our own and
I think final earthly home at last. Be very near to me beloved, if
you can . . .'

Una had not been back there long before she was asked to
translate the 'Don Camillo' stories of Guareschi into English, and
agreed readily. Work was to be one of her weapons against a 'well
of loneliness'. On April 30th she wrote to the BBC offering to
translate the play *Il Dio Vivente*, although Andrea had resigned
from the BBC at the end of 1948.

Felix Hope-Nicholson remembers how he went to Greece for a
year in 1949, when it was only possible to take £25 out of the
country. Almost inevitably he ran out of money, and managed to
obtain a job for a few months in order to get himself to Rome. On
arrival he wrote to Una in Florence to ask her to lend him some
money, and was surprised to receive an express letter back from
her saying, 'I make it a rule never to lend money. I suggest you get
back into the sterling area as soon as possible.' This made him
conclude that Una was not only 'tough' but 'mean'. What he
perhaps understandably failed to appreciate was the nature of her

attitude towards money. 'Neither a borrower nor a lender be' was heavily ingrained in her, and was an attitude of great carefulness left over from the straitened circumstances of her childhood. 'I have passed through all the vicissitudes that range from actual poverty to financial ease,' she wrote, but added, 'I have never yet saved money and I have never been in debt.'[14]

Her two extravagances had been buying books and clothes, and during John's lifetime, expensive presents for her.

In 1950, when Una had been back in Italy for over a year, Jacqueline Hope, who was visiting Rome, spent a day with her. As well as her translating Una was rediscovering her interest in art, and buying pictures, particularly Stuart portraits. Jacqueline was an expert on seventeenth-century paintings, and they spent time discussing and viewing these, enjoying each other's company. It was the last time they were to meet.

Vita Sackville-West was also in Florence in 1950, where she met Philippe Jullian to discuss a biography of Violet Trefusis, but it seems unlikely that Una met her other than by accident, as they had never been in the same 'set', despite Vita's willingness to speak on behalf of *The Well* at its trial twenty-two years earlier. Vita, Violet, and Virginia Woolf had all been 'closet' inverts, lacking the courage and honesty of Una and John.

Una kept busy, 'leading my own life in my own way' regardless of convention or appearances, often wearing 'an old sweater and a pair of old breeches'[15] when she felt like it, as in the photograph taken at Levanto. In addition to art and translating, Una's deep love and understanding of music, particularly opera, stood her in good stead. She had long ceased regretting her own, and took pleasure in a fine voice, especially if combined with stage presence. She was both appreciative and discerning as an opera-goer. She also had, as Micki Jacob testified, 'a gift for friendship, real loyal, unselfish friendship . . .'[16] which also stood her in good stead.

At this time Una was receiving warm, affectionate letters from Andrea, written from the headquarters of the British Military Mission to Ethiopia, where 'Bull' Turnbull had been sent. Usually these letters ended, 'Love and bless you, darling, Andrea.' Their relationship had improved with the years. Letters from Evguenia, usually asking for extra financial help above the continued allowance and Una's supplementary 'gifts' three times a year, were not so pleasant. Evguenia, after a brief spell in the United States Army, had hastily married a Russian called Vladimir Makaroff, who worked in Wall's meat factory, while she worked at the BBC. They were living in a flat in Hampstead in 1950, when Evguenia wrote asking Una to 'lend' her £3,000 with which to buy a boarding house as 'security for the future' as 'the thought of growing old without any security . . . is frightening . . .' She was forty-six at the time, and both she and her husband were in full employment. Una declined to assist over and above her existing commitment to Evguenia, seeing in this scheme another non-starter like the shop in Paris, or 'studying' at Oxford. Evguenia pleaded that 'You seem to disregard the fact that she [John] in her lifetime was inordinately attached to me, and promised me more than once that I shall be well provided for after her death.'

This had been true in the early days, but she knew full well the terms of John's last Will and its intentions, which Una had carried out with fairness and indeed generosity. John had spoiled her, 'in various little ways . . . because she knew I was pure, innocent, and straightforward,' she argued, adding that, 'John if she were alive would have come to my rescue.' She traded on the situation and twisted the facts as much as she could, even telling Una that 'my life with my husband is far from harmonious.' Una replied:

> I have studied your two letters carefully. I shall not attempt to deal with . . . your enumeration of promises that John never made . . . But as regards your renewed request that I should enable you with use of my capital to buy a house and launch a boarding establishment, I will remind you that in all the nine years that you were associated with us John always flatly refused to finance any of your impractical plans in which – knowing your nature – she had no confidence at all. She helped you, out of her affection and compassion, by giving you an allowance yearly, and this I have continued to do since her death . . . adding considerable cheques every year as presents . . .

Whilst claiming poverty, Evguenia was careful not to reveal either her own or her husband's income, despite Una's inquiries. Later she tried to persuade Una to pay off a large overdraft. Una replied:

> I must say I do wish you would drop this line of sentimental appeal to my emotions: there is really nothing at all to touch anyone's heart in the fact that you have deliberately tried to impose upon me liabilities which you incurred not only without my knowledge but in spite of my clearly writing you that I would not be responsible for anything of the kind. Nor would such a situation have appealed to John, who had the strictest notions of integrity . . . I have already made you a payment of £150 this year in addition to your regular allowance . . .

Nevertheless Una made a further 'extraordinary' payment of £150, but had to inform the bank that she would not be responsible for any further overdrafts of Mrs Makaroff's.

Some months later history repeated itself, and Una replied:

> My Dear Evguenia,
> Your letter just received has completely amazed me. How in the world could you bring yourself to do anything so dishonest as to incur a short time debt of nearly £500 when you had no funds to meet it . . . Moreover, honestly, it offends me that you should enlist John's memory in sentimental implications that she would approve of your incurring debts and would wish me to meet them . . . you have done a deliberately dishonest thing, trading consciously upon the vague hope that when faced with an emergency, I would 'pay up'. And this after in addition to your allowance, I had in the . . . last year made you very considerable presents of money.

This kind of situation was to recur over the years, Evguenia never satisfied and trying various wiles to obtain more from Una than John had intended her to have. Una resisted the more outrageous demands, but remained generous beyond the call of duty to John's wishes.

In the spring of 1951 despite feeling 'disinclined for life', Una went to hear her 'most beloved of all operas', *Parsifal*, performed at La Scala, Milan. It lasted from 8 p.m. to 1 a.m. with two short intervals. She had booked to hear every performance, and to stay in a hotel near the opera house. Apparently by chance, she met in the same hotel, the Regina, the bass singer Nicola Rossi-Lemeni. She had first heard him on the radio, singing in Verdi's *Requiem* on the fiftieth anniversary of the composer's death, and had been enchanted by his voice. It was one of those meetings which was to be decisive and fruitful for both parties.

Nicola Rossi-Lemeni was at that time aged thirty-one, having been born in Istanbul in 1920, of an Italian father and a Russian mother. He had at first studied law, then devoted himself to music from 1943, making his operatic debut in 1946 as Philip II in *Don Carlos* in Trieste. He had then been immediately engaged by La Scala, and was at the beginning of a very distinguished career when Una met him. She was impressed by the 'uniquely beautiful'[17] quality of his voice, his dynamism, and his dedication to his art.

Una was a 'striking-looking woman', he told me, which is not surprising as she noted in her daily letter to John that she 'went in my new tweed and your evening cap – silk shirt and bow tie . . .' He was curious and, after learning who she was, was introduced to her. He was as impressed by Una's musical understanding and critical faculties as she with his voice, and within five days of that first meeting Una was helping in the preparation of a libretto for the Italian production of Grunsberg's setting of Eugene O'Neill's *The Emperor Jones*. Una's abiding interest in opera was to blossom anew, and she was always at her happiest in the company of creative artists, whether in art, music or literature. She always believed herself to possess 'no inventive faculty' (which was untrue) but her interest and encouragement was a stimulus to those who manifestly did have it, which pleased her.

On March 30th Una told John: 'Today Nicola Rossi-Lemeni and his wife are dining with me at a restaurant and I hope I may get a chance of a rehearsal.' She did, and stayed on in Milan since 'for anyone of my tastes, rehearsals at the Scala with the finest living bass are not to be missed.'

She described Rossi-Lemeni as: 'a simple genial giant with vast shoulders and diaphragm, already getting a bit ample, as do all singers!' He sent her records, and much mutual wining and dining took place. 'Both of them very friendly, and . . . taking me to the rehearsals on Friday and Saturday . . .' she noted. She met his agent and looked at 'all his photographs and notices and I chose two photographs . . .'

This was not just the kindness of a young artist towards an interesting elderly 'fan' but the beginning of a genuine, reciprocal friendship. The *Emperor Jones* libretto took several weeks: 'we are now at Christian names and get on very well together.' She dined with the Rossi-Lemenis when their cousins came, and also met all the production staff at La Scala; and sat with his wife in her box during his performances, and often dined with them both afterwards. Yet despite all this, she could still write to John in July: 'Oh my dear, dear darling: everyone is so dreary compared to you . . . but it *is* better . . . among musical and theatre folk . . . something to *do* when the devil of depression and restlessness possesses one . . .'

She stayed in Milan attending performances, and telling John: 'Nicola sang better than ever; he was stupendous – *and* his acting!' until the Rossi-Lemenis left Milan for a trip to Brazil. She would not see them again until they opened in Rome in December.

Una was to travel extensively in following Rossi-Lemeni's career, hearing opera in Rome, Milan, Venice, Verona, and in many parts of Europe and America. It was to lead her to many unexpected places, and she rarely missed any of his many performances. She attended his American début in San Francisco as Boris Godunov in 1952, when the critics compared him to Chaliapin; and his début at the Metropolitan Opera House in New York in 1953, in *Faust*, *Don Giovanni* and *Boris Godunov*. Through him she was to meet many opera managers and composers, Tullio Serafin, Pizzetti and Renzo Rossellini, amongst others; and she was also to be involved in the making of long-playing operatic records. Rossi-Lemeni was to become, in Una's own words: '. . . the dearest of my friends and his career the prevailing interest of my old age.'[18]

# 18

# *The Way of Loneliness: Later Years (1954–62)*

Ten years on from her sense of 'utter bereavement' after John's death, Una had returned to Florence and made a new life for herself, taking up again with old friends, making new ones, and developing her interests. She was happy to join the ranks of foreign nationals who made their home in Italy, as she had always loved it and there was little to keep her in England. Her only post-1949 visit to England occurred in January 1953 when she came over to hear Rossi-Lemeni sing Boris Godunov at Covent Garden. There were decreasingly few people to see even though she still kept in touch with many if only by Christmas card.

Yet despite all this activity – itself a safeguard against despair – she still trod 'the way of loneliness', and knew that refined sense of irreplaceable loss which is reserved for widows who are not 'merry' and never remarry. In 1951 Una's maid Prinetta had left her and she engaged Nada Vadi, a simple peasant girl who was to stay with her for the remaining twelve years of her life. She knew little and Una taught her everything, including how to cook, but she was to prove as invaluable as had Mabel Bourne in Rye.

Una's life when she was at home consisted of modestly entertaining and being entertained by friends; translating, writing letters to the living and to John; keeping abreast of contemporary fiction; the radio and cinema. Her pleasures when away from home were centred in art and music, the twin interests of her youth, so that in a sense she had come full circle. She had long ceased to have any personal ambitions in either, but was keen to use her knowledge to help others. Rossi-Lemeni opened the Chicago Lyric Opera's first season in 1954 with *Don Giovanni*, and Una was there in her role of enthusiastic supporter. Later he was frequently to partner Maria Callas[1] and to record several operas with her,[2] to Una's delight.

Unexpectedly, after a gap of forty-one years, Una's plaster cast of her marble bust of Nijinsky was found in a second-hand shop in Cecil Court, St Martin's Lane, by Lydia Sokolova, an ex-ballet dancer, who recognized both its subject and sculptor. Subsequently it was put on display in the Diaghilev Exhibition in London, between October 1954 and January 1955. Una was informed of this, and after the exhibition bronzes of the plaster were cast, one of which now resides in the Dance Centre in New York. Madam Sokolova kept the plaster cast until she died, bequeathing it to Richard Buckle, who later gave it to the Theatre Museum[3] where it can still be seen. Una's life in the years since its sculpting had changed out of all recognition, as had the world itself, and it must have seemed strange to her to be reminded of it. It is one of her finer works, and stands as a monument to the sculptor she might have become, in different circumstances.

Also in 1954, as if to emphasize the shifting sands of time, her old friends Colette and Lily (Countess) Clermont-Tonnerre both died. She was beginning to have the daunting experience of outliving many of her friends and contemporaries. She had not courted life after John's death, and at times it seemed a heavy burden; but she mostly accepted it with a good grace and tried to make light of it. The photograph of her in the company of Tullio Serafin and Rossi-Lemeni taken in Naples during this year shows a smiling and sociable woman in her late sixties, who still takes trouble with her appearance. It is interesting to note also that she is still wearing the rings John gave her, and John's own bracelet.

John Gielgud, meeting Una in Florence at this time, recalls that:

> She invited me to her flat near the Ponte Vecchio, showing off
> a picture which she claimed to be a Botticelli and begging me to
> go and see the San Niniato Church. She was . . . in collar and
> tie with a tweed suit. 'I always dress like this in memory of
> John,' she said, and presented me proudly with a copy of 'The
> Well' which had just been re-published in England to her great
> satisfaction. She talked rapturously of Rossi-Lemeni . . . she
> travelled wherever he was singing, and godmothered his
> children . . .

This description of Una's physical appearance differs markedly
from that in the photograph already mentioned, but she obviously
suited her clothes partly to the person or the situation. The
reference to the Botticelli is interesting. Una was a keen and
knowledgeable art critic and believed that the 'Madonna and
Child' she had discovered and bought was a Botticelli. Felix
Hope-Nicholson thought she had been duped by 'a clever forgery'.
Even experts can be fooled, so it is possible that he was right, as
neither the antecedents of this picture nor its subsequent history
are known. Una also showed the picture to Micki Jacob, and told
her: 'It gives me great pleasure, and when I've finished with it,
the Cancer Research will benefit'; but whether they ever did is
uncertain, as there is no mention of it in Una's Will. She also had
a Bellini, and a number of other valuable pictures in her collection; loving to have beautiful things around her, and having an
eye for a bargain in pictures as in clothes.

Going to La Scala in 1956, Una met Micki Jacob in Milan. In
the course of conversation they recalled John's ready laughter in
response to certain anecdotes, then Micki commented on Una's
current busy activities, to which she replied, 'It fills in the time.
Something to do – oh, it interests me, but chiefly it's a means to an
end.' After this, Micki Jacob wrote: 'Una Troubridge, with her
knowledge of music, art, and literature, with her ability to *use* that
knowledge, commands my admiration; while her ability to make a
new life for herself, to be . . . amusing, interesting – and interested in you! – adds to my affection and respect for her.'[4]

Una covenanted Evguenia's allowance, renewing it every seven years. Evguenia's various self-induced monetary misfortunes and appeals to Una for extra help were virtually habitual, but in 1956 although she was taken genuinely ill she maximized her demands and exploited the situation. Una wrote to John on October 11th, 1956:

> . . . a very small tumour has been removed, with assistance of a temporary colostomy, she may recover entirely and never look back . . . In her letter there is the usual appeal, to sentiment: of course she may die 'and go straight to dear Johnnie . . .' again I wonder why, when after 9 years of abominable cruelty, she left you even when you were in extremis and came to me directly after your death to ask 'what she was going to get' of your money . . . Of course I will help her, in Christian charity, but like, or trust or have more to do with her than I must . . . NO . . .

It is a strange coincidence that Evguenia should suffer the same illness as John, even a mild form of it; and it is significant that despite 'Christian charity' Una's innate distrust of her is as strong as ever. Their value-systems were so different: Una lived essentially within a framework of Christian ethics, whereas Evguenia was an amoral opportunist.

She was ill again in 1957, hospitalized for two months at St Mary Abbot's, then convalesced at Seine-et-Oise, and Una paid some of her 'additional expenses', but as usual Evguenia was not satisfied. Later, when Evguenia was dying, Una answered her appeals for additional money, although she had a working husband who was both legally and morally responsible for her. After her death, Makaroff was to sell the 571 letters, postcards and telegrams from John to Evguenia, which she had carefully kept and catalogued, to a London bookseller, Bertram Rota, who in turn sold them to the Humanities Research Center at the University of Texas, where they now reside. Whether or not Una ever knew of this is uncertain, but it is probable that she did not.

In the winter of 1957 Una finally left Florence and went to live in a flat in Rome, at 3 Piazza di Novella, opposite Rossi-Lemeni and his family: his wife Virginia Zeani, a noted soprano, their child, and Rossi-Lemeni's parents. As Rossi-Lemeni explained: '. . . she

305

lived my life and became attached to my family . . .' She was almost an adopted member of the Rossi-Lemeni family, which gave her life both a framework and a purpose. There was a reciprocal affection and affinity.

Rossi-Lemeni himself recalls: 'what it meant to me, the encounter with Una – how much I learned from her in all dominions of human knowledge about art, history, literature and life . . .'[5] She was, he said, 'a walking encyclopaedia', and he was 'very flattered by her admiration'; 'her opinion meant a lot to me, and she was an inspiration.'

As well as being devoted to his singing, Una encouraged his writing, and pushed him to participate in a poetry competition which he won, subsequently publishing five volumes of poetry.

She settled herself into her Rome flat with her maid, Nada Vadi. This was to be her last home, and it contained the many relics of her life with John. Some of its furniture, pictures and ornaments had been in many of their homes, and she had scrupulously kept John's personal items: cuff-links, watches, lighters . . . In addition, there were her latterly acquired pictures and upwards of 4,000 books, the gathering of a very literate lifetime. Una had many of John's photographs about her including one by her bedside, and one in her living-room in front of which she placed fresh flowers every day. This ritual, like the writing of her 'Letters to John', had become a permanent part of her life. She was careful with money but never frugal: 'If money is available, let it by all means be spent, but never in a manner or degree that can involve present or future anxiety,' she wrote. 'For me, the house that is small enough to be kept in perfect order by service that does not strain resources; for me the clothes, the books, the ornaments that can be paid for within at most a month of purchase. The holiday that does not paralyse future finance, the luxuries that leave a margin that is in itself the greatest of all luxuries . . .'[6] Her 'margin' was quite wide, and she could well afford the international travel and opera-going which was her main luxury. She had never lived in Rome before, and had only pleasant holiday memories of it. It was thus relatively 'neutral' ground and she could build up her own associations with it. She saw much of the Rossi-Lemenis and when their only son Alessandro was born in

1958 she acted as his godmother and grew to be very fond of him. She referred to Nicola as 'Nika' and they often discussed 'mystical problems, and oriental religions' in which they were both interested; and she also, he told me, talked much of John, and of episodes from her own life. Like Una, Rossi-Lemeni was a keen collector of pictures, antiques, and arms and weapons, and they often went together to the flea market in Porta Portese at 6 a.m. on Sundays in search of bargains. If they found a picture which they believed to be a genuine bargain, such as a 'Van Dyke' which was too expensive for either to purchase alone, they bought it together, Una to enjoy it in her lifetime and Rossi-Lemeni after her death. It was an amicable arrangement which worked well. Una also built up a good collection of reliquaries, many of them authenticated.

In 1958 Pizzetti's opera *L'Assassinio Nella Cattedrale*, based on Eliot's *Murder in the Cathedral*, was premièred at La Scala. It had been specially composed by Pizzetti for Rossi-Lemeni, and was dedicated to him. He sang the principal role of Thomas Becket. The work was a resounding success and was performed in Florence, Naples, Palermo, Venice, Genoa, Barcelona, Rio de Janeiro, Buenos Aires and New York. It was even performed in the Vatican in the presence of Pope John XXIII. For Una, this part was Rossi-Lemeni's most perfect role, and she missed only its South American performances. T. S. Eliot was also greatly impressed, and wrote to Rossi-Lemeni: 'in no production of the play . . . have I had an archbishop who looked more like my conception of St Thomas of Canterbury . . . I shall never hope to hear a finer rendering of the part than you gave at the first performance.' Three years later Una was to fly to New York for only the second time in her life (as she did not like flying) to hear this opera performed at Carnegie Hall. She was then seventy-four, and it was to be her last major trip.

In 1959 Una tried to publish some of John's unpublished short stories, and also had her biography of John – hand-written in hard-cover exercise books – typed, at what she considered to be the 'outrageous' cost of 84,000 lire. In due course it was sent to the Heath Agency. After the death of Evguenia, the last of the three potential libellees, it was now safe to publish it. Besides, Una herself was then seventy-two, and all the events long passed; and no one else had offered to write a 'Life' of John in the intervening years. It was finally published in 1961, and one of the people to whom Una sent a signed copy was Micki Jacob, inscribing it, 'To our very dear and very faithful friend.' The recipient was pleased.

It was to remain the only book about John for nearly fifteen years, and an invaluable source book for all future writers. In what it does *not* say, it tells us as much about Una as about John, although she remains ostensibly a self-effacing and elusive figure. The book remained unrevised from 1945, presumably because none of the facts of John's life or death had altered. Only Una's own life had altered and, as she emphasized, it was John's and not her own life that she was writing. After its publication she wrote in her 'Letter to John' dated January 12th, 1962: 'I have had a magnificent criticism in *Books and Bookmen*, a page and a half by Mrs. Robert Henry, with Buchel's portrait, with a splendid appreciation of your genius – a vivid defence of *The Well* and warm praise of my book. – It has made me very happy!'

Apart from this backward glance, Una's life went on as before. She was as keen on art as ever, and proud of her own collection, as the photograph of her pointing at her Bellini in July 1961 clearly shows. She looks quite contented, and with a nice little touch of vanity still cares enough about herself at seventy-four to wear earrings. She was as actively interested in opera as ever, attending a party in Rossi-Lemeni's home after the opening night of the world première of *View from the Bridge*, the opera composed for and dedicated to him by Renzo Rossellini. Through Rossi-Lemeni Una knew Rossellini, the director of the opera in Rome, Riccardo Vitale, and many other prominent musical people. Rossi-Lemeni himself could not emphasize too much, 'how . . . Una was important to me and how our friendship was absolutely unique . . . We shared the same interests for art, for antiques, for religious and philosophical problems – it was a constant contact and she was for me an endless source of knowledge and inspiration . . .'

He also spoke modestly of 'an exaggerated importance that Una gave to me,' adding: 'You must understand – For Una there were three "idols": Nijinsky, Radclyffe Hall . . . and me!'[7] Una had enough of the artist in herself, and enough innate generosity of spirit to appreciate and encourage great artistry in others.

'Allowing for the passing of years, I have remained in almost all things the same person,' Una wrote in 1962. 'My eyes are still grey, and if my hair has long since become a better match to them, that was only to be expected . . . and one's face merely becomes steadily less attractive . . .'[8] This is representative of Una's 'philosophical' attitude to ageing: a non-emotive matter-of-factness. Neither 'change and decay' nor death was feared or unwelcome. It had seemed ironical to her that during the previous nineteen years 'no life is so immune [i.e. from death] as that which seems intolerable', and that despite her medical history she had survived so long, so that in 1962 she was 'in as good health as is consistent with my age . . .'[9] All the same, she told John on January 18th, 1962: 'I am very far from well . . . my back and loins are so stiff and painful since my fall and in the mornings when I first leave my bed I can hardly stand or walk. My legs are increasingly weak . . . I have sudden momentary amnesia of things I know perfectly well . . . is all this merely that I am unduly old for 74?'

At seventy-five Una was busy revising old autobiographical sketches written in the twenties and thirties, and writing new ones. Although these were largely about people and events rather than her own intimate feelings, she was leaving behind her a body of organized material in either conscious or unconscious anticipation of a future biographer. Although it is not unusual for people in their seventies to put their papers in order, it is unusual for them to leave such detailed records for posterity, and it is significant that she left extant letters and diaries which she could equally well have destroyed. By contrast, Alice B. Toklas at seventy-five was writing a commissioned cookery book, later to become controversial for its marijuana cookies!

By 1962 Una had heard Rossi-Lemeni sing 'upwards of 500 performances', with, if anything, increasing enjoyment. In her essay about him written that year, her final tribute was: 'I hope there may be singing in the future life and that I shall still hear Nicola Rossi-Lemeni!'[10]

# 19

# *The Blessed Goal:*
# *Rome, 1963*

It is just possible that Una had a premonition in 1962, when revising her papers, that she might not live for very much longer, and that what was not done then would be left undone. At the beginning of 1963 the sand was beginning to run rapidly out of the hourglass, and 'the blessed goal' of what Una confidently believed would be ultimate reunion with John came into sight after nearly twenty years. She had several more falls, as old people so often do, and broke her elbow painfully as a result of one of them. It was slow to heal, and she felt very weak, and slept even more badly than usual.

On January 26th, 1963 she wrote to John: 'Evening: 7 oc of a long day that began at 5 a.m. I have been entirely alone . . . I *must* try to take up life again . . .' and on February 12th: 'My darling, I had a hateful night. Slept 10.30 woke at 12 – nausea, malaise and every nerve on edge . . . Eventually slept again for a while . . .' The writing becomes as she herself does, '*very* weak and shaky,' and she was understandably 'terrified of being aged and infirm . . .' Some days were better than others, but often: 'Out of doors I felt so shaky and weak that I was afraid to walk . . .' Hunting for bargains in the flea-market with Rossi-Lemeni became increasingly difficult, but she was loath to give it up.

310

In March she had to admit to John: 'Unless the cold breaks I shall not go to Porta Portese tomorrow – it is pneumonia weather and crazy to go and loiter there . . .' In the event she was in 'a low state' and did not go to Mass either. She still kept up her correspondence, and told John: 'Natalie has sent me a number of a Paris periodical *Adam*: "A World Tribute to Natalie Clifford Barney." It seems she is now 85! No special mention of Romaine who must be even older – all very foolish really. Why should the world make a tribute to Natalie? No mention either of Valerie Seymour or you or *The Well* . . .'

Rossi-Lemeni was often away, or at rehearsals when in Rome, and Una spent much time alone at home, cared for by her maid, Nada. At times, she told John, 'tremors much accentuated and can really only write comfortably after a drink!'

At last, reluctantly, she rang up Dr Pennington de Jong, as she was feeling very ill. He arrived the following day and examined her thoroughly, pronouncing 'His verdict: I am sound in wind and limb. My trouble shock from the fall and mismanagement of the broken arm . . .' He put her on a course of vitamins, and she consoled herself that 'One does know *one* thing: if a doctor has the vaguest suspicion . . . of cancer every kind of test is begun within 24 hours . . .' It was to prove a false consolation.

Her mind began to work backwards, recalling more easily the distant than the immediate past. On March 5th she noted: 'Anniversary of my father's death 55 years ago. He was not a man one could ever forget . . .'

On March 8th, writing to 'my beloved' she noted: 'my 76th birthday . . .' Nicola gave her 'a beautiful madonna in crystal', her maid gave her napkins, Paola and Xenia (Nicola's parents) 'a big pot of tulips', and 'Andrea and "Bull" . . . cabled.' The Rossi-Lemenis invited her to supper to celebrate both her birthday and the arrival of Virginia's parents from the country.

Shortly after this her old friend May Massola, then seventy-two, was in Rome for ten days, and visited her. They had known each other for fifty years. News of other friends continued to reach her: her old friend Kathy (Lady) Dorchester, had lost, within forty-eight hours, both husband and lifelong 'friend' Betty, and Una wrote in 'Letters to John': 'I think much of poor Kathy who

'*Widowhood*' (1943–63)

begins – as I did 20 years ago, life *alone* – but at any rate she can't have to face – at 72 – what I saw ahead of me . . . but God tempered the wind and sent me Nicola and his needs and his career and his strange affection for my aged self to provide a motive for existence . . . Kathy's Odyssey is unlikely to endure for many years . . .'

Her own was nearer its end than she knew. In April she began to feel worse, weak and lethargic: 'I am calling de Jong as . . . I feel not only house-ridden but potentially bedridden,' she wrote to John. The doctor put her on to some soporific drugs which prevented her from writing coherently, then arranged for her to go into a Rome clinic for ten days in May for tests. Virginia Rossi-Lemeni told her: 'You must never feel alone . . . you have always got us, and we shall always be near you.' This left Una 'deeply cheered and comforted'.

She asked Dr de Jong and the neurologist at the clinic, Dr Germano, to be perfectly honest with her about her condition. They both assured her that, after tests, there was nothing organically wrong with her, and Germano offered to treat her in the clinic for a month for 'nervous exhaustion'. Una declined, was collected by her maid, and went gladly home. One after-effect of her broken arm that worried her was, as she told John: 'my third finger of left hand has thickened and I can't get my wedding ring [i.e. John's not Troubridge's] on again. I took it off as soon as I broke my arm and thought the swelling would go but it hasn't. I think I must wear it as you did mine, on my little finger.'

The tremors, falls and weakness continued during the summer, with a steady loss of appetite, and fluctuating good and bad days. At times her speech centres were adversely affected. In July her doctor said that she was 'much improved', and continued treatment as before, but advised her to take three cocktails a day instead of two! Andrea was concerned at having no news from Una and at the shakiness of her last letter, and wrote to Rossi-Lemeni to inquire after her, offering to come if she was really ill. Nada refused to go away on holiday and leave Una. The Rossi-Lemenis were away first in Naples and then in Verona and Una was left much alone despite occasional visits from other friends. On August 12th, 1963 Una wrote in her letter to John: 'Your birthday my

312

darling. I sent Nada to get flowers. I am house-ridden and I could not get them myself. Alone all day . . .'

On August 29th she wrote: 'I seem to be losing strength . . .'

The entries become short and less legible, the last being written on September 5th, 1963. Few people outside Rome knew of her illness. Lovat Dickson, her literary executor, had seen her only once since 1961 and her death when it came took him by surprise. Rossi-Lemeni and his family were close at hand throughout her illness. 'She was at the end happy . . .' he states with conviction. On September 17th Una made her last Will, revoking the one previously made in 1960. Like John's it was made a few days before her death and was witnessed by a doctor and a nurse. The signature is shaky and barely legible, symptomatic of how very weak she was at the time.

She appointed Harold Rubinstein and Lovat Dickson to be her executors and trustees; and left the latter 'all my literary property and rights including therein all my manuscripts . . . whether of my own authorship or acquired by me under the Will of the late Marguerite Radclyffe-Hall . . .' Dickson was charged to ensure that 'no use shall be made of the property . . . bequeathed to him or any part thereof in any way detrimental to the dignity and nobility of purpose that distinguish the work of the said Marguerite Radclyffe-Hall,' and that no 'expurgated or abbreviated edition', of her works should be published. It is significant that even on her death-bed Una's chief concern was for the fate of John's works, and to ensure their safety in reliable hands. The exception to this literary arrangement were her own diaries, which she gave Rossi-Lemeni the right to 'destroy . . if in his sole and absolute discretion he thinks fit'. In addition she left to him all the arrangements for her funeral and burial. Her Charles Buchel portrait of John she gave to the National Portrait Gallery, who accepted it; but sadly it resides in a hanging room with other pictures rarely if ever on view to the public. Una left £2,000 and her pearl necklace and pearl and pearl-and-diamond earrings to Andrea; and £2,000 to Cancer Relief, London. Always generous to those who served her well, she left a handsome annuity to her maid, Nada Vadi. She directed that her remaining property be sold, and that the residue of her total estate be given to the

Community of the Poor Clares at Lynton. There was no mention of the Botticelli, so presumably she had either already disposed of it or had found it to be a forgery after all. Her effects totalled £57,274. 13s.

On the evening of Wednesday September 24th Rossi-Lemeni visited Una, then went home leaving her in bed, intending to call again the following morning. Later, at 11.15 p.m. Una died in the arms of her maid, Nada. The death was registered with the British Consul in Rome by Remo Morbidelli, the funeral directors, and the cause of death was stated as secondary cancer of the liver. News of her death did not reach London for five days, the first brief obituaries appearing in both the *Daily Telegraph* and *The Times* on September 30th. A longer notice appeared in *The Times* on Tuesday October 1st, giving details of her family background, marriage, 'lifelong friendship' with Radclyffe Hall, the trials of *The Well*, and a brief note of her post-war residence in Italy. Romaine Brooks saw a notice in the Italian newspapers and sent it to Natalie Barney in Paris.

Una had not, in fact, given any specific burial instructions to Rossi-Lemeni, and despite her deposition to Harold Rubinstein nineteen years before had never mentioned any desire to be interred in England. Rossi-Lemeni remarked: 'She always told me that she wasn't at all concerned about what happened to her after death. "You could throw me in the sea!" she said.' It fell to him to decide what to do, so he bought a plot in the English Cemetery in Rome, in the 'Catholic Foreigners' Section D of the Anglo-American area, and was granted the necessary Concessionary Rights on October 10th, 1963. It was, in fact, a site she 'chose' herself, as when visiting the cemetery with Rossi-Lemeni shortly after his mother's death, she remarked, pointing to a spot in the shade of a tree, 'Well, if you want to bury me, I wouldn't mind being buried there.' Una's mortal remains were laid to rest under a marble slab with grass surrounds, simply but tastefully executed. Rossi-Lemeni explained how he came to select the wording: 'I knew all about her life and her problems – on her tomb I wanted to leave a sign that could recall Radclyffe Hall – it was important, but it was not so simple . . . I found the solution consulting Radclyffe Hall's Bible; on the front page Radclyffe Hall wrote, "There is no death," and this phrase is engraved on the memorial stone of Una's tomb, signed Radclyffe Hall.' Una would have been pleased that he had taken so much trouble to find something appropriate.

Dr Arangio-Ruiz, Una's Italian lawyer, contacted her executors, and probate was duly granted. Una's original burial instructions to Rubinstein were found unopened in the safe of her English bank at Minehead, but she had already been buried in Rome and they doubted the wisdom of moving her, due partly to the time-lapse since the 1944 instructions. As a compromise, they agreed to have a memorial tablet inscribed at Highgate as she had wished: 'Should I die abroad and . . . it . . . prove impracticable to bring my body to the vault, I desire the same inscription exactly to be placed *on* the vault at Highgate, but with place of death and burial added, the whole thing preceded by the words "And to the memory of".'

The tomb at Highgate was later vandalized, and has subsequently fallen into a sad state of disrepair. Una remains in Rome in a well-tended grave shaded by trees. Una's daughter Andrea died in a car crash in 1966 at the age of fifty-six; and her only child, Nicholas Vincenzo Troubridge Warren, Una's last direct descendant, joined a Cistercian order at Nunraw in East Lothian, where he is a priested monk known as Father Martin. 'I hardly knew Una,' he told me, adding that both his mother and aunt Viola were 'exceedingly reticent about her'.

'The feeling of affinity with a fellow human being, of instinctive and unfailing sympathy . . . is a very mysterious phenomenon even when it is felt for a living . . . and personal acquaintance. It becomes even less easy to understand, when this feeling . . . selects as its objective a man or woman whom, in the nature of things, one can never have met in this life . . .' Una wrote in her 'Post Scripta to Black Charles' (Charles II), adding that there is also something 'that arouses in one a vital pleasure when that person is praised or appreciated, a deep resentment when he or she is misjudged or misunderstood.'

Such sentiments are also felt by the biographer who has been close to his subject in a strange 'posthumous friendship'. But he must also ask himself, in the final analysis, 'Of what significance was her life, and for what should we remember her?' The answer to this question is as complex as the individual concerned. 'Nothing ever happens but the unexpected!' Una declared on one occasion, and certainly her own life bears out this statement.

Though fortunate in the social and (later) financial privileges she enjoyed, she also managed, through her innate radicalism and courage, to liberate herself from the tyranny of other people's expectations. She was prepared to face censure and disapproval, and to hazard all for love. She was never a woman to do the 'expected' if it did not accord with her own wishes, and she was never hypocritical. She had certainly not 'expected' to give up her art, separate from her husband, become the feminine half of the most famous lesbian couple of the century, have her name twice splashed across the newspapers in sensational court-cases, or to lead such a wandering life. Undoubtedly the twenty-eight 'middle' years of her life were the most important and interesting of all, the fulfilment of her being.

It is tempting to wonder what she might have been without John. She had the ability to become a serious sculptor, painter or book illustrator; she possessed an intellectual, refined mind, and very considerable linguistic and musical talents. She could have become involved in theatre or opera production; in publishing; or have taken a degree in humanities, languages or fine arts. With such a gift for friendship she would have been a natural diplomat or courier. She numbered amongst her friends or acquaintances many of the famous people of her time in art, music, literature, theatre, the press, and even politics. Perhaps she might have become famous for a salon, like Natalie Barney.

Yet, for all her qualities, abilities and independence, she was primarily a feminine woman who wanted to love and be loved. That was, for her, *the* ecstatic experience. Of all her talents, that for loving, refined as it was by suffering, was the most developed of all; and love and John were for Una inseparable. She wished to be remembered for loving John, or as she expressed it in understatement, as 'The Friend of Radclyffe Hall'.

# Notes

NB    Place of publication for works cited is London unless otherwise specified.

## 1   Childhood (1887–1900)

1   Her birth was registered by her mother on September 19th, 1933, on the authority of the Registrar General.
2   Autobiographical essay, 'On Being Ill'. Unpublished and undated.
3   Ibid.
4   Ibid.
5   Sir Charles Petrie, *The Victorians* (Eyre & Spottiswoode, 1960).
6   Robert Surtees (Durham historian) to Sir Walter Scott, February 1807.
7   Henry Taylor, *Autobiography*, 1885.
8   Robert Southey. Letter dated January 4th, 1826, referring to *Quarterly Review*.
9   Taylor, *Autobiography*.
10  Radclyffe Hall. Notes to Psychic Records, January 3rd, 1920.
11  Ibid.
12  Ibid.
13  Una Troubridge. Essay on 'Oysters', 1944.
14  Henry Taylor. Letter to Mr Edward, May 20th, 1881.

*Notes*

15  Ibid.
16  Henry Taylor. Letter to Mr Edward, September 30th, 1882.
17  Lt-Col. T. Crump, Superintendent of the Corps of Queen's Messengers. Letter dated October 18th, 1982.
18  Autobiographical essay, 'My Pets'. Unpublished and undated.
19  Autobiographical essay, 'The Dancing'. Unpublished and undated.
20  Sir Edward Poynter. Letter from Albert Gate dated January 26th, 1894.
21  Autobiographical essay, 'My Teachers'. Unpublished and undated.
22  Autobiographical essay, 'A London Child'. Unpublished and undated.
23  Autobiographical essay, 'I Remember'. Unpublished and undated.
24  'A London Child'.
25  Ibid.
26  Autobiographical essay, 'Visitors'. Unpublished and undated.
27  Autobiographical essay, 'Christmasses'. Unpublished and undated.
28  Radclyffe Hall. Notes to Psychic Records.
29  Radclyffe Hall. Note 3, sitting of October 18th, 1919.
30  Radclyffe Hall. Notes to sitting of May 21st, 1921.
31  Autobiographical essay, 'On Bores'. Unpublished and undated.
32  'Visitors'.
33  Autobiographical essay, 'Beds'. Unpublished and undated.
34  Autobiographical essay, 'The Play'. Unpublished and undated.
35  Autobiographical essay, 'Conscience'. Unpublished and undated.
36  'Visitors'.
37  'On Being Ill'.
38  Autobiographical essay, 'Calling'. Unpublished and undated.


## 2  Youth (1901–7)

1  Autobiographical essay, 'My Teachers'. Unpublished and undated.
2  Autobiographical essay, 'I Remember'. Unpublished and undated.
3  Sir William Richmond, R.A.
4  Notes to the Psychic Records, March 23rd, 1921.
5  Sir Charles Petrie, *The Victorians* (Eyre & Spottiswoode, 1960).
6  Autobiographical essay, 'Calling'. Unpublished and undated.
7  Felix Hope-Nicholson.
8  G. F. Watts, R.A. Letter to Una, dated October 11th, 1900.
9  Mrs Emily Muirhead Campbell, related to Beatrice Stella (Mrs Patrick) Campbell.

318

10   Autobiographical essay, 'A London Child'. Unpublished and undated.
11   Presumably the doctor.
12   Mrs Emily Muirhead Campbell.
13   Royal College of Art. Report for the Session 1900–1901.
14   F. Brown, *South Kensington & its Art Training* (1912).
15   Royal College of Art Report 1900–1.
16   Ibid.
17   Associate of the Royal College of Art.
18   Royal College of Art Report 1900–10.
19   Ibid.
20   'My Teachers'.
21   Published by Arrowsmith in 1925.
22   He was probably another friend of Harry Taylor's.
23   Fred Terry. End of letter to Una Taylor, dated May 29th, 1907.
24   One of the most loved dancers of her day and a founder of modern British ballet.
25   The Empire Theatre, London, 1907.
26   Adeline Genee. Letter to Una Taylor, dated October 3rd, 1907.
27   Thomas Brock. Letter to Sir Edward Poynter, dated February 24th, 1906.
28   Ivy McKay. Letter to Minna Taylor, from 83 Warrington Cres., London W2. Undated.
29   Minna Taylor. Undated statement referring to loan from Una to Viola, etc.
30   Royal College of Art Report 1900–10.
31   Radclyffe Hall, *A Saturday Life* (Arrowsmith, 1925).
32   Radclyffe Hall. Notes to Psychic Records, January 3rd, 1920.
33   High cravats.
34   Radclyffe Hall. Notes to Psychic Records, June 12th, 1920.
35   This may refer either to Troubridge's niece or to his aunt Louisa.

## 3   Marriage (1908–12)

1   Autobiographical essay, 'Christmasses'. Unpublished and undated.
2   Mabel Veronica Batten, née Hatch, Minna's first cousin.
3   George Henry Batten, Viceroy of India.
4   For full details see chapter 6, My John.
5   i.e. Una and Viola.
6   Autobiographical essay, 'Hero Worship'. Unpublished and undated.

# Notes

7 Radclyffe Hall. Notes to Psychic Records, December 27th, 1917.
8 R. Lovat Dickson, *Radclyffe Hall at the Well of Loneliness* (Collins, 1975).
9 The most famous of whom was Elizabeth Fry (née Gurney).
10 Laura Troubridge, *Life Amongst the Troubridges: Journals of a Young Victorian 1873–1884* (John Murray, 1966).
11 Admiral Troubridge's obituary, *The Times*, January 30th, 1926.
12 Autobiographical essay, 'Beds'. Unpublished and undated.
13 Julia Neilson-Terry. Letter to Una Troubridge, 1908.
14 Radclyffe Hall. Notes to Psychic Records, December 27th, 1917.
15 Felix Hope-Nicholson, grandson of Laura Hope (née Troubridge).
16 Edith Mary Duffus, Ernest Troubridge's first wife.
17 'Christmasses'.
18 By one of their descendants, who wishes to remain anonymous.
19 Sir Edward Poynter. Letter to Una from Como, dated August 28th, 1910.
20 Radclyffe Hall. Notes to Psychic Records, December 27th, 1917.
21 'Christmasses'.
22 Lord Fisher. Letter to Una, dated December 17th, 1910.
23 This information comes via Laura Hope's granddaughter, Mrs Jacqueline Lancaster.

## 4   The Melting-Pot (1913–15)

1 Diary, January 14th, 1913.
2 Troubridge's childhood nickname, which Una used for him.
3 Hugh Crichton-Miller. Letter to Una dated May 20th, 1913.
4 Diary, July 4th, 1913.
5 Una Troubridge, *The Life and Death of Radclyffe Hall* (Hammond, 1961).
6 The *Daily Malta Chronicle*, May 6th, 1914.
7 Radclyffe Hall. Notes to Psychic Records, December 27th, 1917.
8 B. W. Tuchman, *August, 1914* (Constable, 1962).
9 Admiral Troubridge's obituary in *The Times*, January 30th, 1926.
10 'A Thumbnail Sketch of the Rt. Hon. Sir W. Churchill, K.G. & Admiral Sir Ernest Troubridge, R.N. in 1914.' Written by Una in September 1962.
11 Ibid.
12 Ibid.

## 5   The Game of Love (1915–16)

1   Una Troubridge, *The Life and Death of Radclyffe Hall* (Hammond, 1961).
2   Ibid.
3   Radclyffe Hall. Poem 'Reincarnation' from *A Sheaf of Verses* (John and Edward Bumpus, 1908).
4   *Life and Death of Radclyffe Hall.*
5   From *The Forgotten Island* (Chapman & Hall, 1915).
6   *Life and Death of Radclyffe Hall.*
7   Ibid.
8   Radclyffe Hall. Poem 'Moth to the Flame'. No known publication.
9   *Life and Death of Radclyffe Hall.*
10   Ibid.
11   Radclyffe Hall, *The Well of Loneliness* (Cape, 1928).
12   Ibid.
13   *Life and Death of Radclyffe Hall.*
14   One of Ladye's favourite phrases.
15   *Life and Death of Radclyffe Hall.*
16   *The Well of Loneliness.*
17   *Life and Death of Radclyffe Hall.*
18   Radclyffe Hall. Notes to Psychic Records, May 15th, 1918.
19   *Life and Death of Radclyffe Hall.*
20   Radclyffe Hall. Proceedings of the Society for Psychical Research, Vol. xxx.
21   *Life and Death of Radclyffe Hall.*
22   Radclyffe Hall. Notes to Psychic Records, June 13th, 1917.
23   See further details in chapter 6, My John.
24   *Life and Death of Radclyffe Hall.*
25   Ibid.
26   Radclyffe Hall. Notes to Psychic Records, September 10th, 1919.
27   Radclyffe Hall. Notes to Psychic Records, March 13th, 1918.
28   See chapter 7, Psychic Phenomena.
29   *Life and Death of Radclyffe Hall.*
30   Radclyffe Hall. Notes to Psychic Records, November 15th, 1916.
31   Radclyffe Hall. Notes to Psychic Records, December 31st, 1916.
32   *Life and Death of Radclyffe Hall.*

## 6   My John

1   These records of sittings with Mrs Leonard date from mid-1916 to mid-1921, and now reside with the Society for Psychical Research.

## Notes

2 Marie Visetti to Jane Caruth, March 3rd, 1944.
3 Alberto Visetti was a successful singing teacher, numbering amongst his better-known pupils the soprano Agnes Nichols. He was also attached to the Royal College of Music as Professor of Singing.
4 This must have been destroyed as no trace of it has ever come to light.
5 Radclyffe Hall, *The Forgotten Island* (Chapman & Hall, 1915).
6 Radclyffe Hall, *Twixt Earth and Stars* (John and Edward Bumpus, 1906); *A Sheaf of Verses* (John and Edward Bumpus, 1908); *Poems of the Past and Present* (Chapman & Hall, 1910); *Songs of Three Counties and Other Poems* (Chapman & Hall, 1913); *The Forgotten Island*.
7 *The Forgotten Island*.
8 Ibid.
9 Ibid.
10 She was only a mild gambler, it was John who occasionally gambled heavily.
11 A fellow invert, author, and friend of theirs after 1930. See chapter 13, So Vast a Need.
12 An American, famous for her Paris salon in Rue Jacob for over sixty years, and for her many love-affairs, especially with Romaine Brooks, René Vivien and Dolly Wilde, Oscar's niece. She died in February 1972, aged ninety-five.
13 Evguenia Souline, a White Russian. See chapter 13, So Vast a Need.
14 Radclyffe Hall, *The Well of Loneliness* (Cape, 1928).
15 Una Troubridge, *The Life and Death of Radclyffe Hall* (Hammond, 1961).
16 All these photographs are in Una's *Life*.
17 Ethel Mannin, *Confessions and Impressions* (Hutchinson, 1930).
18 In *The Well of Loneliness*.
19 Ibid.
20 All quotations in this paragraph are from *The Well*.
21 Letter to Cassell's setting out the theme of *The Well* prior to publication.
22 Dr Harry Benjamin, *The Transsexual Phenomenon* (Julian Press, New York, 1966).
23 *The Well of Loneliness*.
24 C. N. Armstrong and A. J. Marshall, *Intersexuality in Vertebrates Including Man* (Academic Press, 1964).
25 *The Well of Loneliness*.

## 7 Psychic Phenomena (1917–21)

1 Una Troubridge, *The Life and Death of Radclyffe Hall* (Hammond, 1961), pp. 57–60.
2 Ibid.
3 Ibid.
4 Ibid.
5 Ibid.
6 Ibid.
7 Ibid.
8 Notes to sitting of October 12th, 1918.
9 Ibid.
10 Notes to sitting of July 6th, 1918.
11 *Life and Death of Radclyffe Hall*, p. 59.
12 Ibid.
13 Notes to sitting of January 23rd, 1918.
14 Notes to sitting of June 19th, 1918.
15 Notes to sitting of March 27th, 1918.
16 Ethel Mannin, *Confessions and Impressions* (Hutchinson, 1930).
17 *Life and Death of Radclyffe Hall*, p. 59.

## 8 Our Union (1917–21)

1 Una Troubridge, *The Life and Death of Radclyffe Hall* (Hammond, 1961).
2 Radclyffe Hall, *The Well of Loneliness* (Cape, 1928).
3 As she told Lovat Dickson later.
4 Derek Llewellyn-Jones, *Everywoman: A Gynaecological Guide for Life* (Faber, 1971).
5 Shere Hite, *The Hite Report* (Corgi, 1977).
6 Ronald Pearsall, *The Worm in the Bud: The World of Victorian Sexuality* (Weidenfeld & Nicolson, 1969).
7 *Life and Death of Radclyffe Hall*.
8 *The Well of Loneliness*.
9 Toupie Lowther. One of Ladye's friends, and later of John and Una.
10 *Life and Death of Radclyffe Hall*.
11 See chapter 14, This Agonized Bliss.
12 A proposed psychic newspaper, which never materialized.
13 Diary, February 4th, 1917.
14 Written in January, 1916.
15 Diary, April 19th, 1917.
16 Diary, April 26th, 1917.

17  *Life and Death of Radclyffe Hall.*
18  Radclyffe Hall. Notes to Psychic Records, May 24th, 1917.
19  Radclyffe Hall. Notes to Psychic Records, June 6th, 1917.
20  Diary, Sunday, June 3rd, 1917.
21  Diary, June 5th, 1917.
22  Diary, June 6th, 1917.
23  Diary, August 21st, 1917.
24  Diary, June 18th, 1917.
25  Diary, September 16th, 1917.
26  Diary, October 6th, 1917.
27  Diary, October 10th, 1917.
28  Radclyffe Hall. Notes to Psychic Records, September 12th, 1917.
29  Ibid.
30  Ibid.
31  Diary, August 28th, 1917.
32  Radclyffe Hall. Notes to Psychic Records, May 2nd, 1917.
33  Diary, September 9th, 1917.
34  Diary, September 24th, 1917.
35  Diary, September 21st, 1917.
36  Diary, October 21st, 1917.
37  Diary, October 22nd, 1917.
38  Diary, November 7th, 1917.
39  Radclyffe Hall. Notes to Psychic Records, November 22nd, 1917.
40  Radclyffe Hall. Notes to Psychic Records, January 23rd, 1918.
41  Radclyffe Hall. Notes to Psychic Records, January 23rd, 1918.
42  Diary, December 10th, 1917.
43  Diary, December 23rd, 1917.
44  Radclyffe Hall. Notes to Psychic Records, August 28th, 1918.
45  Una Troubridge. Autobiographical essay, 'My Teachers'. Unpublished and undated.
46  *The Well of Loneliness.*
47  Una Troubridge. Letter to Jacqueline Hope, dated January 28th, 1918.
48  Diary, January 3rd, 1918.
49  Diary, January 30th, 1918.
50  Radclyffe Hall. Notes to Psychic Records, December 27th, 1917.
51  Radclyffe Hall. Notes to Psychic Records, June 19th, 1918.
52  *The Well of Loneliness.*
53  Radclyffe Hall. Notes to Psychic Records, May 15th, 1918.
54  Diary, March 24th, 1918.
55  Diary, March 29th, 1918.
56  Diary, April 13th, 1918.

57   Radclyffe Hall. Notes to Psychic Records, November 5th, 1918.
58   Diary, May 22nd, 1918.
59   Diary, June 18th, 1918.
60   Radclyffe Hall. Notes to Psychic Records, June 26th, 1918.
61   Diary, June 28th, 1918.
62   Mrs Henry Sidgwick. Member of the Council of S.P.R. and widow of one of its founders.
63   Diary, August 16th, 1918.
64   Diary, August 25th, 1918.
65   Radclyffe Hall. Notes to Psychic Records, October 12th, 1918.
66   Diary, December 13th, 1918.
67   Diary, December 19th, 1918.
68   *The Times*, November 19th, 1920. 'Slander Action Radclyffe-Hall v. Fox Pitt.'
69   R. Lovat Dickson, *Radclyffe Hall at the Well of Loneliness* (Collins, 1975).
70   Radclyffe Hall. Notes to Psychic Records, March 26th, 1919.
71   Radclyffe Hall. Notes to Psychic Records, March 26th, 1919.
72   Diary, March 7th, 1919.
73   Diary, March 5th, 1919.
74   Radclyffe Hall. Notes to Psychic Records, April 19th, 1919.
75   Radclyffe Hall. Notes to Psychic Records, April 30th, 1919.
76   Radclyffe Hall. Notes to Psychic Records.
77   Diary entry, June 2nd, 1919, written by John in Una's absence.
78   Radclyffe Hall. Notes to Psychic Records, July 2nd, 1919.
79   Radclyffe Hall. Notes to Psychic Records, August 2nd, 1919.
80   *The Well of Loneliness.*
81   Radclyffe Hall. Notes to Psychic Records, May 7th, 1919.
82   Radclyffe Hall. Notes to Psychic Records, April 30th, 1919.
83   Diary, September 13th, 1919.
84   Diary, August 18th, 1919.
85   Diary, November 11th, 1919.
86   Diary, December 1st, 1919.
87   Diary, January 27th, 1920.
88   Radclyffe Hall. Notes to Psychic Records, March 9th, 1921.
89   Diary, March 5th, 1921.
90   Diary, June 11th, 1921.

**9   The Marriage of Pen and Paper (1921–5)**

1   Notes to Psychic Records, March 17th, 1920.
2   Diary, August 28th, 1921.

*Notes*

3  Notes to Psychic Records, August 2nd, 1921.
4  Notes to Psychic Records, 1919.
5  Diary, October 20th, 1921.
6  Ibid.
7  Diary, December 6th, 1921.
8  Una Troubridge, *The Life and Death of Radclyffe Hall* (Hammond, 1961).
9  Radclyffe Hall. Notes to Psychic Records, April 21st, 1920.
10  *Life and Death of Radclyffe Hall*, p. 69.
11  Radclyffe Hall, *The Well of Loneliness* (Cape, 1928).
12  Vere and Budge were another lesbian couple, friends of John and Una.
13  *Life and Death of Radclyffe Hall.*
14  Ibid.
15  Radclyffe Hall. Notes to Psychic Records.
16  Meryle Secrest, *Between Me and Life*, a biography of Romaine Brooks (Macdonald & Janes, 1976).
17  Fifth written but fourth published, as 'After Many Days' was never published.
18  Diary, April 9th, 1925.
19  Diary, July 6th, 1925.


10  **The Palace of Truth: Stephen (1926–8)**

1  Una Troubridge, *The Life and Death of Radclyffe Hall* (Hammond, 1961).
2  Ibid.
3  Ibid.
4  Ibid.
5  Ibid.
6  Ibid.
7  Radclyffe Hall. Letter to J. L. Garvin, July 15th, 1928.
8  Una's elder sister had married first Maurice Woods, then Garvin.
9  *Life and Death of Radclyffe Hall.*
10  Radclyffe Hall, *Poems of Past and Present* (Chapman & Hall, 1910).
11  Radclyffe Hall. Letter to Evguenia Souline, 1934.


11  **Trials and Tribulations (1928–9)**

1  Michael Howard, *Jonathan Cape, Publisher* (Cape, 1971).
2  Radclyffe Hall to Garvin, July 15th, 1928.

3    James Louis Garvin. Editor of the *Observer*, 1908–42.
4    Una's diary, July 27th, 1928.
5    *Jonathan Cape, Publisher.*
6    Ibid.
7    *Daily Express*, November 17th, 1928.
8    Vera Brittain, 'A Case of Obscenity?', 1968.
9    Ethel Mannin, *Confessions and Impressions* (Hutchinson, 1930).
10   Una Troubridge, *The Life and Death of Radclyffe Hall* (Hammond, 1961).
11   Ibid.
12   Ibid.
13   Ibid.
14   Ibid.
15   *Confessions and Impressions.*
16   Naomi Jacob, *Me and the Swans* (Kimber, 1963).
17   *Life and Death of Radclyffe Hall.*
18   Ibid.
19   Ibid.
20   Notes to Psychic Records, 1919.

## 12    In Sickness and in Health (1930–33)

1    Essay entitled 'Post Scripta, Black Charles'. Unpublished and undated.
2    Laura, Lady Troubridge (née Gurney), wife of Sir Thomas, Ernest's elder brother.
3    Diary, May 4th, 1930.
4    Diary, July 1st, 1930.
5    Letter to Audrey Heath from Paris, dated March 14th, 1929.
6    Una Troubridge, *The Life and Death of Radclyffe Hall* (Hammond, 1961).
7    Ibid, pp. 102–3.
8    Diary, December 28th, 1930.
9    Diary, January 7th, 1931.
10   Diary, January 8th, 1931.
11   Diary, March 5th, 1932.
12   Diary, April 28th, 1932.
13   Diary, April 25th, 1933.
14   Autobiographical essay, 'On Being Ill'. Unpublished and undated.
15   Nijinsky went mad and spent many years in a mental institution.
16   Who wishes to remain anonymous.

### 13  So Vast a Need (1934)

1  See *The Sixth Beatitude* by Radclyffe Hall (Heinemann, 1936).
2  Una Troubridge, *The Life and Death of Radclyffe Hall* (Hammond, 1961).
3  Ibid.
4  Ibid.
5  Ibid.
6  Radclyffe Hall to Evguenia Souline. Letter dated November 27th, 1934.
7  Radclyffe Hall, *The Unlit Lamp* (Cassell, 1924).
8  Radclyffe Hall, *The Well of Loneliness* (Cape, 1928).
9  Radclyffe Hall to Evguenia Souline. Letter dated June 10th, 1935.
10  Radclyffe Hall to Evguenia Souline. Letter dated November 2nd, 1935.
11  Radclyffe Hall to Evguenia Souline. Letter dated December 8th, 1934.
12  Radclyffe Hall to Evguenia Souline. Letter dated July 31st, 1934.
13  Radclyffe Hall to Evguenia Souline. Letter dated December 4th, 1934.
14  Una Troubridge. Essay, 'Beds'. Unpublished and undated.
15  Quotation from Radclyffe Hall's short story 'Miss Ogilvy Finds Herself' (1934).
16  Quotation from *The Well of Loneliness*.
17  Una Troubridge. Essay, 'On Being Ill'. Unpublished and undated.
18  Radclyffe Hall, *Adam's Breed* (Cassell, 1926).
19  *Life and Death of Radclyffe Hall.*

### 14  This Agonized Bliss: the Bitter Cup (1934–5)

1  Radclyffe Hall, *The Well of Loneliness* (Cape, 1928).
2  Ibid.
3  Radclyffe Hall to Evguenia Souline. Letter dated December 15th, 1934.
4  Naomi Jacob, *Me and the Swans* (Kimber, 1963).
5  Radclyffe Hall to Evguenia Souline. Letter dated December 17th, 1934, recalling this time.
6  Una Troubridge, *The Life and Death of Radclyffe Hall* (Hammond, 1961).
7  Ibid.
8  Ibid.

9   Radclyffe Hall to Evguenia Souline. Letter dated August 7th, 1934.
10  Ibid.
11  *Life and Death of Radclyffe Hall.*
12  Ibid.
13  Una Troubridge. Essay, 'Gabriele D'Annunzio and Radclyffe Hall'. Unpublished and undated.
14  Radclyffe Hall's poem 'A Complaint', from *A Sheaf of Verses* (John and Edward Bumpus, 1908).
15  Radclyffe Hall to Evguenia Souline. Letter dated June 7th, 1935.
16  Radclyffe Hall to Evguenia Souline. Letter dated August 7th, 1934.
17  Radclyffe Hall to Evguenia Souline. Letter dated December 1st, 1934.
18  Radclyffe Hall to Evguenia Souline. Letter dated December 8th, 1934.
19  Radclyffe Hall to Evguenia Souline. Letter dated December 4th, 1934.
20  Radclyffe Hall to Evguenia Souline. Letter dated December 17th, 1934.
21  Radclyffe Hall to Evguenia Souline. Letter dated October 22nd, 1934.
22  Quotation from *The Well of Loneliness.*
23  Radclyffe Hall to Evguenia Souline. Letter dated April 9th, 1935.
24  Radclyffe Hall, *The Sixth Beatitude* (Heinemann, 1936).
25  Radclyffe Hall to Evguenia Souline. Letter dated November 8th, 1935.
26  Radclyffe Hall to Evguenia Souline. Letter dated November 10th, 1935.
27  Radclyffe Hall to Evguenia Souline. Letter dated July 1937.
28  Letter from Harold Rubinstein to R. Lovat Dickson, early 1970s.

**15   Our Long Pilgrimage Together (1936–40)**

1   Radclyffe Hall to Evguenia Souline. Letter dated June 28th, 1938.
2   Una Troubridge, *The Life and Death of Radclyffe Hall* (Hammond, 1961).
3   Ibid.
4   Ibid.
5   Ibid.
6   Radclyffe Hall to Evguenia Souline. Letter dated July 25th, 1937.
7   *Life and Death of Radclyffe Hall.*

8 Radclyffe Hall to Evguenia Souline. Letter dated August 28th, 1937.
9 Radclyffe Hall to Evguenia Souline. Letter dated June 28th, 1938.
10 Radclyffe Hall to Evguenia Souline. Letter dated August 2nd, 1938.
11 Radclyffe Hall to Evguenia Souline. Letter dated January 28th, 1939.
12 *Life and Death of Radclyffe Hall.*
13 Ibid.
14 Ibid.
15 Radclyffe Hall to Evguenia Souline. Letter dated April 26th, 1940.
16 *Life and Death of Radclyffe Hall.*

## 16 Much, Much Stronger than Mere Death (1941–3)

1 Una Troubridge, *The Life and Death of Radclyffe Hall* (Hammond, 1961).
2 Ibid.
3 Radclyffe Hall to Evguenia Souline. Letter dated August 25th, 1941.
4 *Life and Death of Radclyffe Hall.*
5 Ibid.
6 Una Troubridge to Evguenia Souline. Letter dated January 14th, 1942.
7 Una Troubridge to Evguenia Souline. Letter dated January 16th, 1942.
8 Una Troubridge to Evguenia Souline. Letter dated January 22nd, 1942.
9 Una Troubridge to Evguenia Souline. Letter dated January 26th, 1942.
10 Una Troubridge to Evguenia Souline. Letter dated February 9th, 1942.
11 *Life and Death of Radclyffe Hall.*
12 Ibid.
13 Naomi Jacob, *Me and the Swans* (Kimber, 1963).
14 *Life and Death of Radclyffe Hall.*
15 Ibid.

## 17 Utter Bereavement: Early Years (1943–53)

1 Naomi Jacob, *Me and the Swans* (Kimber, 1963).
2 *The Times* obituary notice, Monday October 11th, 1943.

3 Una Troubridge, *The Life and Death of Radclyffe Hall* (Hammond, 1961).
4 Ibid.
5 Ibid.
6 Unpublished autobiographical essay, 'War in the City of London'. Dated 1962.
7 Marie Visetti to Jane Caruth. Letter dated March 3rd, 1944.
8 Unpublished essay, 'Oysters'. Probably dated 1962.
9 'War in the City of London'.
10 Radclyffe Hall's.
11 R. Lovat Dickson, *Radclyffe Hall at the Well of Loneliness* (Collins, 1975).
12 *Life and Death of Radclyffe Hall.*
13 Ibid.
14 Autobiographical essay, 'On Spending Money'. Unpublished and undated.
15 Autobiographical essay, 'Clothes'. Unpublished and undated.
16 Naomi Jacob, *Me – Yesterday and Today* (Hutchinson, 1957).
17 Unpublished essay, 'Nicola Rossi-Lemeni'. Dated 1962.
18 Ibid.


**18 The Way of Loneliness: Later Years (1954–62)**

1 In *Don Carlos, The Barber of Seville, Anna Bolena,* and others.
2 *Norma, I Puritani,* etc.
3 On May 13th, 1976.
4 Naomi Jacob, *Me – Yesterday and Today* (Hutchinson, 1957).
5 In a letter to the author, dated August 18th, 1982.
6 Unpublished essay, 'On Spending Money'. Revised 1962.
7 All extracts from a letter to the author, dated November 18th, 1982.
8 Unpublished essay, 'Conscience'. Revised 1962.
9 Unpublished essay, 'War in the City of London'. Dated 1962.
10 Unpublished essay, 'Nicola Rossi-Lemeni'. Dated 1962.

# Index

# Index

# Index

# Index